BARING MY SOUL

Kenny Thomas

A Horney Media and Publishing & Kenny Thomas Music Limited
Publication

Published by Horney Media and Publishing and Kenny Thomas Music Limited in
2021

ISBN: 978-1-739868-208
Also available as an e-book

www.horneymediaandpublishing.com
www.kennythomasmusic.com

Mum always told us she came over on a banana boat.

It turned out to be true.

In July 1962, Maria de Los Angeles Montesdeoca Santana left her homeland of Las Palmas, Gran Canaria, to follow her beloved elder sister Soledad and her husband José to search for a new and better life in the United Kingdom. Sole had gone before to save up enough money to fund Mum's passage.

In the decade or so after the Second World War many families from Commonwealth countries made the journey to Britain. Italians, Greek Cypriots, Ghanaians and Ugandans followed suit. In short, the country had been running out of men.

That wasn't Mum's story.

Gran Canaria was not the place you may know today. Allied to the evil dictator General Franco who had been seriously aligning himself with Hitler, this was a poor country and a hard life. Mum already had three brothers who had died.

Her childhood was a poor, arid existence without toys – she used a stone in place of a dolly and was soon scrubbing floors day in, day out under the very strict eye of a nasty stepmother who destroyed the photographic past of the family and often hit her around the head so hard she remained deaf in one ear for life. Her own Mum had passed away shortly after her birth.

Mum and Sole were extremely close – Sole was the mum whom Mum never had. When *she* left for England, it was inevitable that my mum would follow.

Auntie Sole and Uncle José settled in Portland Place, London, where they worked for the philanthropist businessman and his wife, Sir Isaac and Lady Wolfson. They managed to find my mother suitable lodgings and employment in Central London. She was here to stay.

But they didn't speak any English.

By the time she met my dad, she was working in a café in the West End of London. Dad – Ken (Big Ken!) – was a plasterer whose first marriage ended in the late-1950s. By the time I came along I already therefore had two brothers in Gary and Steve from my dad's first marriage.

He was a good-looking guy – quite definitely a ladies' man once upon a time. He loved his music – big jiver on the dance floor, always twisting and throwing girls in the air and catching them on the way down. But that was just for show. My Nan Ivy once told me that after his divorce he was lost until he met my mum. That probably explains why he went to the café every day where Mum worked, eventually telling one of the other girls, 'I really like her. I would like to take her out on a date.'

In later years he reflected how crazy this was on both fronts.

'She didn't know who I was, and she couldn't speak English,' he would frequently recall.

In a different time, these things worked. Mum's English slowly improved, and Dad stopped throwing the other girls around. They married in February 1967 at a registry office to keep the Home Office happy. I suspect in that era they were not alone in doing so.

The Vatican posed a potential problem but finally, after months of waiting, a canon lawyer in Rome declared Dad's first marriage null and void, judging it invalid sacramentally. They were eventually able to marry the way Mum wanted it, at St. Aloysius in Euston where I was later baptised. At this stage Mum was a devout Catholic and Dad a Protestant.

The missionary priest Dan Magill, who dedicated his life to building irrigation and infrastructure in Africa, presided over the ceremony. It was *his* first wedding. He stayed friends with our family all his life. He had made a good start.

And in those roots and before my time, you will probably find the beginnings of my spirituality.

Mum was incredibly religious. Everybody always said that if you wanted to meet a saint then it was her – simple and holy with never a bad word spoken behind her back.

Of course, I had yet to meet them. I would only learn this and see this love for my own eyes in time.

Then everything changed.

Dad killed a cat.

With that, Kenneth Mariano Miguel Thomas was born.

23:45. Thursday 12 September 1968.

Liverpool Road, Islington, London.

I am in an incubator having arrived two months early. I have a one-in-three chance of survival.

Dad ran over a cat.

The chaos of that car journey and the panic that ensued meant that Mum went into labour and November became September. In an instant, it begins. My life starts with that clear reality that our existence is very fragile. Over the years I have constantly lost people and my quest to ask, 'What is the truth?' became relentless.

Theoretically that begins here, though of course we cannot know for sure how important those first moments on the planet really are. Are there early feelings of detachment from having been heart-to-heart with your mother's *heartbeat* for seven months – and then nothing? Tubes are hanging out of you through a plastic box. Does isolation begin here or is it too early? Has solitude cast its die, or would life's experiences be responsible for that?

There is one aspect of my early years which everybody close to me struggles to understand. My memory is extraordinary. As I grew older, I started to question whether my recollections were actually something I had compiled from my imagination or whether they were some sort of sign.

Mum and Dad were stunned that 'Little Ken' could easily recall buildings, layouts and events from as far back as the age of two. Rock'n'roll memoirs are notorious for their gaps in the memory. I seem to remember everything.

The truth is that we were also a family of stories and constantly reminiscing. That is less common today as society breaks up and the digital era means many moments are instantly disposable, but crucially growing up in that period meant that those who weren't haunted by it were always telling lots of World War Two stories. My grandad's brother Ernie *had* seen it all from Dunkirk in 1941 to El Alamein, Tobruk and Monte Cassino. Grandad himself rescued many people from the rubble of bombing air raids on London. These experiences and the level of suffering he witnessed shaped his life. Atheism was the only belief system that he could entertain.

My grandmother talked often of hiding under the bed during the Blitz. Of course it scared her, but it made her tough and formed a strong character. Her attitude was simply to get on with it and do battle. Life didn't give you time to crumble. All the family, to this day, say that she made you feel like a Thomas!

I almost made it my mission to extract as much information as I could, as though I would be the custodian of family history. Even as a kid, I knew that there was limited time to get the maximum information from those whose better years had passed before I was born but whose knowledge was invaluable. I always wanted to know more from Ernie. I would often sit down with him and ask him to tell me about his wartime experiences. Poignantly, he told me of his (Army) friend who popped his head agonisingly too high above the trenches one day whilst shaving. He died instantly from a sniper's shot. Ernie never forgot the shrill of his scream until his own dying day.

Dad often told me of the morning after Archway was flattened in London. 'We must never forget' was very much the sentiment of my childhood. Events were still very close to my parents' and their parents' generation.

We laughed, too, and messed about. Boy, did we laugh. Going to Nan's to eat pie, mash and liquor was great, and during the war years she was Dad's sparring partner when he took up boxing at a very young age! Always mischievous, she would often place me in her shopping trolley and pull me down the road and round the corner. Of course, one day when I encouraged her to go as fast as she could, the wheel broke and that was the end of that!

Memories, therefore, as with many families at that time, were in our make-up, but my ability to recall pretty much anything seemed almost loose wiring to my parents.

Even to this day, my friends in the building game call me the Snag-meister. I can go into sites that they are working on and spot detail the naked eye has missed. Rooms and buildings dominate much of my recall.

So do people, obviously. At the age of two I can still visualise Jackie – a friend of the family, who would later teach me to swim – picking me up in her Morris Minor in the brightest of London sunshine.

'Close the curtains,' the young me kept crying out.

'There are no curtains,' she replied.

The fact that this is such an insignificant anecdote makes it significant in itself. How was I able to channel these very distant and early memories?

At two, little Sandra arrived – my new sister was on time. No cats had fled the scene in the preceding hours.

I can vividly recollect feeling jealous – I was no longer the centre of attention. It was not long before I threw a Tonka toy at her head, denting it and resulting in a trip to hospital. She still has the scar and I have always regretted it, and much later would come to ask myself if in fact I was a bad kid growing up. In time, I hope you will see that I was a good kid who did some bad things! Yet, at the age of four I had become territorial! I did of course have someone to play with and became very protective of her. I knew we were different, though. She couldn't be controlled and was a free spirit. Always from an early age, I had that little voice in my head that slightly just reined me in. Because I had questions.

By the age of five, though, those doubts really began.

Isolation did take hold.

Aunt Sole was dead.

It was five o'clock in the morning on 30 November 1973. I was asleep in Mum and Dad's bed. Mum staggered heartbroken to her feet. So began the darkest and saddest of days.

7

Cancer had beaten her. She was just 39.

I didn't discover until late in my teens that the radiotherapy tore her apart. Though I learned that only after, an angst had risen in me and planted the seed of medical uncertainty and distrust. It would never leave me.

Aunt Sole doted on me. It was like having another mother. She was the one who would frequently rubber-stamp my Canarian roots. I was always little Mariano to her. Her death tore the family apart as individuals, but united us in our grief.

Of course, this was my first experience and questioning of mortality. And so young, too.

Innocence ended. Spirituality began.

'Where is she now?' I would ask Mum.

'Her life has changed not ended' was the considered, delicate but beautiful response.

For the first time, I understood there wasn't a forever here on earth. From Mum's words, I also took that there was something else that *is* forever.

At five, I became serious, and I remain so. I began to understand that I feel different, and I am different. A potential outlier.

Often I have failed to enjoy life's good moments because I am still lingering on the answer to the previous question, which inevitably brings the following one. As soon as I asked myself what the truth was, I had assigned myself to a life of pursuit – so very far away from any definitive conclusions at this point.

As I write now, my mind is locked onto a cold winter's playground at St Ignatius Primary School in Stamford Hill, London. I am standing in the same spot where Alfred Hitchcock received his Jesuit education. I am watching classmates play together in the chilling air. I am not part of it. By choice.

I am alone, contemplating the spiritual world… at the age of five.

On a Sunday I had the option to stay at home with Dad or go to church. I mostly chose the latter. Dad was a self-professed Protestant and a Freemason. There is no ideological position more dramatically opposed to Mum's Catholicism. In later years, I would ask Dad what exactly was it that he was protesting against, and he was unsure of the answer, but he was certain that protesting was a good thing.

As a teenager I would get into some heavy debates with him about his Masonic affiliation. He was uncomfortable with my questions about this ancient gnostic sect, and it frustrated him being unable to provide me with the answers. After all it was a secret society and revealing those secrets carried a death penalty. Not wanting Dad to be found hanging from Blackfriars Bridge with symbolic bricks in his pockets like the Italian banker Roberto Calvi, I decided to do my own research into the so-called *Brotherhood*. Dad would say that it is not a secret society, but one that has secrets. My answer to that was that if a society was good and true then it would not need to have secrets and its truth would be out in the open for all to see. This always touched a nerve; I would then make a swift exit out of the door knowing that I had pushed things a bit too far.

Mum never Bible-bashed and Dad respected her faith. At marriage, he had to agree not to be a hindrance to her religion and that their children would be brought up in the Catholic faith. He made sure that he stuck to his word, though his own appearances at church were confined to First Holy Communions, confirmations and maybe the odd Christmas Eve Midnight Mass.

Around me there was always a religious ethic, whatever that religion was. Mum was maternal to everyone, especially the latchkey kids whom she would see coming home from school and without food. She often took them in.

One Christmas, a Jamaican family near us lost their dad. He alone had been bringing up the two brothers and sisters. Three of his children were old enough to do their own thing. Dad suddenly announced, 'We're having Johnson over for Christmas. He will have dinner with us, we'll buy him gifts and he will be part of our family that day.'

This was never to parade. It was who they were.

To me, this was authenticity in action.

9

I could see very early on that Mum was very different to almost everyone around – her upbringing obviously had been, too. I regularly watched how people interacted with her and I just didn't see many of the flaws I saw in other people – including my beloved dad.

She really was a woman of prayer.

But with my innocence turning to awareness after Sole's death, Mum's heart was broken. She remained that kind person – more than ever in fact – but we saw a shadow of whom she had been.

And Dad, knowing her best of all, was concerned.

One day he literally pulled a rabbit out of a hat.

In fact, it was more a canary.

We were taking Mum home. Uncle José had already headed back there after Sole's death, working ships in and out of Gran Canaria. Her passing had destroyed him, too. The coast was clear now as well – the stepmother had died and just her sister Eulalia (Auntie Lala) remained.

The truth is that London was now home for Mum and a change of scenery didn't bring anybody back. She did love being home on an island you would not recognise from the tourist destination it is now. Dad, though, struggled to get work.

He had made a very brave decision. He loved it there and if job prospects had been better, it is quite likely they would have stayed. Yet, it *was* alien to everything he knew. When he wasn't working, his life had been running the boxing gym at Alexandra Palace in London – a place like no other where he was the glue, taking so many errant kids off the street and giving them purpose, focus and community. He talked one notorious knife-wielder off a bench on our estate and into the gym, offering the choice that he could stab Dad there and then, which would have life-changing consequences, or meet him outside the flat the following Monday and learn how to box. He chose the latter. This was his loving, giving side at work, but also his fearless nature.

I don't think Dad even considered the impact of taking such a massive part of his own life away by moving. So many people came through his doors at the gym – such camaraderie and so many lessons of life were born there. Plus – we could all see the respect and gratitude from every one of the kids who turned their lives around in that building when they had been living in a world where there was no respect to them and where they showed none back.

As a child it *is* an adventure playing on the beach all year round, speaking Spanish and really tasting freedom. Indeed, I felt very Spanish before I went. I was Mariano to Mum's side of the family. That spirit of adventure got me into the odd scrape, too. I got busted for shoplifting in the supermercado! Mind you, back in the UK, I had become a little mischievous, once playing hairdressers with my sister, getting the scissors out and cutting off a large chunk of her hair. I then hid the evidence in the cabinet. I knew I had done wrong.

I was soon learning that your actions could have very big consequences – nearly killing half a dozen nuns. Mum used to hang the washing out on one of these Canarian flat roofs. Below was a terraced area where the habited nuns would sit. Just about strong enough to roll over this large piece of masonry and trying to coerce my sister into helping me, I knew it was naughty but still pushed the stone over the ledge, smashing in pieces as it hit the ground, nuns scattering everywhere.

Naturally, when the knock on the door followed, Dad freaked out. Six-year-old nearly arrested for nun-slaughter.

It was logged, though – actions have consequences.

But then there were my brothers – who were always my brothers despite living with Dad's first wife and their mum out in Enfield. We talked all the time, and they were often around at weekends. The notion of half-brother just didn't exist – so close were the family.

I missed them. He missed them. They missed us. We had tried to fill a hole by going back to the place of Mum's origin, but Dad hadn't thought it through. Everything that was our stability was back in the UK – except Sole, who wasn't coming back at all.

Dad then got sick with shingles, but above all I was home*sick* for Dad's mum and dad, too. Nanny Ivy sent me a box of 7" vinyl so I could play her music when I was in Las Palmas. I had learned so much from my nan in particular – real life skills like cooking and cleaning, but also the ability to laugh and do so out loud. Nan was by far the funniest in our family – so much so that I always took my mates to see her first when new people came into my life and often would pull a sickie off school just to see her. Nan would say to my mum, 'I thought you said he was ill. Within an hour of you dropping him off to me he was as right as rain.'

You couldn't fool Nan.

Old school, in that she would send me down to the bunker to get the coal, but smart, witty and contemporary enough that she was the best of my mates. When there is a void in your life as we experienced with Sole's death, hindsight tells me that you need that family humour more than anything.

In short, the move to Gran Canaria turned out to be a disaster.

We are now effectively homeless.

Less than one year on.

And miles from anywhere. Dad's plan had massively backfired. We stayed with Nan and Grandad for a short while and then we were placed in damp temporary housing in Almington Street, off Hornsey Road, Islington.

Some undesirable people live in the same building. We have no bathroom, just a small kitchen and a toilet. We take a bath in a tub. Luxury is not only being back near Nan and Grandad, but also going round to theirs for a *proper* bath. Our spirit is not broken, but in reality we have gone backwards.

Early on, I witnessed Dad standing at the bottom of the stairs to the building with a baseball bat. At five and a half feet and with a shoe size of six, you wouldn't give him much chance, but he never knew fear. He calmly put Mum, Sandra, and me in the car, dropped us off at Nan and Grandad's house for the night, and then went back to deal with them. I am not sure what he did but there was no more trouble from them ever again. I would learn that he would always find a way.

This was new. Really new – so different from our previous house on Widdenham Road, Islington, when Nanny Ivy and Grandad Alf were next door, and Dad's sister Marie with my cousins Barbara, Jackie and Lee were living below. That was old-school London but with family at its core. This move *home* was going to either make us or break us.

Dad was delighted to be back in regular touch with my brothers and his sons from his first marriage. He made sure that one of the first things he would do was to take me to see my first football match at Highbury. My Grandad Alf, who was himself a good footballer when he was young, used to go and watch Arsenal play regularly in his earlier years and was a passionate supporter of the Gunners. Grandad was not a very tall man but, being a good carpenter, he made himself some wooden blocks which he would wrap up in a small bag and take to Highbury and stand on them to get a better view of the game.

One of my few memories from that first match was watching Terry Mancini run around the pitch and thinking that he reminded me of that funny man I used to see often on TV called Max Wall.

Tragedy struck, though, and that was to have a lasting effect on my life. My brother Steve was getting massively into mopeds which were then a lot more powerful and borderline on a par with motorbikes. He was heading over to us one day from Enfield to show us his first proper set of wheels, when he never showed up.

My other brother Gary, however, did.

'There's been an accident,' he began.

'Some old boy pulled out, didn't look and has gone straight into the side of Steve.' He was lying in the road for an hour and a half and has broken his femur. For the next two years he was in and out of hospital and to this day, still cannot extend that leg. When he was released, he made the pin into a plaque which adorned his wall for some time! All I remember is that Steve seemed to be in hospital forever and had every kind of operation done.

When he recovered, obviously he and the world of motorbikes parted company.

As a family, we had to get back to what we knew and that meant family and boxing. Dad was straight to where he left off and by the age of six, I was begging him to take me to the gym only to be told that I was too young at that stage.

Apart from being that father figure to hundreds of young lads whom he took off the streets and showed discipline and rules to, Dad was the business in the ring, too, winning 90 of his 112 fights and going up against some of England's best boxers. My cousin Lee was already following in his Uncle Ken's footsteps. Lee boxed for the Finchley Boxing Club, a stylish southpaw with a vast number of contests under his belt. I sparred with him once in later years, and, although he took it easy with me, I did my best to avoid those fast, heavy hands. Eventually at the age of seven, I was allowed to go and watch the big boys whack the bags. My initial shyness at being surrounded by such huge men meant Dad had to give me a smaller punchbag in the office, so my training began there.

Wherever life plants you, you do your best to grow, and it was finally the move to the Hillside Estate on Stamford Hill that shaped me. It was tough, as our short-term accommodation had been on our return, but it was here that I would live until around the age of nineteen, after which it was condemned and pulled down. Formative years.

I already had a lot more questions by the time we moved there. Now I began to have experiences to sit alongside them. Broadly speaking, these fell into three categories. The diversity of culture – which led to music and, at first-hand, crime, survival instincts (and therefore staying streetwise).

Suddenly, I was living a Catholic upbringing alongside Jews, Jamaicans, Africans, Indians, Irish and Pakistanis. We lived in and out of one another's houses and, in our new group, got on as one. It was on this council estate that I would meet my best friend for life, David Sassoon. My Jewish brother from another mother. Ironically his mum was named Angela like mine.

Dave was a very funny guy who enriched my life at every stage. As I discovered music, he would be around – the first to listen to the record with me. He would also alert me to new songs, and between us we built up quite a record collection. We both shared a deep love for Stevie Wonder. We were soul brothers in every sense of the term.

We hadn't lived on the estate for very long when one day Dad leaned over the balcony and shouted out to all of us kids playing outside.

'Who wants to do some boxing?'

'I do – I do – I do,' came the quick responses.

16

He cleared the furniture out of the way and about eleven of us crammed into that small living room. Dad produced some boxing gloves and for the first time those kids experienced sparring. We each took turns and slowly got a chance to take on everyone in the room. My sister Sandra and I kicked things off, and then it was Reginald against Johnson, Johnson against Maria, Tony against Reginald, Maria against me. The only thing that got hurt that day was the ego of us lads because we all got beaten, hands down, by Maria Murray.

She wiped the floor with the lot of us.

Alicia Murray (Maria) and Reginald were the children of Gladstone Murray, a big, powerful man from Barbados. He was called *The Shark* when he was younger because of his ability to dive deep into the sea back in Barbados and hold his breath for an enormous amount of time in order to find pearls. Well, this was the story we were told, and like so many anecdotes on the estate you never knew what was true or what was said just to excite the imagination. However, this story *was* indeed true when one day, with our own eyes, we watched him swim two lengths of an Olympic swimming pool underwater.

This was life on the estate!

We had nothing, but we were rich in so many other ways.

Dad was all about the boxing gym. That was his life. He ran the Alexandra Boxing Club for almost 30 years, teaching the *noble art* to so many lads. Although I thought his matchmaking skills were not as good as his boxing ones. Putting a fight night together is no easy task, you need a certain number of bouts to make a show, and that show must go on. Sometimes I was convinced he cut a few corners.

There were at least three times when I looked across the ring at my opponent and thought, 'He is bloody massive... there is no way he is my age or my weight.'

They *were* much older and way heavier, but it is too late when the first bell is about to go. You have to get on with it.

When my good friend Jimmy Lazarou was having a fight, about an hour before the weigh-in, he was sitting at a table when

Dad turned up with a massive jug of water and several bank bags full of 50p coins.

'Get that down your neck, Jimmy,' Dad told him.

'You're kidding me, Ken,' Jimmy replied.

'No, you've got to make the weight or the bout is off, so drink that water and stick those coins down your pants. Don't worry, one of our guys will be over by the scales and will keep an eye on things,' Dad assured him.

Jimmy struggled to drink the water but somehow managed to get it all down. He shoved the coins down his pants, hoping that they wouldn't be noticed, and made his way to the scales. He was bursting for the toilet and his pants looked big, but he made the weight.

The bout was on.

This was Dad. A right character but with a big heart – and a bag of coins.

My friends were from such diverse backgrounds – Eric Johnson, of Jamaican descent, whom I met at school, was one of the dearest. We were soon joined by Steve McMullen (Muttsy), of Irish roots. As a trio, this would form a core friendship at secondary school and beyond.

Eric and I would go on to make mischief at break times where, in a very busy environment, we were briefly entrusted to run the school tuck shop!

You were given this huge responsibility for approximately a week. We were lucky to last that long.

We hit the cash'n'carry store on the way to school then transferred their stock into ours. By the end of the week, we are called into the school office. The numbers no longer added up.

They were not daft at Catholic schools – they kept a keen eye on what you were doing.

'We have no proof,' the lecture began. 'All we know is that the takings are down by half, and it doesn't make sense because everyone still seems to be getting their fill out of the tuck shop.'

We were never ever let near it again.

'I'll get Bertha out!' shouted Mr Lawrie Leslie.

Bertha was a giant-sized plimsoll, an instrument of terror, used occasionally by said teacher to bring us into line.

Lawrie Leslie used to be a professional footballer, the goalkeeper for West Ham.

Big hands, a big heart and a very big plimsoll.

There were two Kennys at my school, Black Kenny and White Kenny. When the two Kennys got into a fight once during a PE lesson, Mr Leslie fetched Bertha out of the cupboard, and in front of all the other pupils gave our butts an old-school spanking.

It worked.

He had my respect, and he was one of the few teachers there that I was very fond of. When I heard in recent years that he ended up in a nursing home and eventually passed away I was genuinely sad. He was a legend on the pitch and at our school.

Another whom I liked was Mr Dominic McKenna who taught us Sociology. His lessons were the ones I enjoyed the most. He was passionate about teaching, very animated, funny, loud and he had a fiery spirit. You could always hear his voice bellowing down the corridor.

'Get outta here!' he would shout if he caught us sneaking about when we should have been outside in the playground.

You didn't mess with Mr McKenna.

But once again, he had our respect and he was loved. This was how it was done then.

He eventually left teaching and became a priest. I know this because some years later I bumped into him at Allen Hall Seminary in London. He still had that cheeky glint in his eyes, and no doubt he is at a parish somewhere now giving them Hell... fire and brimstone.

When the pressure was on, it was Eric and Steve who lent me their course notes so I could blag my way through the final exams.

Together, we channelled our creativity into other places. In addition to the music, we would write poems. These were not the kind of verse that school taught you. We carved out the hysterical rhyme market! Often the teachers would be the subject of our 'work'. Indeed, we were summoned again when one of the books was discovered. Punishments – we were banned from a subsequent school trip – but we did earn a trip to the office of Mr O'Brien, the deputy headmaster. Here you were offered either a letter home to your parents or the cane. I always chose the letter home, knowing that I shared the same name as my dad as in Mr K Thomas, so intercepting the letter became one of my newly acquired skills. On this occasion Mr O'Brien made his offer but it was actually a trick question. When I chose the letter home, he told me that this time I would be getting both: the cane and a letter home. The only other thing you could guarantee from a visit to his office was that you would always find my good friend Vincent Lynch standing outside waiting for his just deserts. If getting the cane earned you air miles, that would have been a right result for Vincent, because he was a frequent flyer.

My book of poems was sadly surrendered!

The key, though, is that I neither was devastated by the lack of class excursion nor succumbed to the supposed discipline that authority was meting out. I had already worked stuff out and school's inspiration only really came in the friends I made and through my own learnings, being able to see through things to what I thought was the truth, rather than a botched-together, often at times intellectually flawed state-imposed narrative.

It inspired me, but only because it made me seek alternatives.

And Mum and Dad were very supportive, making me believe that anything was possible. Church, too, rather than school, was the benchmark of morality and understanding. For sure, I still had a million questions there, but I looked towards Sundays with trust, and Monday to Fridays with suspicion.

However, violence, aggression and racism were also my neighbours – a blueprint for multicultural Britain. It was a mini-society to feed off for all its cultural richness such as food, particularly Myra's chicken soup, salt beef bagels or the smell of jerk chicken, ackee and salt fish temptingly wafting out of a nearby flat together with the Ghanaian influences, as well as the Indian food, Freddie Sassoon and his obsession with chillies, and because of Mum, most of my friends ate calamari at our house for the first time in their lives.

Then there was the storytelling and that cross-section of religious beliefs, but I also saw many black and Irish friends fall victim to violence at the hands of the police. I witnessed sexual assaults and I knew exactly who was committing the burglaries. You also learned when to say nothing and what the parameters were.

By seven, I took part in my first boxing gym show in Highgate. This is an illegal meet before you get your medical card, and you go three rounds with your opponent and there is no winner or loser. Yet around me I was observing street fighting and petty theft that I knew instinctively not to bring my boxing to. *My* fighting had context – a physical version of rules, regime and discipline to accompany the mental path that my natural probing instinct and spiritual mind were taking. Healthy body, healthy mind – it has often been said. That is the root of the young me.

So, I learned fast and studied hard. Very early on at Hillside I came home from school one day to be asked by a rather out of breath and very sweaty, small-time crook on the estate if I would just look after 'his girlfriend's handbag for him' until he came back for it later that evening. The penny dropped. I was grateful to say goodbye to naivety early.

Then, on Sundays, I *did* take that path to church. It became the focus of the week. All of the experiences of school and the estate could be processed there and then. Instantly I took church seriously. From the moment I first attended, I had all the questions and none of the answers, and not because I was sceptical or disbelieving. I always believed and still do. There was just a lot to learn and so I began to form many friendships with the priests that outlived almost all the other experiences in my life.

Wherever life plants you, do your best to grow.
And I was making friends – the best of friends…

5 Till Death Do Us Part

My dear friend David Sassoon passed away just a few years ago. As everybody tends to say these days – taken way too soon. I remain devastated he is no longer here.

Everything that happens from this point in my story… Dave was there or thereabouts. From the moment we moved onto the estate, we were inseparable. Like plenty of kids did back then, we cut our fingers together and made a pact. Soul brothers, now blood brothers. His Nan 'Myra' in effect became my third grandmother! His mum 'Angela' and his Auntie 'Freda' were, and still are, family to me. We *were* joined at the hip.

One day, from across our gardens behind the flats, I asked him his name and we simply hit it off. Polar opposite in so many things and especially the genetics of our forefathers, our friendship was instant and durable.

Like many on the estate, his own arrival is a story in itself and each of my friendships took my outlook on life towards these different philosophies. My Muslim friend Bobby Islam taught me a lot about respect and tolerance, which I observed from how he was with his dear mother, and when he spoke about his beliefs. Around Bobby and Derrick Woods (a Seventh-day Adventist) I became less judgemental and more accepting.

But Dave's grandfather Peter Spigelman was a Polish Jew who had managed to get away from the Nazis by fighting for the Polish Free Army, only to be eventually captured by the Russians, earning him a free holiday in Siberia. After the war, he went back to his village where none of his family had survived. (Dave and I secretly called his grandfather 'Pope John Paul II' because of the uncanny physical resemblance.)

With jokes about Germans very much part of the armoury of that first generation post-1945, he was very quick to address context.

23

'Not every German is a Nazi,' he would say. 'And not every Nazi is a German.'

This statement left a lasting impact on me. I was still looking for the truth, but it shaped the rhetoric for me. So honest and dignified, despite everything. From that point on, I placed to one side many of the stories and attitudes to the war. I attempted to understand it.

My dad also went to do some building work for a Jewish lady and when he came home, he told me that he sadly could see her faded prison camp number tattooed on her arm. From that moment, I never lost sight of the fact that a human being could try to reduce another human being to just a number.

The Jewish influence was massive on my upbringing. I think that outside of New York and Tel Aviv we had the biggest such community in the world. On one occasion later in life, I was walking home and had to turn the car alarm off for one of my neighbours. Rules meant that on the Sabbath he couldn't hold certain things, like car keys, or keep them in his pockets. He was an Orthodox Hasidic Jew. His vehicle was going mental and there was nothing he could do because of his beliefs. I had to step in, go into his house, grab those keys, turn it off and then place them back in the house to put the neighbourhood out of their misery.

When you reflect, you can very easily say that 'if hadn't been for such and such, things might have turned out differently'. We never get that chance in life to know. But it all starts here. That Jewish perspective was insightful, and my best friend and I had common ground.

Dave and I were all about the music.

Of course, there were roots at home. We were always surrounded by something playing. Dad was massively into Johnny Mathis and Matt Monro; Mum loved her Spanish rhythms. Both loved the album *1,000 Volts of Holt* by the Jamaican singer John Holt, most famous for his massive hit 'Help Me Make It Through the Night'. We were introduced to his music by our good friends Rudy and Nancy Murdock (may they rest in peace). Many a weekend we would visit the Murdocks in Borehamwood, Hertfordshire, where reggae music would play late into the night and would dance, sing and burn off all that youthful energy.

They were special times.

For the young Kenny Thomas, John Holt hit the spot.

From that moment on, there was no stopping Dave and me. Music of many origins was always pumping out of the flat – that heavy reggae beat never too far away. Your ears would always follow the base of whatever sound system was rocking. (By the 1980s reggae and the Notting Hill Carnival in London were massive – a real breakthrough moment when Aswad hit Number 1 with 'Don't Turn Around' after performing for years. Suddenly – but not suddenly at all – they were mainstream.)

By eight and nine I was devouring a Stevie Wonder *Greatest Hits* album and we both all but lived at R&B Records – the store opposite the estate.

The smart amongst you will have already concluded that obviously I would be hanging out at an R&B record shop. I hate to break it to you gently but with her love for lovers rock and his for jazz-funk, this middle-aged Jewish couple running the place were not defining my genre just yet, despite its name.

But every time I walked in, they would have put something aside and greet me with the words 'I've got another record for you'. Yes – Rita and Benny were a massive influence!

That was R and B Records!

Rita and Benny.

Stevie, to this day, stands tall. It was as though he held a tuning fork in the same frequency as my soul – even at such an early age as this. But I was hooked – totally transfixed. With no ambition whatsoever other than personal fulfilment, and reaching into an emotional void that all these spiritual questions were opening up, I of course began to replicate the sound of the artists that I was starting to love.

Singing along to records soon led me to church groups and their Amateur Dramatics. Later, Dave and I began buying

25

instruments. In time I went from mimicking to listening to all the elements of a hit record, but I always locked into the voice. That understanding of tone and accent even extended into shouting down the corridor at school parodying the teacher.

I even thought I had mastered my own mum's voice once and rang up the Head of Year, Mr Griffiths, to explain my absence from school. Using my best Spanish accent, I was convinced that I had pulled it off. Half an hour later, Mum rings me to ask why I am at home, to which I protest, only to be told that Mr Griffiths had just called her at work, informing her that I was doing bad Mum impersonations. I had to get to school sharpish. When I arrived, he tried to tell me off, but couldn't conceal his laughter, only to concede with, 'You know what, Kenny, just forget about it.'

But the signs were all there from the spoken to the sung word. The vocal was king.

At this stage I was learning through imitation.

The young Kenneth Mariano Miguel Thomas was taking the first steps to becoming Kenny Thomas himself.

Self-awareness was growing. My ability to express myself had found an outlet. I was still watching and observing but I was not that isolated five-year-old staring at my classmates in my playground in the aftermath of Aunt Sole's death.

Through music, friendships, my family, the boxing club and the church, my roots were on an even keel. These were elements I was largely in control of. They still posed a lot of questions, though. But then, of course, events impact on you and there is very little you can do about them. They shape you, too, and leave you with dozens more unanswered dilemmas.

I am partly talking about the estate. At eight, I saw the police taking a guy out of his flat one day with a massive bag of white powder.

Women on the game within earshot of our home were normal, too.

By the age of eleven, I witnessed my first gun and drugs for myself, invited one Sunday to come and sit in a car with two older Jamaican friends who decided to skin up a joint. They then locked the doors and windows and proceeded to fill the car with smoke. It was like the dance floor of an 80s nightclub in there. I couldn't see a thing. Despite saying that I had to leave and not be late for my mum's Sunday dinner, they just laughed and said, 'No, man, you're staying right here with us.'

Windows up, guard down, I breathed in far too much. I was stoned for the first time!

Mum was waiting at home for me, cooking a roast. She, too, was preparing a joint for Dad to carve up.

Needless to say that, by the time I got home, I had worked up a colossal appetite to eat all of her culinary delights.

I never felt intimidated by my community. It certainly had edge, but it also meant that everyone was watching out for you. It all merged into the background. I didn't lack empathy. I just saw it so often I became desensitised.

And the boxing kept me sharp – I had my wits about me.

I was bullied for a short time at primary school by this big lad who would constantly kick me in the shins. Originally, I thought I would let it ride and see if I could connect with him – beat him with words over fists, the mind over body.

It didn't happen.

My dad told me that there was only one way to deal with this – next time go for him. And it would stop. So, when he started in the corridor, I did, overpowering him, but leaving both of us stunned that I had actually done it. I went from being bullied to bully vigilante – and guess what? – I became best of mates with my previous aggressor.

I also saw Dad cry for the first time – these moments were quite rare in that generation, so much so that you never forget it. We both sat there together, on a May bank holiday weekend. I knew Dad was tough but had a soft heart and I saw it beating with emotion the day George McKenzie from the gym was killed. He had been a close family friend who used to go with Mum to bingo. He was killed by a young lad; his body was placed on his bed and his flat was then set on fire.

At the trial, George was portrayed very negatively as a homosexual – his death a result of self-defence. With no witnesses to the event, we only had the killer's words to go by. The judge told his *attacker* that '*he* had suffered a terrible ordeal' and suggested he 'go home and try to forget about it'.

Years later at a friend's wedding in Brighton, I got chatting to a guy who happened to have gone to the same school as George's killer. Asking what had become of him, he told me that he had heard that the guy ended up in a prison in Thailand, allegedly convicted of a murder over there. How true that is, I will never know, but I like to think that justice caught up with him and he finally ended up where he belonged.

Everything happens for a reason. Often that takes time to evaluate. We have a built-in mechanism that repairs itself, if you like. And the only way to understand it is to go through it, not to attempt to circumvent it.

But my intellectual radar *was* engaged.

As well as my own studying and the church, I took so much from an elder generation, absorbing something that is probably lost today.

Storytelling – just like Nan and Grandad.

I *loved* being around old people – especially the cyclist George Irving.

George told proper old London stories. Sometimes he slept in his shed on the allotment, a stone's throw from his own back door. An eccentric for sure.

In my teens, I would often visit him – just to listen and learn. I don't know if I had a sense of history that this generation had something special, in both their style of narrative *and* the narrative itself, and that this was about to be lost.

In George, I witnessed something I still ponder to this day – an NDE.

Near-death experience.

He died in hospital. Dr Logan confirmed it to him.

Then he rejoined us.

He was not the same person afterwards admittedly, but every time that I visited him, his story never deviated. He had crossed the line and been to the other side. I knew he was not talking to me from his imagination but from his experience, even though his wife Mary constantly said he should shut up and I should take it with a pinch of salt. But nobody spent more time with him than me at the end.

And he told me that he could see the doctors around him (when dead). Some people walked right through him. He was standing beside one of the doctors looking at an old man's body lying there, and that old man was George.

He was outside of himself looking at himself lying there.

When better, he placed a picture of the Sacred Heart of Jesus by his fireplace, given to him by one of the priests from St

Ignatius Church, and often pointed to it, saying, 'That man there is the saviour.'

Of course, we ultimately lost him. The legacy was the near-death experience. He *lived* for some time after he died. But he lived on forever with me, fond of saying, 'Don't say you can't, boy, say you can.'

Nothing was impossible in his eyes.

The consequence was that he was never scared of death. It left me fascinated.

Somewhere in those years, Dave's father Freddie and I connected and were having very deep, heavy conversations. In business, he had a million get-rich-quick schemes. In life, he had a huge knowledge of Kabbalism from his grandfather who was a Kabbalist, long before Madonna got a whiff of it. I wasn't necessarily subscribing to everything he taught me, but I was feeding off the different influences which would influence the Kenny Thomas that you now think you know.

Of course, to engage in music, I needed more than just my voice.

Church was the obvious forum for both my spirituality and my understanding of rhythm. In time, wherever I was in the world, I would find a Mass to attend. I would also realise that, for the most part, the religious experience as a whole was stuck in the 1960s.

I was often being pushed forward for solos and people would mention my voice, but I never had desires on being the star of the show. I just wanted to be part of it. The church's am-dram was very, er, *churchy*, and the folk band played those typical songs written in the mid-60s with that Yiddish feel to them. I did my best to adapt the vocals in my own way. The reality was that I was singing along to everything, again mimicking, but now Al Jarreau and Johnny Mathis. I began learning acoustic guitar, and then bought my own which I eventually flogged to Dave. I eventually fell out of love with it as an instrument as the Commodores next took centre stage and as an altar boy, music, timing and performance accompanied everything. I knew the rituals and all the seasonal variations inside out – the waft of the church incenses an ever present. In short, I was into the smells and bells.

At fourteen, I also discover the most amazing private library in Hackney which I visit religiously, so to speak. Owned by my now lifelong friend Michael Moore, who at the time was writing his PhD in Natural Law, he was an intellectual giant, who made time for the young me, and never tired of the millions of questions I needed the answers to. I borrowed many books from his library, and his wise but gentle influence on me continues to this day.

The church and other places of learning outside of school begin to take over and yet comedy, whilst often falling foul of the Church through Spike Milligan and Monty Python, remains massive in my household. The conversations that I am having with Father Deryck Hanshell teach me further humility and calmness. He became a spiritual father to me, and I a spiritual son who was in much need of guidance.

I would often offload the contradictions that were building up around me.

'You wouldn't believe what I have got up to this week,' I would begin.

Upon finishing my litany of errors.

He would reply whilst never judging, 'Kenny, welcome to the human race.'

Father Claudio Rossi was another beautiful human being – gentle, strong-willed and knowledgeable. I feel his presence immediately when I think about him. And Father Peter O'Reilly, a soldier in the Second World War, was one of life's roughest diamonds but your archetypal parish priest, a man of great virtue and so kind to the poor and homeless.

But it was not just the people I looked up to who cast influence. I allowed the unknown in, too. So, when religious groups would come to the flat, I would invite them all in however big their party.

31

It has become standard fare to mock Jehovah's Witnesses coming up your path, but I would be meeting them halfway down the garden – much to Mum and Dad's irritation. Then, once I got them in, I would hit them with all the historical and theological inconsistencies I found in their teachings and leave them sweating when they couldn't provide me with the exact date for the end of the world.

I loved the debates, and believe me, you had to get up early to turn me! But at least hey, I kept them in so long they weren't knocking on your door at the crack of dawn with a pamphlet entitled 'Awake'.

I look at the Carmelites, an order in the Church with its roots stretching back to Old Testament days. I still have regular contact with that faith. At fifteen, I take myself to stay with Cistercian monks in Leicestershire for a few days. I am prepared to explore, to understand all religions and all possibilities.

The influences are so strong that I consider abandoning everything – including my music – and I begin to seriously consider entering a monastery. Later, after my pop chart career, a strong rumour circulates that this in fact did happen when the hits stopped. On neither occasion was this the case. I just realised that in fact I had two callings in life.

Philosophy needed a soundtrack. I took up the trumpet at school much to the delight of my parents and less so the neighbours on the estate.

In the process I am exploring music that is both in the mainstream and not, whilst expanding my search for truth. I both sought out and formed naturally great friendships with the priests which stand to this day with those who are still alive. These were pivotal moments.

Against the backdrop of my personal development and self-discovery, I suppose that every generation witnesses something similar to what happened next. Other influences come into your life through technology.

The arrival of the Sony Walkman was a game-changer.

Dave and I would plug our earphones into our identical Binatone portable cassette players, the only Walkman at the time with two earphone sockets. So, when his batteries died, he would plug into my machine for some more uninterrupted musical pleasure. We would each make tapes or chuck in one we had purchased and then listen on repeat. Stevie Wonder's 'Hotter than July' and anything by George Duke dominated. We had gone from blasting it out across the flat and the estate to sharing the intimacy of searing vocals and heart-wrenching soul music, but doing it together as best friends. The Walkman did that.

We both saw the posters going up for the new Earth, Wind & Fire album *Raise!,* and that became the longest two weeks of our lives waiting to hear 'Let's Groove' before obviously we knew it existed. Lovers rock – as it was called – was a massive genre of black music for a while, too. If a popular hit came out, within three weeks someone would have given it the lovers rock treatment. The influences were rich and everywhere.

Of course, we did also blast the music out, too – Mum and Dad owned an Alba stereo system. That meant we became obsessed with those long 12" records that they used to put out in the 1980s, adding minutes and huge instrumental sections to your favourite hit records, and learning every single word to what we thought were classics like 'Rappers' Delight' by the Sugarhill Gang, given to me on vinyl by my cousin Lee.

The Walkman, too, had a knock-on effect. Roller skating was massive in that decade, and roller skating *with* the Walkman – kids, look away now – was the coolest thing on the planet. Dave, Derrick, Bobby, Johnson, Tony and I would hit the road and skate all day. Later, we would be joined by James with a massive 'ghetto blaster' on his shoulder. Pumping out pure soul grooves, in search of the smoothest tarmac and the steepest hills, occasionally hanging dangerously onto the open back of the old Routemaster bus until the conductor lost his rag.

Music was driving everything and connecting me to an outside world which the advent of the CB radio – a classic 80s gimmick – only enhanced.

'Fourteen for a copy,' I would announce on Channel 14 to whoever was out there.

It turned out Bandit was.

My handle (name) was 'Stink Bomb'.

We would 'pick a window'. That means choose a channel and talk for hours.

'Bandit, do you copy?' I would say night after night until somehow I managed to bump into Bandit himself in South Tottenham on an 'eyeball' (meeting) with another guy called 'Tank'. At first, I didn't know who he was. After months of speaking to him on the CB radio I was expecting him to be some young white guy. Instead, he was much taller than me (most people were), older, too, and of Ghanaian descent.

This was James. We formed a solid friendship and from that moment on we, too, were inseparable alongside my relationship with Dave.

James and I dubbed ourselves 'The Terrible Twins'.

In those early teen years, electro music also arrived and with it, a body-popping explosion and a surge in breakdancing which meant all the lads on the estate would meet after school most nights and get some serious carpet burn!

We were stunned – speechless, in awe – when we saw the first moonwalk, credited to Michael Jackson around the release of the multi-selling *Thriller* album rumoured to be the first pop video to have over one million pounds spent on it with its *An American Werewolf in London* feel. But it was not Jacko who brought us the walk, it was Jeffrey Daniels from the band Shalamar, whom I was delighted to meet and share the stage with later on in life and who brought us this revolutionary new move. That *Thriller* release was the next game-changer. All of us on the estate waited every day for new music, but the anticipation counting down to this was worldwide.

Occasionally I will still do the odd bit of body-popping to amuse my kids. I enjoy seeing them laugh at me and my rusty moves which used to be cool 40 years ago. Somehow they know that their old man is not quite right in the head, but it is quality entertainment.

You have me, the young Kenny Thomas, there in a nutshell – truth-seeking and unlocking a spiritual awareness, growing up a Londoner but half-Spanish in a crimeridden but bond-forming and multicultural environment with survival instincts aplenty, discovering music and dancing through friends *and* technology and expressing it and the spoken word through, mimicry, roller skating and CB radio.

Oh, and the boxing, too!

By 1980, disaster struck with the fire at Ally Pally. Years of history gone, the future uncertain – memories ashen-stained in an instant. Dad and I were devastated – remember, the day after we returned from the Canaries, he had been back on his old stomping ground. From the ashes the phoenix rises, and nothing ever destroyed us for long. The gym area had to be moved into Palm Court and then eventually to the old BBC bar, part of their old studios. Just like my nan taking me down Holloway Road, that sense of nostalgia always beat a drum in my heart.

When it came to entering secondary school, I really did do something which everyone considered extraordinary. Almost all my friends made the obvious choice to transfer to the local Thomas More School in Wood Green. I wanted to challenge myself so split ranks, taking two bus journeys to Cardinal Pole, Hackney, where I would know nobody on day one except one other lad. My parents didn't stand in my way. They knew even then that I was my own person. Most nights, Mum would have to come in very late and tell me, 'Kenny, you need to go to sleep now, you can't stay up reading all night.'

I had books sprawled across the bed, flitting from one to another reading huge amounts of philosophy and theology: I couldn't get enough of it. I wanted to acquire knowledge of as many subjects as possible. I realised that the mind was able to store as much information as you were prepared to throw at it. As odd as it seemed, they respected that.

On holiday in Bude, Cornwall, at the age of twelve we were camping near a religious group. Making fleeting friends on such a trip, suddenly the group broke up when some of the kids announced that they had to go off for a community meeting in one of the tents.

They kept saying to me phrases like 'now since we know the truth' and since that was all I wanted to understand, I became interested. At every kick-about, I kept asking myself *what* they knew. But I also felt something was not right as if they had been sold *a* truth, if not the definitive absolute one. They attempted to get my sister and me to take some of their books and suggested that we should all meet up back in London after the holiday so they could tell us more about 'their truth'. My dad was having none of it. The children seemed very indoctrinated – almost cult-like. I just took them at their word, but it left a lasting effect on me. How, at the same age as me, did they think that they had arrived at all the answers?

I became even more focused – on a mission. There were only two roads ahead – one good and one bad. A quick fix with instant gratification versus a tougher one.

What was the truth in *everything* – philosophically, theologically and politically? And in any other way I had not yet had the life experience to consider.

I knew life was transient and short-lived but what was the order of the universe? Or on an even deeper level *who* was? I consumed more and more books whilst understanding that in effect I was living two lives – street versus Church. On the horizon the superficial nature of much of pop, which I loved but in time came to feel a little uncomfortable with, was running headlong into my beliefs and desire for answers. Yet the two would have to sit side by side. They defined me.

When I look back now and reflect, this encounter was a massive turning point. The truth is that the questions were mounting, and my reaction and overanalysis of this group was just the end of a big build-up of similar thoughts. They didn't teach me anything new. Their significance really serves only to confirm that there was an end of the line – an actual objective truth. They knew it. Or so they told me. I was still searching.

It wasn't just that holiday which was an eye-opener. Returning home brought *home* the hierarchy, tyranny and codes of a complicated estate like ours.

Our flat had been burgled.

The attempted robbery was interrupted by George Irving. Two guys menacingly and swiftly exited the building both holding large knives. George quickly got out of the way, managing to avoid being seen and therefore any form of confrontation.

The reality was stark: we avoided coming back to a house clearance. Every bit of furniture, white goods and all of our personal possessions were lined up and ready to go.

But everyone knew. Everyone knew who. And then I knew.

Code and betrayal.

Nobody grassed.

They got in with the keys.

There had been one spare set in my sister's bedroom, casually swiped before we left. The premeditation and planning kill you. Then the acceptance of being able to do nothing about it stays with you forever. You learn to live with it, but it sits on your shoulder. Only recently and therefore many years later I ran into the person who took the keys. I just gave them a hug!

You may well wonder how much of this rubs off on you – obviously I was on the Canarian Most Wanted for theft of lollies in Las Palmas, and bad habits never die! So I do confess to pinching the odd Duracell from Woolworths *but* only in aid of the very needy cause. Dave and I had to keep our Walkmans going. The Artful Dodger in me was short-lived – one of Mum's friends from church, who worked in Woolies, told her. A telling-off was duly administered and my days of light-fingered theft came to an end. One good thing was that my mum never told my dad about this.

She wasn't a grass either.

Crime was always in our midst. I became accustomed to seeing knives but not carrying one. Seeing a gun in someone's flat was both scary and a natural progression of what was going on. In such an environment, the line was being crossed all the time. I also saw the huge scorch mark on one of the guys' heads the day after a 'drug-fuelled' game of Russian roulette with the blank round skimming him. Even empties can do a lot of damage.

But my childhood *was* normal. I always stuck to my mum and dad's moral code, if exploring my own thought-process and Dad's work ethic.

Industrial since the age of sixteen, he was nothing but a grafter, and good at it. When I went on to have hits, that never left me. I would often sneak off from record company duties and go to help a mate do up a house.

Morals should be consistent; thoughts are entitled to change and should. Dad always told me to tell the truth even if gets you into trouble, and generally if I haven't, it has gone wrong. Tell a lie, he would say, and you can't keep up with it.

Yet, of course, people are defined by their actions, and he was true to his word. I vividly recall him tracking down a man who owed him a few grand and being told that he had no way of paying Dad back.

'I don't even have a pound note in my pocket right now,' he said.

'You can't go around with no money in your pocket, that's not good,' Dad replied, abandoning the debt, and then he reached into his own pocket to give him something.

That was Dad all over.

He could be tough, too. I set a bush up in flames on the eve of my twelfth birthday. Three fire engines burst onto the scene to put it out before it could set all the cars directly next to it on fire. Dad gave me a hiding. No presents the next day. There were consequences for your actions.

We would camp out on the allotments behind the estate and make racing karts from scratch, each of us trying to take the other out, with one kid making some *Ben-Hur*-type contraption with perilous nails and spikes sticking out of it. Dad was not impressed with that – 'madness!' and 'dangerous!' he yelled.

Dave Sassoon attended the Victoria Club, a Jewish youth organisation on Egerton Road. He really wanted me to come there with him, but there was one small problem, which he overcame by renaming me Kenny Goldberg! I knew enough about the Jewish faith and when I wore a kippah I looked the part and pulled it off. We had some great times there. Many of the friends I made at the Victoria Club were very surprised years later to learn that I was not actually Jewish after all. One of them still insists to this day that indeed 'Kenny is Jew-ish'.

By thirteen, I had my first Saturday job at my Uncle Leslie's car showroom on York Way, King's Cross. I loved working for Les. He was a good man with a good heart, plus I got the chance to sit in the driving seat of the E-Type Jaguar he had on show.

Then later I began working in a garage for an old guy who lived in Tottenham and had been a car mechanic for years, and I guessed I would learn a trick or two for the days ahead when I could own my own vehicle.

I worked alongside a very violent, rough lad, who was around fourteen years old. He was from a completely dysfunctional background. His rhetoric was constantly aimed at his obsessive desire to kill someone and not in a throwaway tone. It was the mainstay of his conversation and he meant it.

I don't think I was in any way ignorant of the pitfalls of life at this point but obviously I had a lot to learn, and the old guy took my naivety on by announcing that the following weekend he wanted the violent lad and me to work at his house and not at the garage.

The following Saturday I turned up and grafted hard, moving loads of junk and car parts out of his garden with the other lad. Towards the end of the day during one of the tea breaks the old guy revealed to me that he and the other lad had a sexual relationship going on and that they both wondered if I was interested in joining in.

'That's not my thing,' I told him.

'You guys crack on, good luck,' I told them.

And I left.

On the way out he tried more than once to touch me on my crotch, but I swiftly dodged it and pushed him back.

Whatever he was thinking, I only had one thing on my mind – you're going to get sorted.

Within minutes of returning home, Dad was marching straight back out of the house again, into his car and tore round to the guy's house. I remember Dad holding him by the throat, off the ground, pinned up against the wall. The rest of it I will leave to your imagination.

His actions have nothing to do with his ability to fight and the years at the boxing gym. He simply had a sense of old-school justice about him. Undoubtedly the most fearless man I have ever known. Just like the guys at the flat, he took them on because he felt a two-versus-one scenario was simply unfair. This had everything to do with justice, and today I often see Dad when I look in the mirror. But the boxing probably saved him from a certain death in the Korean War. He grew up with National Service compulsory and being part of the Army boxing team, he narrowly avoided being sent and condemned there. At the time he was stationed at the Tower of London in the Royal Fusiliers (City of London Regiment). He vividly recalled the Kray Twins looking down from the top of the moat jeering at him. Dad had been a PTI (Physical Training Instructor) in the Army and was training other soldiers in the moat at the time.

He was a great wind-up merchant, too – especially to Mum, who would always bite. If you mispronounced a word, he would repeat it for fun and leap onto all the little nuances. At the gym as the matchmaker for all potential boxers he would forever pull their leg. One lad, who had been battered in a really tough bout, was so put off by it that he avoided the gym for weeks. Eventually he came back in to see my dad.

'I've been thinking about quitting,' the young fighter confessed. 'But I am going to carry on.'

'That's great,' Dad replied, 'because I've got some good news for you.'

'Really, Ken, what is it?' he asked.

'I've got you a rematch.'

The kid never returned.

He had also suffered and at divorce hearings in the 1950s to his first wife, he won both the case and custody in a verdict that was extremely rare then – namely that he had suffered mental cruelty and was therefore damaged and emotionally wounded in the relationship.

I was very much aware of the contradictions in my world. My spirituality was already a massive part of who I was. Yet, on my doorstep lay the underworld that I learned to turn a blind eye to. It's what you did – old-school London with its morals and codes. It was exactly that – secrets where truths were implied and not spoken of, morals where you didn't grass and go to the police… where there was nothing worse than a grass and you took what you knew to the grave.

At school, too – where aside from the Church you might hope you had the best shot at the answers to the truth – I began to dismantle the narrative. In time, I would only remember the teachers I recalled fondly and once resorted to avoiding the strict wrath of the Maths teacher by setting off the fire alarm on the way to class because I didn't have the completed homework in hand, causing an evacuation in the process. I soon worked out what was essential and what was hot air. 1066 taught me a lesson. Every schoolchild back then was learning about it. I could see its irrelevance bar one lasting value. I worked out pretty sharply that history was often written by the winners.

I therefore realised what could largely be discarded in life. Biology, for example, irritated me. I found it incredulous that evolution, a theory, was passed off as scientific fact, and that the teacher had no answers for my questions. Surely the teacher must have been fascinated by it once in her life to study it. Quite likely at university she conducted her own special area of research for which she had a passion. Now she was just trotting it out. I concluded that for the most part human beings are not happy with a mystery, uncomfortable with the unknown or that which cannot be fully known. They want all the answers and they want them now.

I knew, too, that many teachers had in fact just never left school. They attended then went back to teach churning the same narrative that they were fed. Many wouldn't survive on my streets.

I was soon understanding that Catholicism was one of the religions that truly analysed itself, where critical thinking *is* encouraged. Sociology did draw me in but generally I realised that school was not going to teach me the things I wanted to know and that the only way in which I would learn about life was to hang out with older people who had experienced a bit of it and were not serving up the same agenda from the curriculum.

I just about went along with it but educated myself at home – by the age of fourteen reading up on The Illuminati, the Alta Vendita Lodge of the Italian Carbonari movement, and various other secret societies. I got hooked on Darwinism and *The Origin of Species*, devouring an eight-hour set of lectures that scientifically destroyed his theory on a number of levels, especially genetic entropy, whilst exposing the underlying racist eugenics that flow from it. The actual title of Darwin's book, forgotten now by many, is *On the Origin of Species by Means of Natural Selection, or the Preservation of Favoured Races in the Struggle for Life*. I always had a problem with the 'favoured races' part. A book written by a white English man, published in 1859, when slavery had only been abolished in the UK some 26 years earlier. Something was inherently wrong with this title and the mindset of the man it came from. The idea of 'favoured races' is the very thing that led Darwin's cousin Francis Galton to coin the word *eugenics* to describe efforts at 'race betterment'. These erroneous ideas end up only with division and wars. I was having none of it.

When it came to O-Levels – perceived as the standard – school sent home a letter to my parents saying that I might not do so well unless I knuckled down, preparing them for the worst.

So, in effect, I made a mockery of the whole thing because I simply went round to my friends Eric and Steve who were performing slightly better and were happy to lend me their coursework.

Three months of pooling notes meant that I walked away with seven O-Levels and, despite my certainty that beyond the need for Maths and a passion for poetry this was all a bit of a waste of time... I still went back for more.

You will notice that at no point do I express the sentiment that I lived for my musical classes during my education. You may wonder, too, why I even went into the Sixth Form, albeit for just a brief time. The latter provided structure whilst I didn't really know what my next step was in the real world where you earned money. The former bored me to tears.

Music at school was a nonsense – steeped in theory and classical pieces, and without relevance to what had taken root in my soul. I already knew that I wanted to be a writer of songs. Buying and swapping new music plus discovering the previous decades and idols like Donny Hathaway were my course content. My tutors were my circle of friends, David Sassoon, Derrick Woods and James Williams-Baffoe, especially Derrick who was older than me and had a vast knowledge of soul, funk and reggae. Through him, we had access to the music of the past and his finger was always on the pulse of the present. Derrick's elder brother Keith introduced me to Dubwise, bands like Black Uhuru, King Tubby, Scientist, Mad Professor. These were the Reggae Sunsplash days, where Gregory Isaacs, Sugar Minott, Eek-A-Mouse and Yellowman reigned supreme in the dance hall, often with Sly and Robbie providing the rhythm and production. I went often with Keith and Derrick to a blues party; my entry was allowed only because I was with them. The sound system would be kicking, and various guys would get on the mic and throw down some serious toasting and chatting.

Another big influence on me would come in my early teens when I spent many a weekend for sleepovers at the home of the Sharma family in Hornsey, North London. Sanjay was a friend of mine from my dad's boxing club and a handy fighter he was, too. I loved spending time there, plus I had my eye on the girl who lived next door to them, hoping she would be my first girlfriend. That never happened, but the thought of it kept me motivated. Sanjay and his friend Lawrence, another boxer, were into their soul music and had a great collection of vinyl. It was here that I discovered for the first time The Whispers, Michael Jackson's *Off the Wall,* and records like *Back Together Again* by Roberta Flack and Donny Hathaway. They also introduced me to more jazz-funk, Narada Michael Walden, 'Dancing in Outer Space' by Atmosfear, and the Brit funk artists Light of The World, Begger and Co, Central Line and Freeez. This was a great place to be with beautiful people, the best Indian food and new musical discoveries. Sanjay and I would eventually lose touch when he stopped boxing and knuckled down into his studies. It is a good job he did, though, because he is now one of the UK's leading Professors of Cardiology. In recent years we have made contact again. I got to meet his wife and daughters and he even wired me up and stuck me on the treadmill to check out the old ticker.

At fourteen I learned to drive. John Harris, my cousin Barbara's husband, would pick me up from my nan's in his Mini and we would head off to an empty industrial estate. There I learned how to skid and perfect a wheel spin. John also got right into CB radio and adorned his car with a big mag mount antenna and off we went with James to CB fairs, engaging in eyeballs and convoys.

The 80s were such a great decade.

The disc jockeys on BBC Radio London and naturally the many illegal pirate stations around the capital at the time all provided a steady flow of new sounds. Radio London was an extraordinary station. It was the BBC *local* station for the city, but it bore no resemblance to any other aspect of BBC local radio with its lost dogs and gardening phone-ins. At the helm was Tony Blackburn, fulfilling his passion for soul music having played in the mainstream and public eye for so many years. Alongside him was Robbie Vincent who would work for them during the week and at the weekend would take his big box of records onto the biggest radio station of the day – BBC Radio 1.

It jarred with everything that national network was putting out prime time in the week with its *Top of the Pops* image in tow, but for me, for us, for our estate, there was a now legitimate platform for what was already going on in the clubs and might sometimes take months to cross over into a hit. It was Robbie whose jingle said, 'If It Moves Funk It' – so we did.

With our ears close to the ground and tuned into the scene there was no getting away from the fact that there were certain DJs who were well ahead of their time, and no one more ahead of all of them than DJ Froggy. He was the first person in the UK to own a pair of the now legendary Technics SL-1200MK2 turntables. He knew his soul music and he knew where the scene was heading. He worked both at Radio 1 in the late 1980s and Capital Radio on a Saturday night with 'The Froggy Mix'. Steven Howlett aka DJ Froggy … a DJ legend RIP.

Suddenly we were hearing music months before anyone and anywhere else, and we were overjoyed to see an underground record that we knew break into the charts. In the early 80s I observed the New Romantics. I had watched punk from afar. Mainstream radio served up a diet of 'white' music, but I couldn't help be drawn to the soul and its various guises towards the end of the decade, that moved beyond body-popping, the electro sound, and began to embrace Marshall Jefferson, Frankie Knuckles and Steve 'Silk' Hurley, from the Chicago house scene. That genre was captivating. A game-changer. For a while, imitating the scissor movements of jacking our bodies was the latest obsession. I even injured my left knee in the process. I shouldn't even have been in clubs but had been going since 1983 when a nod and a wink to 'friendly' doormen got me in well underage.

From here, I started to understand about sampling. Almost every song on the radio for a time seemed to be borrowing influences and chunks of other hits.

In some form it was always 'soul' music for me. The day Nat King Cole passed away is one Mum always told me about. She loved him, too, as he had sung many songs in Spanish, as did Matt Monro, but there were tears in my mum's house that day. I knew instantly why. The best singers were so from the heart, and it resonated a spiritual tie-in. I felt it was music in its purest form.

By the time I came to writing down pop lyrics and then reproducing them vocally, a soulful-sounding voice unsurprisingly emerged from within. But I became encyclopaedic

– almost trainspotting, too – cross-referencing producers, drummers and bass players, logging the lot.

I am often asked where I got my voice from. Although Mum had a lovely singing voice and often sang Spanish songs to me as a child, I would have to say it primarily came from my dad. I remember him singing some of the old crooner songs in the bathroom and on the building site, and the tone of his voice is the same one I have today, even more so as I have grown older. I am sure he could have been a singer had he had the inclination and the opportunity, but his first love was boxing.

It wasn't just music radio, the club scene, or the influences of the estate. London had a speech station (which is now national) called LBC, which I listened to with Dad. The spoken word and conversation were also very important and a form of learning. The dial was a lot less congested then – it was Capital, Kiss as a legal or pirate, Horizon, Solar, LWR, BBC London before it became GLR and then LBC. For the latter, the average man in the street had a voice. It was CB radio but less of a cult.

I was also given four TDK cassette tapes entitled *Proofs of a Conspiracy* by someone at a convention I attended. I don't think anybody else was doing this at my age! Their narrative left me speechless. They outline what would happen in the next 40 or 50 years on the planet such as the deliberate break-up of the nuclear family, the relationship of the West versus the radical religious ideologies of the Middle East and, of course, wars, economic crashes, false flag events, Masonic globalism and ultimately the imposition of a New World Order, a Socialist police state, leading to political tyranny and quite possibly World War Three. Heavy stuff!

Almost everything they predicted has happened.

There was, of course, a long way to go. I couldn't write a song. I didn't have a clue how to get into the business – and I was still going through with the notion that, to satisfy society, A-Levels needed to be completed, even though I can vividly recall being around my friends' houses, feeling locked in the system and thinking that this was just not going to go anywhere. *This* kind of education was not for me.

The only thing that I knew for certain was that I wanted to be in music. In whatever capacity, I didn't know. Making it, being around it, I wasn't sure. Some of my older friends started going to 'Soul Weekenders' and were privileged to go to a club called Crackers, on Dean Street, London. They told me all about the soul and jazz-funk scene and this only further stirred up my imagination and made my gradual introduction to clubbing inevitable.

Dougies nightclub in Clapton, All Nations in London Fields and The Four Aces on Dalston Lane were local to me, so they were a good starting point. Then came 100 Club, Le Beat Route, Websters in Tottenham, swiftly followed by Camden Palace, Café de Paris, The Wag, The Hippodrome, Limelight and Legends. This was where my friends and I cut our teeth, so to speak, in preparation for what was to come, as we made our way into the 90s.

DJs themselves were starting to become as important as the tracks they were playing. I was blown away by the skill and timing of it. It all morphed into the epic main room at the Ministry of Sound by the early 90s. I couldn't have known or dreamed that venues I frequented would end up hosting me.

It didn't take long for the penny to drop in the Sixth Form. One day, I simply walked out and never went back. How many times have I heard the saying, 'School, the best days of your life'? Complete rubbish! I hated that place. The best *day* of my life was when I stepped out of those gates for the last time. I would get my life skills elsewhere.

I like to think nowadays that I got my education from the 'University of Experience' where the only way to learn is the hard way.

I also had my first serious girlfriend, Barbara. You may not be surprised that the middleman who introduced us was one of the Jesuit priests, Father Claudio Rossi. Things were going well with Barbara until we had our first couple of teenage tiffs and her mother banned me from the house. Not one to be deterred by the ban I waited at night until I knew her mum and dad were asleep. I then climbed up the drainpipe and in through her bedroom window. Risky stuff! Out of a movie!

The problem back then was that if you told me I was not allowed to do something, I became even more determined to do it. This works only until you get caught. The ban was eventually lifted and a normal service resumed. We stayed together for a few years, but in the end, it was my sister Sandra who ended up marrying her brother David!

David became a massive musical influence on me and introduced me to the much deeper levels of jazz fusion in artistes like Herbie Hancock, Weather Report, Chick Corea, Stanley Clarke and gospel music from the likes of Eddie Holman, whom I would later gig with. We would often visit his friend Brian Buchanan, a champion bodybuilder, and spend hours listening to this kind of music. It was a real education for me, introducing me to a deeper level of jazz fusion.

When, many years later, I was lucky enough to meet Herbie out in LA, I got him to sign an autograph for David. A small way of saying thank you for introducing me to the music of a genius.

Within two months of storming out of education, I was working – as a first-grade bank clerk mostly distributing the post at the Williams & Glyn's Bank, St Mary Axe, situated in the Baltic Exchange. The first day I walked in with absolute shiner from a boxing match. A black eye was not a good look for the front desk of a City bank, so they felt they had better start me off in the post room!

That meant I got to know everyone. In truth, I really enjoyed my first taste of working life, but I also knew that I was still inside some sort of restrictive system, an institution, not too dissimilar to school.

I didn't last long. Somebody picked on me at an office party, and I had a go back at them, over-delivering with an attempted punch straight out of Dad's gym. It was a rare occasion when those instincts manifested themselves outside of that environment. I had so much energy back then that I didn't know what to do with it. Boxing taught me discipline, not ill discipline, and how both to win and to be a good loser. Not on this occasion. The manager called me in. I had to endure the

49

banking disciplinary procedure and was put on six months' probation.

I did stay on for a while and then handed in my notice. In truth it helped me – I soon realised that this was not where I wanted to be at all. I was just passing time.

I still needed to work obviously, and almost blindly found myself in no time at all working at an accountancy firm next to Smithfield Market near Farringdon Station in London.

I knew already that I had to be wary of not falling into something for the sake of it and it then becoming the status quo and therefore overrunning in my life. This job outstayed its welcome immediately!

So, I rang Norman Saxon, a close friend of mine since the age of sixteen, whom I also met via Fr Rossi's introductions, and undoubtedly one of the most intellectual people I have ever met. He created the opening for me.

Just like Dave Sassoon he was a soulmate – if not the same sort of soul man – and we would talk philosophy and theology, dogma and doctrine, Thomas Merton and Jimi Hendrix, for hours and equally not at all at times.

'Do I have to work here, Norm?' I asked him.

'It's your job,' he replied matter-of-factly.

'What is to stop me leaving?'

'Have you signed a contract with them yet?' he enquired.

That was that.

'Anyone want anything from the shops?' I asked one lunchtime.

And got up and walked out.

Never to return.

I was home by the time they called, and I told Mum to tell them that I wasn't coming back.

They were not happy, but neither was I.

That's why I left.

I had no intention of going back there to work off my two weeks' notice.

'But he's owed wages,' someone in HR protested.

I told Mum to tell them that they could keep it.

Employment and I were not going too well.

Next, I took a temporary job for some weeks at the Wellcome Institute in Euston where I used to have to go down to the vaults of the building which stored thousands of books and bodyparts, preservered in formaldehyde, of people who had died from unexplained tropical diseases! Often I would spend my lunch hour down there walking around eating my sandwiches and studying the cadavers. The human body fascinated me – a work of art right there.

I didn't last long at Butonia either – the biggest button company going. Any button on any garment in the UK probably came from there. After sticking this one out for two months, I couldn't take another button. And they were paying buttons, too. So once again, in my own unique but unorthodox style, I walked out of there one lunchtime, too, jumped onto the Number 76 bus taking me back to Stamford Hill, never to return again to the world of buttons.

It served as a focus – a reminder that I was only doing this to just about pay my way until I could break into the music business.

Around this time Dad temporally lost his mind. Well, that was Mum's opinion, when he decided that he was going to take up skydiving. In his mid-fifties by then, I guess he wanted to have one last go at recapturing his old airborne Army days while he was still young enough to do so and mad enough to do it. He duly signed up at the A1 Skydiving Centre in Huntingdon along with one of the other lads from the boxing gym, did his aerial training and he was off. Every weekend he would set off for Huntingdon and we would spend the day nervously waiting for a phone call from him to say that the parachute had opened, and he had made it safely back to earth.

On one occasion my friend Steve (Muttsy) was over at our flat on the estate, and Dad was telling us about the wonderful experience of the moment the chute opens and you are up there enjoying the view. Dad then went on to ask us if we had the courage to do a parachute jump. Of course, without hesitation and driven by our young egos we responded with an absolute, 'Yes, no problem, we could do that with our eyes shut.'

51

'OK,' he replied. 'Then I will pay for you both to do the training and we can all do a jump together.'

That was it: Steve and I had been viciously coerced and led into one of Dad's traps. Pride was not about to let me and Muttsy back out of it now. Dad booked us in and a couple of weeks later we went with him to the centre, did a day's training and the following day would ascend 2000 feet into the atmosphere in a cramped Cessna aircraft and hopefully not plunge to a certain death. On the day of the jump, to say that Steve and I looked a little green-coloured was an understatement. It was nerve-racking. On the way to the aircraft, Steve revealed to me that he had never been in an aeroplane before. I turned to him and said, 'Are you telling me that you've never been in a plane before, and the first one you're getting into you're going to jump out of it?... Muttsy, that is insane.'

We took off; it was noisy and there was not another word uttered from Steve or me for fear of vomiting. Dad had a nice little grin on the go, enjoying every second of our suffering and misery. At 2000 feet we circled for what seemed like an eternity and then Dad shuffled towards the small open door. He was given the signal to go and as he jumped out you could faintly hear him shout 'Geronimo!' What a nutter. Steve was slowly dragged to the opening and most impressively threw himself out, hoping the universe was on his side that day. I was last to go, sitting there with my feet hanging out of an aeroplane, and my first time was something that I will never forget. One last quick *act of contrition just in case* I was about to meet my maker, and I was out. 1000, 2000, 3000, check... I looked up and there it was, my parachute had opened and all was well. The view was, as Dad had forewarned, amazing! Or should I say 'Outstanding'.

I made it back to terra firma, not very far from the huge X on the ground, right in the drop zone. Dad and Steve were nowhere to be seen as the wind had caught them and, much to my amusement, they had landed a mile away in a cornfield.

It remains one of the best things I did with Dad.

My dream of music, however, was proving a distraction but not yet a reality. Dave Sassoon's dad, Freddie, was a very connected guy with a lot of rhythm about him. I often spent as much time talking to Freddie as Dave, and I recognised early on that he had a good lyric in him.

One day at Myra's house, I had found the courage to tell him that I really wanted to make a record and I loved singing.

He asked me to sing to him right there… in Myra's kitchen…

Then there was a light bulb moment.

'You come with me,' he took charge. 'We will go somewhere tonight.'

And that somewhere was Stoke Newington. To the studio of the world-famous Guyanese-British musician Eddy Grant, former band member of The Equals.

Freddie knocked on the door of Coach House Studios on Osbaldeston Road.

It was the coldest of cold winter nights.

No answer.

We would try again tomorrow.

Walking there again on another bitterly cold night.

We knocked once more. The door was partially ajar.

We crept in only to be greeted by Patrick, Eddy's brother.

'You gotta hear this kid's voice,' Freddie announced. 'We have got to make a record with him.'

So, we did.

9 *A Whiter Shade of Fail*

We had finally left the estate – saying goodbye but not farewell to an enormous chunk of our lives and the cultures that it provided, good or bad. The flats were condemned. The damp, decrepit buildings were so poor that, even though Dad offered to do the flat up himself, he was told not to touch it. This particular part of London was closing.

Removed from that situation now – my goodness, it was the right thing to do. At the time there was a lot of good in that upbringing, albeit always keeping your wits about you. I was sad to leave but everyone had to go. Next stop was Springfield in Clapton, Hackney, about ten to fifteen minutes away – unsurprisingly a slightly nicer part of town altogether, though temporarily devastated by the hurricane of 1987, leaving many of the huge trees in the neighbourhood uprooted and their branches landing in the nearby park.

The same afternoon that I had called Norman and marched off home, I was back working again! Of course, it was again not my dream job, and it actually exemplified the bullshit of industry before I saw it full on in the music biz.

I called Keystone Employment Agency in King's Cross, and they spoke to a company called Auto Magic. Remarkably, they informed me that they were looking for someone like me. It did sound a lot more exciting, but anything had to be better than a job you had barely survived a fortnight in. They asked me to do an interview that day – not that they were desperate or anything. So, I filled the form in and hammed up my CV, upped my previous salary by a grand, and when we got on like a house on fire, they told me they would love to have me on-board and offered me the job there and then. They were a young firm and, even though it was clearly not what I wanted to do, it suited me and I was relatively happy. Of course, in the office I was singing all the time and constantly mimicking the songs on the radio, and they would ask me to do just that. It was as though things were building, where in reality it was only so in my head.

One evening at the Eddy Grant's studio Patrick invited Eddy into the session to take a listen to the songs we had done. Eddy listened attentively and when the songs ended, he turned to me and said, 'You got a very good pop voice.' That would do for me.

I cut two songs.

The first was 'I Wanna Make Love to You Baby', the second 'In My Arms'. I realise of course that the first one is a terrible title, but Freddie did love the ladies! I wanted 'In My Arms' to be the single, but Freddie, having been the person to coin the title of the other song, made sure the cheesy 'I Wanna Make Love to You Baby' became the debut track. We had done the artwork, too, for a single – the front cover was both of the moment and a bit naff. I stood there in a suit wearing a polo neck with two earrings. The shots were taken in Dougies nightclub.

I was at an impasse. Going through the motions at a job where the people were fun, but the fun was non-existent, and then desperately hoping and believing that because I had cut a record and had done so at Eddy Grant's studio that I might just possibly be on the brink … and could walk between two stools and go for it full-time.

I needed some divine intervention.

Patrick Grant took me to meet Matthew Fisher from Procol Harum, the band of that haunting organ on the 1967 hit *A Whiter Shade of Pale*. Well, to my utter disbelief, he agreed to skip the light fandango and do the master edit on the demos. I was delighted and extremely happy to meet someone from such a legendary 1960s band.

He was not just a one-trick pony, though – even though many people will struggle to name many of the band's other hits, his versatility shone through with his work with the soulful New Edition, most famous for the hit 'Candy Girl'. The disc for this was clearly on display on the wall of his home, which is where we went to drop off our masters.

But of course – and I say that years on, having experienced this so many times now – when they heard the demo, they did think I was black.

55

Patrick took the recordings to David Kassner, the son of Edward Kassner, the owner of President Records. The same label Eddy Grant's former band The Equals were signed to in the 1960s. David Kassner heard the songs and simply said, 'Let's do it, let's release them.'

So, we did.

Looking back now, I had done nothing – except experience a recording studio for the first time under the tutelage of somebody related to one of the true greats. I wasn't lost in the dream, but I was tottering between belief and potential *and* the reality that, whilst I had started, I hadn't got anywhere at all.

There was a lot that we did wrong. That cover photo for that first release was too cheesy.

Dad was a great leveller – patient whilst I hoped for something to happen, but also providing the reality check when I had walked out of my third job at Auto Magic and the money was running out, leaving me to become a drain on the home.

There is simply a lot of waiting round whilst you are trying to make it. And you do need a bit of luck and favours. I had *never* personally sent a single demo to a record company. I was being totally led by self-belief, but also that of Freddie Sassoon.

There is no doubt that I was excited at hearing my voice back on a recording – actually for the very first time. I was far from a professional but gaining any experience was vital. I had begun to write a cappella and brought in the odd musician, but it was very early days. Of course, at the time you think this is it. On reflection, you realise how green you were.

I sang once or twice in a club and that 'This Is It' feeling swelled. I felt I was gathering momentum and building reputation. The vibe was good but of course that does not equate to radio play and sales. It was, at least, a start. In the moment, because you *are* progressing, it is very easy to think you are on the cusp of something. The reality is probably that I was on the cusp of the cusp.

For whatever reasons – quality, lack of marketing, being unknown, disinterest from radio – the two songs never even had a chance to bomb. I had gained little experience. I had cut a record. But I remained back at square one. Inexperienced.

I did have the self-awareness to know that I was chipping away. I didn't realise that I was banging my head against a brick wall. Nothing could take away the feeling, though, of handing my first vinyl to my mum and nan – despite its title!

What I understand now is that President Records did not have a clue either – no idea how to promote it and way behind the ball game. They didn't press enough copies, and despite the club scene, I genuinely don't think anyone played it on the radio. I can look for excuses now. At the time, I thought not to wallow or chase it. I somehow realised it was not going to happen.

I must keep busy, I told myself. *Now* was not the moment.

And I did keep busy in many ways. Every other weekend I was away with the Territorial Army. Good character-building stuff! Infantry training, tactical combat, section assault, survival skills, map-reading and first aid, very quickly building up my stamina and fitness to a whole new level. I spent time in Aldershot, Winchester, Woolwich and Pirbright, learned how to use various weapons, like the SLR rifle, the General-Purpose Machine Gun (The Gimpy) and the SA80 rifle, which was being introduced at the time. I marched across Salisbury Plain in the coldest winter, slept in trenches, crawled on my stomach through fields of sheep excrement and pushed myself far beyond what I thought I was capable of, and I met some of the nicest but hardest blokes I have ever known. All in all, this was a great experience, but it wasn't a career move.

Meanwhile, back on Civvy Street, part of me knew that I had to network, even though it was not my instinct to falsify myself in a fake way to advance my career. But of course, I needed to work, too, because this wasn't *working*. Hence Dad's words. So, I did network.

The BT network!

I took a job on at 125 Shaftesbury Avenue in a massive office just to tick over. It was a big place with lots of great people. I enjoyed that space… But of course, I, too, was waiting for that phone to ring.

10 Let There Be House

It is now the end of 1988. I am growing up fast and a little out of control. Music dominates so much of my life without me being in it. I am introduced to the house scene at a night called *Enter The Dragon* at the Park in Kensington. Meanwhile, other friends of mine are throwing shapes on the dance floor at Shoom where DJ Danny Rampling is banging out the latest underground sounds and the UK embraces its second Summer of Love. House music and more specifically acid house are on the rise, and the latter is beginning to cross over into the mainstream. I am well aware of it before it becomes the soundtrack to the end of this decade. Acts like Luther Vandross, Cameo, Cashflow and Anita Baker were my stars of that period, but they would have to concede some of their chart positions for the up and coming artistes of the rave culture. 1988 and 1989 were the equivalent of my parents' 1967!

If you know your music, you will know that 67 was a massive year – indeed Procol Harum's *A Whiter Shade of Pale* was part of that soundtrack. It was also Flower Power, San Francisco, the Summer of Love and drugs.

The house music scene certainly mirrored the latter.

Dad started working on the house of a guy named Barry Stoller who lived not far from us towards Stamford Hill. Barry wrote the famous *Match of the Day* theme tune. He wanted a studio built in the basement of his house and Dad asked me to help him with this. It was messy work, but I enjoyed seeing it coming together from start to finish. Barry became a good family friend and it was he who introduced me to his friend, the psychic Bettina Luxon.

She invited me over for a cup of tea one evening.

I was curious rather than sold on the idea.

'If it's anything like my past, I don't want to know my future,' I began sceptically.

She insisted on giving me a so-called reading. Something a good Catholic boy would never normally entertain. However, curiosity has always been a weakness of mine.

'I see gold discs on the wall,' she claimed.

Well, this wasn't a big revelation as I was working with Barry who happened to be a record producer. Getting a gold disc in my lifetime was a long shot but not beyond the realms of possibility.

'And I see a place with a lighthouse.'

That could have been Puerto de la Luz, where my relatives live, or anywhere in Maspalomas in the Canaries. Or nowhere at all.

I had actually bought a one-way ticket to the Canaries! I wanted adventure and my plan was to achieve what Dad had been unable to do.

I didn't go – not until years later anyway.

'There are going to be some people in your future who are not good – steer clear,' she concluded.

But that could apply to anyone and everyone.

It was apparent that she claimed to know only the futureand if she had been one of those who contacted the dead, I wouldn't have gone at all. That is an absolute no-no for me. Leave the dead to rest in peace, focus on the living. After all, they are the ones to be most wary of.

The experience was interesting, but not my cup of tea. I figured I would just let life unfold and find out things as they happened.

By day, my new boss Peter at BT was both goading and reminding me that I hadn't yet made it – 'When are we going to see you on *Top of the Pops*?' he would frequently ask. One morning he came in to work and said, 'I saw you standing by Leicester Square station about half an hour ago and I thought you were one of the New Kids on the Block.'

Boom boom! I absorbed it all jokingly, but I knew somehow, one day, I would have the last laugh.

He was also a Freemason, and we would get into discussions that led nowhere because of his vow of silence. What really got to him was when I began reading a book by Walton

Hannah called *Darkness Visible*. This book is a superb exposé of Masonic beliefs and rituals, and reveals things the ordinary person would not normally know. Dad was a wind-up merchant, and as the apple doesn't fall far from the tree I am also fond of the same, so some days I would take a photocopy of images from the book, stuff that was top secret, and leave it on his desk before he arrived. This went down like a lead balloon, but he took it well. In all honesty I liked him and it was mutual. Despite our differences he will always be one of the best bosses I had in the 9 to 5 sphere.

But at night, I was always out as the game changed. Suddenly I was not going to clubs anymore but listening to illegal pirate radio for coded instructions to the location of a rave. There was no Facebook back then, kids.

Once you had heard the meeting place (usually King's Cross) you would turn up there, and then someone in the know would reveal the actual venue. At first, a massive field somewhere with a big sound system, and later on warehouses and then we would dance until the sun came up, hoping to avoid any interruptions from the Old Bill. At one warehouse rave, Adamski, probably best known for his collaboration with Seal on the hit 'Killer', turned up with his SQ-80 and his Roland 909 machines and entertained us with some spontaneous noises that my own kids would now never believe I listened to. This was well before Adamski rose to fame and bombarded the charts with those very same noises. He was in from the start and very much a regular.

The music was great, the vibe incredible, plus it was illegal – what was there not to love?

But it was new territory and almost as a rite of passage, I found myself taking LSD. My friend Norman had done it in the 1960s and always warned me to *never* do it. He told me that when The Beatles announced they had experimented with it, it became a landmark moment as though everyone now had a green light, but he reminded me that it was an *individual's* choice to do so even if it was a bad choice.

The five of us set off for Camden Palace on a Saturday night in 1989: Dave, Warren, Larry, Mark and I. The other four had done it before, and now it was my turn to see what all the fuss was about. It was simply easily obtainable and being sold blatantly by some bandana-clad, smiley T-shirt-wearing dealer as you walked into the main room of the club. All I remember from that night – well, at least what I know to be true memories and not some trippy construct from my imagination – was that I danced non-stop and hugged more strangers than I have ever done before. We shouted out, 'Let's go mental!' (careful what you wish for) and we all laughed so much that our sides hurt. We ran the risk of having permanent grin lines on our faces. It is the stuff of teenage folly and, again, pure curiosity, but no cats died in the process.

The last track played by the DJ that night was Soul II Soul's 'Keep On Movin'', a nice soulful touch and a welcome departure from the banging beats of the preceding hours. Dave and I jumped into the back of what we thought was a hovercraft, but was in fact a car, and we all made our way to a kebab shop on the corner of Finsbury Park. I attempted to order some food, despite not feeling hungry at all, but this epically failed. I was unable to rein in my laughter standing there at the counter, primarily because the guy behind that counter couldn't control his face which was constantly changing shape. I abandoned the idea of food and got back into the hovercraft. We seemed to be moving in slow motion as we made our way from North to East London, Young MC's 'Know How' was on full blast and the sun threatened to rise. We then caught sight of a milk float and decided to follow it. When the milkman pulled up outside some flats and went in to make his delivery, we jumped out of the car and helped ourselves to a few pints. It was a strange thing to do, but the whole thing was strange.

Our night, or should I say our morning, ended up sitting by the River Lea wondering why the sky was purple. I eventually walked home, back to Springfield Park and very carefully, in some ninja-like fashion, made it back into my bed, undetected by my parents, and, thinking the whole experience was over, began to wonder why I could still hear music from the Camden Palace, despite the club being several miles away from my home. I was still tripping, and this was confirmed when a police car pulled up into my room. I managed to talk my way out of the situation and avoided arrest. Sleep followed and the following day nothing ever looked the same again.

This was a completely different experience in life, opening up a trapdoor into your subconscious that never quite closes again. Giving the imagination free licence and allowing it to take over your entire headspace can be interesting, but seriously dangerous. Dragging the junk from the basement of your mind up into your new loft conversion isn't a good idea. I realised then that taking a journey into the deepest parts of my head would be best done when accompanied by an adult.

Norman was the first person I called the next day. He wasn't impressed or surprised, thinking that it was a stupid thing to do especially after his dire warnings and having seen the downside to it in the past.

'What's done is done,' he said. 'You've had a look, now leave it there.'

With his infectious smile and contagious humour he called me a *nutter*, and the usual laughter ensued.

And LSD changed the experience. Some of my friends went there and never came back, suffering dangerous long-term consequences from depression, mental breakdown to paranoid schizophrenia. Even though it was against this backdrop that durable acts whom I loved like Soul II Soul emerged, in time I would realise that the illegal rave scene was essentially just a moment in time, but house music, which emerged from The Warehouse in Chicago in the late-1970s, was now reaching a worldwide audience and it was here to stay.

I loved house!

I more than dipped my toe in, though, and its influence remains in me to this day. But, as is often the way, it was a moment of chance that changed everything. They say you make your own luck in life – well, Dad made mine.

One day he got a call at the gym asking if he could take a fighter with him to a boxing show.

'Off the record, he's in the music biz,' the voice at the other end of the line confided. 'He's a manager and looks after some rapper.'

This had nothing to do with boxing. People do like to tell you a little more than they need to sometimes. On moments like this everything can change.

And it did.

Dad met the guy, took him to the bout and of course, en route, bit his ear off.

His name was Steve Finan, though *actually* it was Steve O'Connor, son of the comedian Tom. He had been around show business all his life.

'My son's a singer,' Dad announced.

Poor Steve must have heard this a thousand times and has told me since that he just really liked my old man, so did choose to engage.

'I'd like to hear what he does,' Steve replied more than politely.

Of course, my father was in proud paternal mode here but really was clueless as to Steve's background. When you have been brought up on Jerry Lee Lewis and Johnny Mathis, and there is this boxer in your car managing Monie Love, who is having songs produced by Dancin' Danny D who, in turn, 'penned' the acid house 'classic' 'We Call it Acieeed', Dad must have done very well to keep up with the conversation.

I think also that he saw his chance and, whilst he knew that I could sing, was slightly concerned about the lack of direction in my life. From nowhere, he took charge:

'Come to Sunday lunch next week,' he urged.

'Yeah, I will,' Steve replied.

And to this day I have no idea what prompted him to do so, other than he really liked Dad.

'I like your voice and we should make a record,' Steve announced when I played him my rough demo as Mum was clearing up.

I was stunned – exhilarated. Excited, nervous, over the moon – all of that.

Suddenly, I was in. This felt different to cutting the two tracks with Patrick Grant. That was valuable experience and a dream come true, but was over in a flash and achieved nothing. I understand now that there was no process then. I didn't have proper representation or a plan. We just did it and waited to see what happened. Nothing did.

Now I am almost doing the hard yards, starting to learn about the business. I meet a young producer Steve is managing, called Richie Fermie, who had been remixing tracks for the *Jungle Brothers*. I start going to attend gigs with Steve and he single-handedly connected me to the game. I am introduced to Neneh Cherry who has the massive global hit 'Buffalo Stance'. Then I am taken to Wembley Arena to a concert in April 1990 for Nelson Mandela called *An International Tribute for a Free South Africa*. I get to meet Winnie Mandela, watch Neneh, Natalie Cole, Anita Baker, George Duke and Terence Trent D'Arby perform onstage... Some of these people as you know or might suspect are my heroes. I seriously begin to think that this is interesting. That backstage view. Something I had never seen before.

Then Steve tells me we are going into the studio:

'The quickest way to make a record is to pick a cover,' he tells me.

I am not about to get all artistic on him and argue – plus, even though I have begun writing my own songs some time back, they are an experiment, lacking that final quality and know-how. A work in progress, in every sense. At this point, in everybody's eyes, I am no more than a soulful vocalist, far from a songwriter.

So, smiling but pinching myself that this is happening, I head down to a studio just off the back of Camden High Street where Richie Fermie meets me and we begin to try out our first cover version, laying down a vocal to a Johnny Guitar Watson song called 'Ain't That a Bitch'. The track sounded good, different and very cool, but it lacked that pop edge that was needed to get me onto radio and gain the support of the club DJs. It was a good first attempt, but we needed something a little more special.

It also feels good as an experience – better than last time – as though the time away has done me good. Perhaps, too, I am benefiting from a more professional culture that tells me this might actually be real now. A little older and wiser, too.

Richie Fermie then reached out to a DJ friend of his, Glen Gunner, and asked him what soul track was a guaranteed floor-filler every time he played it out. Glen came back with his 100% no-brainer answer.

It was a track by the *Gap Band*.

'Outstanding'.

I knew the record very well; in fact, it was one of my all-time favourites.

It would be a very brave move to rework that. If you got it wrong it could go down badly with the soul music fans.

But not being one to avoid a good challenge, I was up for it... If you don't have a go you'll never know.

So, Steve booked in a session at Ventura Studios in Acre Lane, Brixton, for me to lay down the vocals. Richie would produce the record, along with Glen Gunner's initial advice and input, therefore crediting him with a well-deserved co-production.

Glen calls on the services of a percussionist he happens to know.

The guy walks in. We get on like a house on fire. He went to town on his congas, adding a much-needed vitality to the record.

We sit back in the studio together listening to the almost finished results of Richie's mastery and he turns to me and says, 'This is gonna be a massive hit, Kenny.'

'Really, do you think so?' I reply disbelieving.

I am not down on my confidence in any way. In fact, it is soaring. I just don't have the hours under my belt to know that with any certainty yet. I had never met him before, but I took him at his word.

It was Shovell, who would eventually form part of the band known as M People, and they would go on to have a string of hits (and much later play percussion on a Barry Stoller track as if my life was joining up the dots). Little did I know that Shovell and I were about to effectively start out together and would be sharing many hours on the road. I had made another friend for life.

But first we had to get a deal, so Steve took me to see Adeva in concert at the Town and Country Club (now the O₂ Forum) in Kentish Town. There I met Ken Grunbaum, the Head A&R man for Cooltempo Records, the label Adeva was also signed to. We spoke very briefly that night... as best you could do at a noisy gig.

I then met Ken again when he came over to Ventura Studios to listen to what was almost the finished mix of 'Outstanding'. He loved the track and was keen to sign it. He spoke to me in an almost father-like way, asking me if I was ready to go for it and put records out. A kind of 'Do you think you can handle it?' preamble. I was up for it big time.

Yes. I had been waiting for an opportunity like this for so long.

I liked Ken from the get-go, and when I had my first meeting with him at Chrysalis Records in Stratford Place, London, he had a massive picture of Marvin Gaye on his wall, which was a good sign and a great start.

Chrysalis Records had masterminded the likes of Go West, Living In A Box and Sinéad O'Connor, to name a few, so they definitely knew how to make hits. But more importantly I was about to sign to Cooltempo, their dance music imprint. They knew how to make good dance music, too, and gravitated towards that soul sound, and above all, with a lot of hard work, they understood how to cross it over into the mainstream charts.

It was a great meeting with Ken and Steve. I liked Ken and it was reciprocated. And everybody loved Steve. This was going to work out just fine.

'We're gonna release this record,' he tells us.

I think he had probably already decided that, so long as I hadn't walked in there with some sort of attitude.

'We're going to sign this and go for it. Are you ready?'

'Born ready,' I replied.

Which obviously was a lie.

I had *never* bombarded record companies with demos. I probably should have. Nobody had heard of me. Now I am in front of the man who is having big hits and making really cool music. No wonder the label was called Cooltempo.

It was simply the most exciting conversation of my life at this point.

Dare I say it, 'Outstanding'.

And that was obviously the name of the track – a massive R&B Number 1 in the States previously, but only charting at 68 in the main chart in the UK back in 1982.

That was the name of the *track* but what was the name of the artist? Even at this early stage, territory was being marked.

'You need to change your name,' I was told.

'It sounds a bit… Thomas Dolby…'

Dolby was not exactly a huge star, perhaps best known for hits like 'Hyperactive', but wow, wait a minute, I am a singer trying to break through. I am me. Kenny Thomas.

'Go and have a think about it,' they urged.

There are no obvious alternatives suggested.

It was my name and I was comfortable with it. Why would I change? Was this control? Was this me being told I am not a person but a product? I didn't get it in any way. Many singers had changed their names, and it probably did make a difference for them. Gerry Dorsey became Engelbert Humperdinck. Reginald Dwight transformed himself into Elton John. Stevland Hardaway Morris is Stevie Wonder.

But for me, I am who I am, like it or lump it.

So ready? No. For none of it.

67

I was still at BT and had booked that one-way ticket to the Canaries to take a timeout and see my cousins. That demo and that conversation changed everything. Steve called me and said, 'Look, you are going to have cancel that ticket and leave BT... this is moving forward... we are going to sign the deal... Hand your notice in.'

Rapidly I was introduced to a really good professional team at Cooltempo with Ken on A&R, Simon Dunmore as the club promoter, Jody Dunleavy as Press Officer, Katie Rennie (now Katie Conroy) in charge of TV, Judd Lander as national radio plugger, Karl Badger on Marketing, supported by Lisa Blofeld, Barbara Dunn, Sarah Simpson, Tony Cooke and Claire Scivier. We would go on to form friendships, socialise together and work hard to make things happen.

I was pretty impressed with what was evolving – and crucially, too, with Steve's belief that the quickest way to a hit was a cover, Simon Dunmore played a crucial role in the choice of songs going forward. His knowledge of soul music was second to none, and he had the right connections to bring in those big-name dance remixes. I *was* lucky enough to be doing the music we wanted to do whilst mindful of that fact that I wasn't quite good enough to write my own material yet.

It is really now starting to take shape. Jody Dunleavy arranged a photo shoot with the DJ, rapper and photographer Normski! It has all gone up a notch. I am impressed with the set-up and filled with optimism. Who could possibly know what might lie ahead? This could go anywhere – back to square one or sky-high.

So, the song had form and presence but had not been commercially colossal in the UK, offering me a fair crack at owning it. The place to start was on my patch – the club scene. I had obviously seen many times – as a consumer – how a record grew and got momentum and, of course, the influence of the DJs. I had been to that many clubs because I was in love with the music.

Now, though, I needed that scene more than ever, and for the first time stepped back from being entertained in it to hoping I would be its entertainment.

The response was massive. And immediate.

'Every time I play it, it is a floor-filler,' one by one the DJs told me.

Perhaps they said this to all the guys.

But it was the only evidence I had to go on.

It *did* feel amazing. I *had* actually made a record, as though the work with Patrick Grant and Freddie Sassoon didn't really count when of course it mattered. These are all stepping stones. Every time I went into the studio, I discovered myself a little more, listening back.

Mum was of course over the moon. Dad was very supportive, too, but very aware of the potential pitfalls of being a popstar. He was excited for me – after all, it was his audacity that had got me here – but he was wary, too.

Through his building work he had run into all sorts of people in the game from Barry Stoller to Pink Floyd where he spent many months building their studios in Britannia Row, Islington. He told me stories of how they would make enormous amounts of noise rehearsing in the studio, and when a speaker blew up it would then be thrown out of the back door onto the growing pile. He became friendly with one member of the band. The others, he said, on most days walked around 'out of their minds like zombies'. Later on, they invited Mum and Dad to The Wall concert at Earls Court. Little did they know then that they were about to witness something that is now a part of rock'n'roll history. I wish I could have gone to that gig.

But nowwas I about to conquer the world?

In short, no.

That feedback from the club scene was incredible but all I had was an iconic minor hit in a soul world. I probably would have taken that when I was listening to Stevie Wonder with Dave Sassoon.

But I did feel close.

Was I about to run back to BT? No. I knew the label believed in me. I *knew* that I had mileage. This was just a glitch.

The facts don't lie, though.

There *was* a long way to go. I was undergoing a crash course in the pop industry. I never felt any sense of entitlement, nor did I possess any unrealistic expectations. I did sense that I might need a little bit of luck for this to really happen.

12 And the Beat Goes On

At this stage there is no album.

Nor is there a follow-up single.

There is no hit. There is no plan. But there is a belief in me which I never doubted. I had blind faith in myself, too, together with the drive and willpower to make music, but now Ken at the label backed me 100%. Like so many before me and since, we just needed a break.

In 1990, the charts were still the barometer. Today, to say you have a Number 1 is still a massive notch in your career and, of course, you can't top that position but some records that were peaking at 20 or 30 then sold more than the supposed big hits of today.

The record company did have ears, though. Your sales success would be the defining moment – it was a business after all and not a hobby, not *their* dream as it was mine. Yet, everything was telling them that my debut single for them was *outstanding* in the clubs. It just hadn't made it to radio.

In other words, it was making it and taking with it a huge groundswell. But it couldn't get through the doors of the mainstream, and that meant Radio 1 or Capital Radio in London.

Remember, too, my live work had consisted of singing in the church group, recording in the studio and nothing else. One night Steve took me to a big club in Hammersmith called the Hammersmith Palais to do a performance to track (known as a PA). The club was absolutely packed to the rafters and this was one of those pivotal moments when I had my first chance to show a London crowd what I was capable of. About 20 minutes before I was due onstage, Steve decided that he would throw me in the deep end without any armbands. He had an innate instinct for all things creative, especially when it came to live work. There were a lot of important people in the house. He wanted them to hear my voice – in isolation and for the first time. A cappella was rare at the time. He knew I needed to make a big impression and he sensed exactly how that should be done.

'When you go out there, you're not going straight into the track. I want you to start singing the verse and bridge of 'Outstanding' and then we will kick in with the track... I need them to hear your voice a cappella, so they know you can really sing,' he took me to one side to brief me.

I had never done this before, but I trusted Steve. He was never wrong.

I went out onto the stage. The crowd were silent, expecting the music to start and wondering what was happening when it didn't. I was given the mic and began singing the first line of 'Outstanding'. The audience went crazy, cheering so loud I could just about hear myself. I will never forget that night. Afterwards, Steve had the biggest smile on his face.

'This is going off,' he told me with his years of experience against my none.

'That was brilliant, you are going to start every PA with that from now on.'

So, I did... Wherever I performed I started with the a cappella and the reaction was always fantastic. Once at the Palladium in Enfield, the DJ Gary Smith planted me in the audience. I stood there like one of the punters as he held the mic out to people in the crowd to see who was best able to sing 'Outstanding'. There were one or two interesting attempts at it, and then he held the mic out to me. As I burst into the first line of the song, you could see heads turning and mouths opening as the penny began to drop. This has to be one of the most novel ways I have ever started a performance.

The record company had me back out often doing two or three promos a night, for which I had no training, and even with my energy levels I found exhausting. With my agent Paul Fitzgerald we made our way up and down the country singing in club after club, being paid just enough money to cover our expenses, and on one occasion getting knocked for £100 by the manager of a club in Penarth. I was never demoralised, only ever more determined. Slowly but surely, I was winning over the audiences, whilst putting up with the odd moment of hostility from a drunk clubgoer who clearly thought it was cool to give the unknown singer a hard time. All par for the course.

I left to spend a few days in Scotland on a promo tour, arranged by a tour manager named Ian Robertson. We drove the length and breadth of the country, sometimes singing in three or four clubs per night. This was the only way I could carve out a fan base and give 'Outstanding' the chance it needed to make it into the charts. The crowds were becoming far more receptive because they were now familiar with the song and its growing support from the DJs up and down the country.

While I was there in Scotland, I received a call from my dad saying that my nan had become unwell and had been taken into Barnet Hospital. The promo tour had one day to go before I made my way back to London. For the next few days, we visited my nan in hospital, not knowing if she would make a recovery. The doctors knew she was very ill but were reluctant to say what her chances were. It wasn't looking good.

On Friday 10 August, Dad took a call from his sister Marie saying that Nan had taken a turn for the worse and they didn't expect her to make it past the weekend.

Dad wept. All of us did.

We all made our way up to Barnet Hospital and I just sat there by her bedside next to my cousin Jackie. I held my nan's hand, watching, praying and occasionally exchanging fond memories of Nan with Jackie. I couldn't believe that one minute I was in Scotland enjoying the gigs and the next I am here. I guess like many grandchildren we think our grandparents are going to live forever. I must have put the thought of losing Nan on the back burner; it was something that was always a long way off, but now that moment had come.

After sitting there for an hour or so I distinctly remember thinking that I really didn't want her suffering over the coming weekend and possibly dying alone in this hospital with no one by her side. We are all here right now. Couldn't God take her now? No sooner did I have those thoughts than she breathed her last, surrounded by her family.

Nan was gone. I was devastated.

Nothing else mattered. Music, records or otherwise.

This is my nan, whom I brought all my friends to see – the lady who was down with the kids and uplifted everyone with

73

her sense of humour. My mates' best mate – the lady my pal Lawrence stole a prize cactus from someone else's greenhouse for.

Everything happens for a reason.

I had had a chance to play my record to her in hospital on a set of headphones – as though someone knew time was against us… As if you were allowed one moment you could share that was going to be life-changing before life changed forever.

And she loved it. Of course, she would have said that anyway. Her support was unconditional so if she said she loved it, she loved it. I take great comfort in the belief that she hung on just long enough to know that I was about to achieve my ambitions, and, even though my world is rocked at this point, I am well aware that many people see loved ones depart with so much unfinished business. If music was to become one of the biggest parts of my life, then at least one of the most important people in it knew that as they said goodbye.

As you will expect by now, every death brings new questions, and each occasion leaves you memories which you can't shake off. When they prepared her body in the chapel of rest, they parted her hair the wrong way. It just wasn't Nan and that upset me greatly. It never leaves you. To this day I have refused to ever enter a chapel of rest again. When I kissed her, she was ice-cold. It wasn't the Nan I recognised. It rocked me, but it taught me. My own family are now under strict instructions that when it is my turn, just close the bloody lid and remember me how I was!

Where oh where did that leave everything that I was on the cusp of? I was that torn apart inside that I couldn't continue but equally I knew that I had to – for Nan. If those last moments resonated as they did then surely the message was to crack on with things.

In a way I was happy that 'Outstanding' had flopped on its first outing. Had it been a hit then I would have had to just get on with it and would have had no time or space to grieve. I guess we have to expect to lose our grandparents someday. I just wasn't ready then. Ivy Thomas was what being a Thomas was all about. I am so glad that I did keep my real name!

But two weeks had passed before we could bury her. Single, I just spent the fortnight knocking around Hackney kicking my heels, devoid of all emotion but ripped, too, of excitement at what may lie ahead musically.

Getting through the funeral was all that mattered. And of course, afterwards you let your hair down a bit as that suppressed build-up of tension that you can never see past finally succumbs to a few drinks recalling plenty of happy memories. The laughter that night just underlined that she was a Thomas.

We retreated afterwards to my cousin Lee's house – this is my dad's sister's son. Despite the occasion, Lee's wife Alison told me that she knew this really nice girl in Barnet and proceeded to invite her round there and then. Not the ideal day to be matchmaking, but I was all for spontaneity.

It was late at night and Alison said, 'I'm going to ring her.' She duly came over.

We hit it off and she was amazing support in that moment and anchored me onto something real when everything else around me, from pop to the value of life and death, was up in the air.

Sophie could not have wandered into my life at a better or worse time.

Things soon were steadying and the two of us were good. A DJ named Leigh Clarke from Northampton was ringing the record company up and telling us that we should rerelease 'Outstanding'. He said it was a floor-filler every time he played it. He was not the only DJ reporting back to HQ about the massive buzz this tune had out there.

My energy levels were up, and I was just about ready for the second attempt at the record.

In fact, the record company believed in me that much and I started to think this might just happen when Steve took the multitrack tapes over to New York to get the hip-hop group Black Sheep to lay down a short rap on the new 12" version. It was half a hit first time around. Now they were seriously investing in it financially and creatively with that vision to pull it off, I really did begin to believe the hard work would finally pay off.

As the bells chimed for midnight on New Year's Eve, 1991 looked full of promise.

13 A Happy New Year?

I had spent the night clubbing with Sophie, her sister Katie and Katie's boyfriend Phil. It had been a while since I had ventured back into anywhere playing deep house music. Phil would become my new partner in crime! Over the next few years, we would go out frequently, *have it large* and come back to an earful from the girls.

I thought I was the bee's knees with my blue Ford Escort and massive, brick-sized Motorola mobile phone whose antenna could take someone's eye out, proud to place it on the bar next to my pint. Michael Douglas in the film *Wall Street* – he started all this!

I drove over to Mum and Dad's that New Year's Day, feeling a bit jaded from my night out. There was bound to be some great Spanish food awaiting me there. As soon as I opened the front door a very sad-looking Mum greeted me and said, 'Your dad has gone to Auntie Marie's house.'

'Your grandad is dying, he's not gonna make today.'

What a devastating start to the year. I had to make for Uncle Leslie's and Auntie Marie's at fast as I could. I grabbed my rosary beads from my bedroom, jumped back in the car and bombed it over to Finchley, praying all the way.

As I opened the door to the house my Uncle Leslie told me, 'He's going now... he's going now.' Then just as I made it to the side of his bed, he left this world.

Nan and Grandad were both gone within months and almost in sync with my fledgling career. He was 81.

He was a quiet man, with never a bad word to say about anyone. I never ever saw him lose his temper. Dad said he only ever saw an anger once with a neighbour when he was a kid. This is quite a contrast to his own father, my Great-Grandfather Alfred, who I was told was also a quiet man until he had a drink inside him and then it was not unusual for him to be out in the street having a punch-up with three blokes at once and laying them all out. He would eventually die from sclerosis of the liver, which is why he and all of his brothers hardly ever touched a drop of alcohol.

Grandad was a great carpenter. I remember watching him work as a boy, sitting there as he sharpened and realigned every tooth of his handsaw and prepared his tools for his next job. Nowadays these saws are just thrown away and replaced immediately. I guess that is more convenient, but it lacks value and tells me a lot about our postmodern culture. Easy come, easy go. Dad always said that Grandad could make a grand piano out of a bathroom door!

He was proud to be a Thomas. His ancestors came up from Helston in Cornwall in the 1800s. Great-grandfather Joseph Thomas was a tailor who settled with his family, first in Wardour Street, London, and then eventually in Islington. Joseph's son Alfred would eventually marry Catherine Anne Tremlett from a well-to-do family that had an ophthalmic instrument-manufacturing business in Stoke Newington, North London. They were, I was told, connected with the building of a church on the corner of Tremlett Grove in Islington, hence the road being named after them. I knew my great-grandmother, Katherine. She lived to the grand old age of 98. I would in later years successfully investigate my ancestry with the help of Great-Uncle Ernie and the internet, eventually meeting up with a branch of the family that now reside in San Francisco, descendants of my Great-Great-Auntie Lydia, who made the journey from Cornwall to Canada, and then to the USA after the First World War.

I loved working on my family tree. This was me all over: history, tradition, connectedness and an attempt at obtaining a glimpse of the various personalities in my inherited gene pool. To what degree is my personality type the result of nature or nurture? I'll never know the answer to this, but me being me, I still want to attempt to find out.

After Grandad's death, I took a few days out, but eventually I had to get back out on the road again. This is meant to be the biggest year of my life and two people who mean the world to me are no longer here to share it. Both gone in months.

I began to dream heavily and vividly each night, which included some very real conversations.

'Nan, we shouldn't be talking,' one dream began. 'You have passed away.'

'I know,' she replied, as we both stood there beneath the trees which lined the front of her house in Finchley.

'I have to go now,' she said, as she turned to stare towards the first-floor bay window of the house.

I looked up and I could see through to the sky. The ceiling and roof had gone.

The morning after that strange dream, I told Sophie about it and I dismissed it as something the mind does when we are experiencing a loss. Although it did leave me with a heavy feeling.

Later that day Uncle Ernie called Dad – could he come round? The ceiling *had* fallen down in that same room.

I know that I was grieving but I didn't find any of this odd. I found it very natural. After all, Nan's life had changed not ended. To me this was evidence of that connectedness that we all have, an invisible reality.

But I had to work. This was my big chance and I must find a way. They wouldn't release 'Outstanding' for a third time. It needed to be now.

And second time around it was different. At the time, Capital FM in London could break you and the DJs were huge stars. To have their support was colossal. Amidst all this, I find myself onstage at Ritzy in Tottenham with their afternoon presenter Mick Brown. I perform and it goes crazy – women are trying to grab me, and I have never experienced anything like this at all. My feet are literally not touching the floor. Security had to pick me up and carry me out of the club, removed for my own safety.

'Listen, Kenny,' Steve Finan smiled, 'that's when you know it is going right off.'

And it was. I had been to so many gigs and seen many bands. I hadn't seen that, and I was in the middle of it and – dare I say so – the reason for it.

79

Next in our sights was Radio 1. If we could only get them to play the record it would be a game-changer. To achieve this some radio pluggers will often make up any old nonsense, just to get one spin on a big daytime show. The radio plugging department at Chrysalis Records were not averse to conjuring up a story or two. They told Simon Bates that I was discovered in a karaoke bar. That was the best they could come up with. It worked and we got the record played.

Steve Finan was not happy. In fact, he was fuming. He told them it was the most stupid thing they could have done. All our hard work and credibility potentially lost in a fictitious crooner narrative on national radio. I would spend the next year or two undoing that story when it came up in interview after interview. They could have just told the truth and let the record succeed on its own merits, instead of throwing crap at the wall hoping some might stick. This led Steve eventually to move my national radio plugging from Chrysalis and put it into the hands of Nigel Sweeney and Jacqui Quaife at the company Ferret and Spanner. They were working the Simply Red *Stars* album at the time, and this proved to be a very wise move.

Hit records happen because of a series of so-called *breaks*. My first *break* on TV came in the form of a late-night performance on *The Hitman & Her,* a television dance music show hosted by Pete Waterman and Michaela Strachan. It was recorded in various nightclubs around the country on a Saturday night, and then broadcast, twice, a few hours later into the early hours of Sunday morning. If you missed being tortured at 1am, then not to worry, it was back on again at 4.

Its target audience was clubgoers, who had had a proper skinful at their local discotheque, followed by the customary kebab. If they managed to avoid a punch-up and a night in A&E, and could remember where they lived, they made it home and were unable to sleep. After all, sleep was for grown-ups.

I wore bright white Levi's 501 jeans with a slicked-back 80s hairstyle. I was fresh-faced and ready to go at Mr Smiths nightclub in Warrington. It was not the coolest TV, but it was a good start. TV was king and I needed to be seen and heard on it.

I am grateful to Pete Waterman for having me on the show. It definitely got me out of the starting blocks and into the race.

We make a pop video for 'Outstanding' – on a shoestring. I had no expectation for its quality, but the guys did brilliantly. It is probably the best video I ever shot – I am a barrow boy at Berwick Street Market. On a sunny day, with Shovell and other friends in tow, we surprise the traders and shoppers with our cameras, truly capturing a moment in time that can never be repeated. Then onto the WAG nightclub in Wardour Street later that evening to shoot the final scenes. I look like the lad next door and the guys made it in such a fun way – probably because the limited budget forced people to produce their best. It also lacked the bullshit of much of what followed when I was a supposed 'popstar'. I seem innocent, humble and natural, and they capture that spirit. Of course, I have never done anything like this before and I am certainly not an actor.

I do that interview with Simon Bates on BBC Radio 1. He is as much of a star as many of the acts he plays. Famous for the *Our Tune* feature where people tell their life stories and pick a song that sums it all up, he ends up hosting the mid-morning show on the network for sixteen years. He has power and influence.

I start to do kids' TV – first on a show called *Motormouth,* interviewed by Andy Crane whilst skipping with a rope I borrowed from the boxing club. The boxing theme and story would be used time and time again over the coming months. It was too early in the morning to be jumping around and sweating under the hot lights in a TV studio, but it did the trick and was different. I remember my friend James telling me that he got home in the early hours of that Saturday morning after being out in a club all night, lay on his bed half-asleep with the TV on in the background, only to see me pop up, hopping away. He had to double take and thought he was hallucinating. No, it was real! In a surreal kind of way. These were the things I had to do back then to get noticed.

I am in with a shot at this. It is 100 times bigger than the first time we released it, and one marker of that is the fact that the nonsense is on a grander scale. I suspect that I know who is feeding it, but I have to tell Bates that I was never a BT engineer *nor* was I discovered at a karaoke bar. The Chinese whispers of PR were already working overtime and not necessarily in sync with me.

Then it happens.

Everything that I had been working for relentlessly, and at this point on autopilot because of the losses of my grandparents, is coming together. One minute you are pushing, working every interview and smiling through every personal appearance. The next you are through the doors and on the other side.

'Outstanding' makes it into the Top 40.

I am blown away.

I am in the UK charts. I make that famous run-down on a Sunday afternoon. Nobody can ever take that away from me. I have made it.

To a certain degree.

I just wanted to *make* music not *make it* itself, but the two do go hand in hand and the record company goes into overdrive. They know that they are getting a return on their investment, and they need the next stage.

Then I get great news from them that the show I watched as a kid, the one I dreamed of getting onto, had invited me for the first of what would end up being nine appearances on *Top of the Pops*.

7 February 1991.

Filmed on the Wednesday, going out on the Thursday. Old-school television – not live. Bruno Brookes, the Top 40 presenter on Radio 1 for much of the previous decade, is the host. Gloria Estefan, The Simpsons, Candi Staton and New Kids on the Block are on video, and I sing 'live' alongside Kim Appleby, Oleta Adams and the Number 1 from The KLF – '3 a.m. Eternal'.

This is colossal. I am tempted to say that it has all happened in one month. It has and it hasn't. It *has* exploded in the four weeks since Grandad passed away but of course, it started way back with all those Stevie Wonder records, Dad's influences, the estate, Dave Sassoon, the local record shop, house music… everything. There is no such thing as an overnight success.

I had no nerves on that first recording of the most famous music show on the planet. If you like, boxing drilled performance angst out of me. *But* I never enjoyed miming. Ever. And that was the requirement of this massive programme. I had to fake it, so I was learning fast – essentially this was acting.

I was a singer and wanted to belt it out live. I occasionally got it wrong. I *wasn't* an actor. My biggest fear was that it would look like something out of a bad kung fu movie where the dubbing was out of sync. I worked on it and eventually got it down to a fine art.

Then we would get shunted around this small studio that looked massive on the TV. I would be singing and the next act would be setting up on the opposite stage – being in a show so mechanically constructed bore no resemblance to the one I had seen every week of my life.

But of course, the next day came and I watched like a viewer, as a fan – as I had always done. I recall that it snowed heavily that night, so not wanting to miss out on the opportunity, my mate Phil and I borrowed his younger brother's sledge and we hit the hills of Barnet. It felt as if I had watched someone else earlier that evening. I would have to get used to seeing myself on TV.

Surreal.

Yet, significant. This was who I was and how I behaved, but I was already making the distinction between 'that is TV, that is my job, and this is me'.

'Outstanding' eventually peaked at Number 12 – my first hit under my belt. I knew that I would have to work really hard now to make sure it wasn't my only hit. Being a one-hit wonder was not for me.

And it was *now* my job. From the record company advance I was being paid £100 a week, eventually supplemented by money made from gigs. It wasn't the *big time* money-wise, despite what many thought, but it was stable and kept me grounded.

Steve Finan was now not only my manager, but he had become a close friend, too, and a mentor, teaching me and preparing me for a time when I would be earning larger sums of money. One day we pulled up outside Chrysalis Records and the car directly in front of us was an old BMW, nothing special and not one that would attract attention.

'Can you see who's driving that old BMW?' Steve asked.

I took a closer look and could see it was Sinéad O'Connor behind the wheel.

'You see, you don't need to drive a big, flash car,' he said.

Yes, I got it: she was a huge star and keeping it real.

Yet, the record company were now starting to call the shots, ringing me saying that I had to attend this and be seen at that, but I knew early on that I did not want to go to the opening of every envelope. At times, I almost succumbed, but that wasn't me, though I could see that it *was* for many artists. I just thought they were all feeding an illusion.

But I worked out how, too. After that first *Top of the Pops* and with the video being played on various other shows, I noticed people were looking at me differently. In fact, they hadn't been looking at all previously. Now, in every aisle in the supermarket, there was someone. Wherever I went, eyes followed. I had been out on the town with a few mates and crashed at one of their flats one night. I made the mistake of heading out early the following morning to a newsagent's around school time – one of those places where they put that odd note up saying, 'no more than four schoolchildren at any one time'. Well, they were all in there.

'You're Kenny Thomas!?' a young lad shouted.

'No, I'm not,' I replied, all embarrassed.

'Yes, you are, you're that singer Kenny Thomas.'

'No, I just look like him,' I said, as I headed for the door to make my escape.

And that was now the norm – and not something I was used to.

Some people wanted it on their terms, of course – a photo in a nightclub or being interrupted when I was out socially with friends, when I wasn't in the mood and might be having a bad hair day. This invasion of privacy goes with the territory, but I always believed that the privilege was mine, not theirs. I am being asked for my autograph – what an honour that is.

Even the record company fell under this spell, though, and you could see it in the cars they sent for you, the outfits they picked and of course the budgets earmarked against your name.

And right now, their priority was where they were going to get the second hit from. It probably reads as bad planning and lack of vision, but they did have the foresight to back me twice on 'Outstanding', so it was something that was hovering in everybody's minds, but we needed to act quickly.

The process nearly destroyed me.

I was given two songwriters to work with who were always reminding me of what I *couldn't* do or giving me songs that were clearly not in my key. As though they wanted me to fail or force me to sing in ways that did not suit my voice. They just couldn't stop knocking me and criticising me. I would drive to work every day feeling sick on the way there and demoralised on the way home. It was an early marker that something as beautiful as making music had its own negativity and nastiness. This experience caused me to start to doubt my vocal abilities and wonder if I really had what it takes to achieve greater success.

My manager then sent me to Sheffield to work with Mike Ward who wrote Alison Moyet's hit 'Weak in the Presence of Beauty', and Eliot Kennedy who was beginning to establish himself as a songwriter and producer. Eliot would later go on to work with artists such as Lulu, the Spice Girls, Take That, Gary Barlow himself, Celine Dion, Bryan Adams, Aretha Franklin, Mary J. Blige and John Legend, winning an Ivor Novello Award and being nominated for a Grammy Award. We became really good friends. His track record, very impressive.

This now just reads as though I am dropping names and song titles for fun. The truth is that it was a massive endorsement from the record company. From day one, they were giving me the best shot at success even if I had to dodge those few bullets along the way.

I told Eliot what had happened with those two guys who just picked the bones out of everything I did, knocking my confidence at every opportunity. After that, I never looked back and I am surprised in myself that they had got to me, but this was new territory and as prepared as I was for life with streetwise skills and a well-researched brain, nothing prepares you for the music business. Eliot had been here before:

'You have an amazing voice,' he told me. 'Don't let people do that to you, don't ever work with people like that. Get in that vocal booth and do what you do.'

I went in, the red light came on, and in an instant I realised that it was wasted energy to worry about what anyone else thought. All it took was one session with Eliot and the positivity he radiates to restore that confidence and belief in myself. There was something very special about him and I told him so.

'By this time next year, you're going to have a massive worldwide hit and be a millionaire,' I said to him.

'Do you think so?' he replied.

'Yes, I'm convinced of it,' I said and I was right. Looking back, I must have sounded like Del Boy out of *Only Fools and Horses*, with my entrenched London accent. Rodney, by this time next year…

I also go to Brixton, South London, to start working with an absolute genius called Ian Green. At sixteen, he was playing bass for Maxi Priest – he was that good. We start working through demos of some potential songs. This was one of the best *hook-ups* songwriting-wise, arranged by Dominic Walker at BMG Music. Although I didn't realise it at the time, Ian was going to play a crucial role in the success that was coming. No crystal ball needed here: this was pure providence.

We are still searching for that second single, though, and if it had the potential to be bigger than 'Outstanding'. Steve Finan turns up one day at Cooltempo for a meeting with Ken Grunbaum. Ken was late, so Steve had to wait in his office for about half an hour. All pretty boring stuff, until Steve noticed a cassette tape in the waste-paper basket. It had the title 'Thinking About Your Love', a demo by the singer Beverley Skeete and written by Mike Ward.

He stuck it in the tape machine and had a listen. There was something about this song, he thought. Although in its present form it needed some serious production changes, it could be the hit song we were looking for. Steve re-presented it to Ken.

It was considered and then for a while the whole idea was abandoned. I didn't like it much. In fact, I thought it was awful. Back to the bin.

Not quite.

Ken became convinced we should give it a go. The song was then recorded by a new group called Higher Ground, again with a female vocal. This was then played to me by Steve and for the first time I could hear what they were all saying. With the right production and my voice this *could* be something very special. It is starting to get interesting and I am warming to the tune. Their demo improved on the first one I heard. Things are moving. Could we advance it further?

I was then introduced to Steve Mac who has a massive hit with Nomad called 'I Wanna Give You Devotion'. At his studio in Chertsey, we begin to get the track together and see if we can get that right balance between a soul record and a pop hit. The one thing that became evident from all of this was that this song was definitely going to work, and it suited my voice.

Ken needed to move fast. He wasn't sure of the direction the track was going in with Steve Mac, so he was still on the lookout for the right fit for the record. Steve went on to become one of the most successful record producers in the UK. Though we would much later work together, it was all about timing, and for Cooltempo it wasn't right at that moment. They had to find a producer for the record and fast.

Two former members of the band Dead or Alive who had a massive Number 1 in 1985 with 'You Spin Me Right Round' are assigned. An unusual fit for a soul singer and a song with as yet no defined production value. But this record needed to be a big hit in the pop charts and pop is what they did best. These guys are good. They cleverly called on the services of a backing vocalist named Tracy Ackerman. Her voice would become as important as mine for the sound of this record.

It is coming together. Piece by piece.

It *was* coming together. We had to play around with the arrangement a little – Steve Finan suggesting previously that I sing a cappella paid dividends here with the hard vocal start on the track – but I began to realise that when there are wobbles in your mind, you can't hit all those high notes. When you are free from negativity, your voice floats you psychologically, spiritually and emotionally to new territory.

And we delivered.

It became my biggest hit, reaching Number 4 in July 1991.

I had cracked it – a Top 5 hit at the second attempt.

'Thinking About Your Love'.

14 Deal Or No Deal (no pain, no gain)

I was in. Accepted. Because I had a chart smash.

But I split critics in two. The soulful voice inside the white man.

Black Echoes, a popular black music and culture magazine put me on the front cover. It was the first and last time that they had put an artist like me on that pedestal. They thought it was a breakthrough moment and maybe it should have been. I later learned that they had never had so much negative mail from people complaining.

I had always bought *Blues & Soul magazine.* The truth is that I was only ever given copies of the teen staple *Smash Hits* in later years by the record company when I was in it. I had no real interest in pop music magazines.

Blues & Soul were honest enough to tell the record company that I would never get a front cover on their magazine. There were clear lines of demarcation.

I am stunned that I was really the first person through which this issue had been put on the table – daft really when you consider how I really was an artiste making music inspired by black music and I loved everything they printed.

But that was how it was.

'We won't be doing that again,' the Editor of *Black Echoes* confided in Steve Finan.

At least I was having hits and we were up and running.

Obviously, this was business and it seemed to matter to everybody else that I was *in,* but I hadn't become any different. In the moment it is often difficult to analyse those changes in others as they are happening, but I was on it straight away – my guard up, to be consistent with the person I had always been. You didn't just get a new set of values overnight.

On 19 June 1991 I am back for a third time in the TV studios of *Top of the Pops.* 'Thinking About Your Love' is sitting nicely at Number 5 in the charts. On that same show presented by Nicky Campbell are Drizabone with Real Love, Rebel MC

89

featuring Barrington Levy and Tenor Fly with 'Tribal Base', Bette Midler with 'From A Distance', and Color Me Badd with 'I Wanna Sex You Up'. That afternoon in between takes and the dress rehearsal, I hung out with Rebel MC and Barrington Levy.

'How many hit records have you had now?' asked Barrington.

'This is my second hit record,' I replied.

'So, where are you living?' he continued.

'I'm still in Hackney, where I grew up,' I told him.

He then warned me, 'You will have to leave there… after you have a hit record, people around you will change, and some of them will be out to get you.'

No one had ever told me things like that before. His experience of fame in Jamaica was not unique. It can be applied to anywhere. Human nature is universal and so with it come faults like jealousy and hatred.

He was right. Many people did change.

So, I continued going to the library, and nipped away to help my mates on building sites! My relationship with the Church was my constant. Father Hanshell would welcome me regularly, and I him. He was a good friend and someone I could offload my troubles onto, always giving me the best advice and direction for life.

He would ask me how the week was, and I would enjoy that opportunity to detach myself from my other reality.

'Well, I spent a day and a half making a pop video,' I would begin.

It wasn't your standard fare. But true.

We *had* made the video for 'Thinking About Your Love' with the director trying to borrow some ideas from the movie *Ghost* which was big at the time.

So, I am standing on a bridge over the River Thames at the crack of dawn and I am partly *ghosted!* A disembodied spirit knocking about, trying to communicate with a girl. Not sure how this related to the song and in terms of special effects they never quite pulled it off. Sometimes it was difficult to translate the idea in a producer's head into reality. Outside it looks more *Mary Poppins* than *Ghost* and a very different London skyline.

One minute I look all ghostly and the next I'm back in my body looking all tangible and heartbroken. Honestly, I look like someone who needs a doctor. Then I am in a house with her. The building is in need of a good roofer because water is pouring in through the ceiling, absolutely soaking the poor girl. Not much I can physically do to help because I'm still detached from my body.

I *was* starting to get the backing in terms of budgets for shoots like this but if you watch it now on *YouTube,* you can quite clearly see it does not stand the test of time, even if the song does. The tech is simply not there. And I am a novice at this.

But this was my dream and I needed to sharpen up in all aspects, especially business-wise, without losing my integrity and becoming the caricature the industry probably assumed I would.

When 'Thinking About Your Love' was being cut, I had only signed the deal to record the one single 'Outstanding' and an option for the album. They just didn't factor in that the first album was going to sell over 600,000 copies, and neither did we.

I'm still travelling every week to work with Ian Green in Brixton. Ian was working with two other songwriters at the time, Kenny Nicholas and Trevor Jacobs. The one great song that came from that collaboration was 'Voices', the title track of that first album. It all started with me doing a beatbox into the mic and then recording layers of individual vocals to make up the chords. No instruments were used on that record, only me hitting an ashtray and utilising other household objects we found in the room. Kenny and Trevor came up with the main melody and lyrics.

Over time it became obvious to me that I really wanted the opportunity to work with Ian alone. He could write songs, produce records, play pretty much any instrument he picked up, and he had a great voice. Together we could make a great album. My gut feeling was telling me this.

'You need to go it alone,' I told him.

'No, I'm cool with how things are now,' he replied.

'Trust me, Ian, if you came to work with me at the studio in Islington, just you and me, we would make such a good album,' I told him. 'Think about it.'

I knew it was a leap of faith for him, but it was clear to me that this was the right thing to do.

Some days passed and then I got a call from him.

'Kenny, I thought about what you said and I'm up for it, let's do it, let's make that album,' he began.

Great! I was really happy. He was the man for the job.

Steve Finan had taken over the Liquidator Studios on Caledonian Road in North London. The studio was owned by the ska band, Madness. This is the place where Ian and I worked hard, day and night, putting that first album together, assisted by the very talented engineer John Lyons. The three of us would spend more time together than we did with our family or friends. We simply had to pull it out of the bag. It was down to us alone to make it happen.

Often I would go stir-crazy. A studio can be a creative buzz or a sterile abyss. Some nights we thought we had written the next massive soul club hit; other days we left, having gone around in circles, convinced that we would never make another smash. That was the process, but with pressure added to it on a level I had never experienced.

Imagine the contrast and the 'journey' of excitement when Steve tells me we are going to cut a record and then, albeit at the second attempt, you watch it grow and climb the charts like the songs you bought and loved, and then you are hearing DJs on the radio and in the club scene championing you in the same way you listened to them as a music fan.

Except now it *is* you.

Then you get a hit. And the game changes. From hope and excitement together with the feeling that it is all new, you get expectation. That intensity can make you thrive or fail, or both at different moments.

Time and timing were everything, too. Unprepared is what we were after the first hits. Steve Finan rushed off to the USA in search of songs for me and came back with a couple of killers, 'Girlfriend' and 'Something Special', but the need to deliver was so great that Ian Green and myself locked ourselves in that studio and would work often into the early hours. This is how it would be for months on end, even coming in to record a vocal on New Year's Day while everyone else was at home reaching for the paracetamol and lamenting the overindulgence of the previous evening.

But with Ian Green I started to find my feet. We rubbed off on each other, sharing the same mindset and vision, crucially scrapping as many ideas as we laid down. I was beginning to understand that part of the process of making an album was leaving out as much as putting in.

That editing was clearly of a different era. There was no auto-tuning which came to light for the general public in the mid-Noughties when it was exposed as being used on TV talent shows. In the early 90s, I am afraid, we were using multitrack and had to wait for the tapes to rewind! Then you would often redo the vocals. An old AKAI S1000 was our sampling unit at a time when the technique was really in its infancy. I wanted to put that stamp on the album. It did of course take days and that equipment is now seen as so primitive. Old-fashioned but dear old analogue has a warm place in my heart.

At the same time, my influences were diverse. Going from fully live instruments, with great musicians on track, to my beatbox on *Voices* and that desire to reproduce almost a choirboy element in the vocal.

Yet it was exciting and magical – the workload was full on. My feet did not touch the ground now that I had this connection. You can perhaps see through the detail in my narrative here how working with the right person transformed me to think that anything was possible, giving that belief to experiment but also that stamina to wait and retake. I was finally at home in the studio. It was a relief to be there, and this ambience and new confidence drove me on to write one of my own favourite recordings in 'Will I Ever See Your Face'. It was just a fictitious little story, but in my own mind was a line in the sand. I could now write as well as sing.

How the mindset can change in the correct environment.

In between, of course, you start having hits in other countries, so your bags are always pre-packed at home and the next plane is just around the corner. You are in and out of TV shows and radio studios, and you don't have time to be creative.

Your career is developing in delay in other territories as they catch up with the UK's early success. Often you don't know where you are going and what you are promoting.

Once I did a gig in London, got in in the early hours, had a quick shower, a change of clothes, had a one-hour power nap on the sofa before the doorbell rang with the driver waiting to take me to the airport. Then, when you landed, you didn't quite know what scenario would await. On a Norwegian TV show, I had to stop the recording halfway through. During the performance two girls were sneaked onto the set behind me and I could hear some unusual shuffling noises that didn't sound like dancing. When I looked around, they had stripped off all their clothes, writhing away, as naked as the day they were born.

I stopped singing and shouted, 'Stop right now!'

The producer of the show approached me looking very annoyed.

'What's the problem?' he asked.

'Not sure what kind of TV show this is, but I'm not into it, and I don't want to be associated with this kind of thing in any way. You did this without asking me, not cool...' I replied.

'Are you OK with the girls dancing behind you?' he asked.

'Yes, but with their clothes on or I'm out of here,' I told him.

We then agreed that the girls could remain on set — dancing was good, nudity was not. We did another recording of the performance and I left.

They never invited me back and I had no intention of returning.

It turns out that the show was very much like the 90s late-night TV show we had here in the UK called *The Word*. An often controversial show, where guests could get away with just about anything.

Was this what was expected of a popstar? I don't think my heroes Stevie Wonder, Luther Vandross and Bobby Womack performed like that. It was certainly not what I was in this for.

I *was* now a regular on TV from the likes of *Wogan* and Jonathan Ross to *Going Live!*, from Andi Peters to *Pebble Mill* at lunchtime. The legendary Radio 1 Roadshow, which no longer exists, was also an absolute must for anyone with releases out in the summer. They, too, were masters of gimmickry. With Phillip Schofield as host, I was flown in once by helicopter to the stage!

Capital Radio's Mick Brown and Pat Sharp were also all over it. It was exciting to hear my music on one of the stations that I grew up listening to. Better than that – some of the top house record producers were starting to get their hands on my music and remix it, like the legendary Frankie Knuckles.

That gave the whole thing new energy. More importantly, it was everything you wanted in that the audience were running with it and doing the work for you.

I knew that these were opportunities that so many people did not get. Publicity was the oxygen of the popstar. Soon, though, you are on a treadmill, and you turn up just expecting to promote and sing and hope that people are inspired to buy the record, but every now and then the little curve ball comes along that gives you a chance to either show your character or fall flat on your face.

I didn't much care for naked dancers in Oslo. Nor did I look particularly good skipping on the children's TV programme *Motormouth* whilst trying to do an interview.

Why? Because they had latched onto that idea that I *was* a former amateur boxer.

I wasn't a professional boxer.

I went to the gym and had the best part of 50 contests. The preceding item to singer, on my CV, did not read boxer. What do you do? You do not want to waste half the airtime by contesting the point, so you go along with it. To this day, some people still believe I was a professional fighter, and some don't believe that I did any boxing at all and that it was another record company concoction.

My book – my truth. And that is it. Despite the rumours and whatever anyone feels to write on Wikipedia.

More to the point, it was way too early in the day to be skipping around on a TV show.

Of course, you are travelling constantly for work but not for life. You don't always get to see a lot of these places. At times it is literally airport, car, dressing room, TV set/venue and then the same in reverse – and that can create pressure, too.

But the speed with which it grew and the lack of preparation for what followed meant that my next release *Best of You* (with Gary's wife Dawn Barlow as one of the dancers in the video) suffered. It had been storming up the charts, peaking at Number 11 but the rush to release the album meant that the singles to promote it didn't achieve the positions they could have, because people bought the CD or LP instead.

Even though *Best of You* wasn't as big a hit as it could have been here in the UK, it did set things up nicely for the album release and it was doing very well throughout Europe. This meant more travel, more TV shows and more people with me on the road. The whole thing was moving along at a faster pace now. It was exciting, and I was determined to do my best to enjoy every minute of it.

Steve made sure I had a road manager to travel with me. For this he called on Monie Love's brother, Marvin Johnson, who became my right-hand man. Often it would be just Marvin and me on journeys, but we were soon joined by two dancers, Sue, who featured in the *Best of You* video, and Julia.

They would perform alongside me on the TV shows. The four of us became very good friends, and when our work was done for the day we took full advantage of any free time in the evenings, seizing those opportunities to socialise in whatever city we found ourselves. If the schedule was too tight and our time limited, we made up for it by getting together back in the UK, pursuing London's nightlife.

So, the overall perception is that you are living the high life – 'the dream' – and at times I guess we were. The only problem I had with *living the dream* is that dreams are for people who are asleep. As nice as dreams are they are not real life.

I was all about being awake. And we had to keep moving.

Steve suggested that I take up the guitar again. He thought it would be a good addition to singing and give me a more credible edge onstage. So, I purchased a lovely semi-acoustic one and began taking lessons to brush up on my scales. It didn't take long before I had to admit to Steve that I really was out of love with the instrument. Plus, all the guitarists I knew were such awesome players I figured it would take me years to get anywhere near their standard. I decided to stick to what I did best.

Singing.

I ended up giving that guitar to my young nephew Nathan Thomas. He was much inspired by seeing his uncle on *Top of the Pops*, plus he hadn't spent years strumming the damn thing in church like I had, so it was fresh and new to him. This turned out to be a wise move because he would go on to master it. Becoming a very good guitarist, singer-songwriter, he eventually signed a deal with Universal Music Publishing. Now *he* inspires *me*.

On some of those promo tours in Europe, I would occasionally get the odd day off here and there and take some time out alone and go walkabout, visiting the great cathedrals of Europe like Notre-Dame, Paris, or the Dom in Cologne. TV shows and clubs were a noisy affair, so I needed some time to be silent, to not think much at all. I found places like the chapel on rue du Bac, Paris, to be just perfect for this. There I was able to recharge, reflect and refocus.

Ask anyone who knew me back then and they will tell you that I was the type of person who was always on the go, 100 miles per hour, places to go, people to see, and this was true to a certain extent. The hidden reality was that I did hit the stop button and got off the hamster wheel whenever I could, but very few people got to see that side of me or even knew it existed.

While we were going all around Europe, 'Outstanding' was doing well in Australia and New Zealand, so I was told, but I never even made it there! Equally, I understand that I have a big following in Brazil! The record company would pick and choose where they sent me. They would swallow the expense, but only if they knew they could claw it back on record sales from those territories.

So, at this point I have had three chart hits, done many clubs gigs with live vocal to backing track, but I have yet to form an actual band, I haven't done one full gig or even hinted at a tour. Then comes what I call another *Deep End* moment.

Steve had a habit of throwing me into them. *Blues & Soul magazine* were celebrating 25 years by having a concert at the Albert Hall in December 1991, and they wanted me to perform on the show. Of course, Steve said 'yes' and now I would have to deliver somehow.

On that bill were Edwin Starr, Will Downing, Freddie Jackson, Lalah Hathaway, Lonnie Liston Smith, Incognito, Mica Paris, Ruby Turner, JT Taylor, Young Disciples and Omar. Not much for me to worry about, then!

To be honest, I am not one for pre-gig nerves, but that night was an exception. It wasn't because I had never even stepped foot in the Royal Albert Hall before... That in itself was mind-blowing. It was because I was told the American soul singer Freddie Jackson would be sitting out there in the audience watching my performance. I had bought all of his records as a teenager and now he was going to watch me sing. This wasn't like stepping into the boxing ring and the nerves associated with that, but it was pretty damn close. I wore a three-quarter-length tweed jacket, handmade for me by the very talented Soho tailor Mark Powell. The shoulder pads were slightly extended to create shape, something the 80s singer Colonel Abrams would have been proud of. I looked the part: externally I was a man on a mission, but internally I felt like a boy who was way out of his depth, but I didn't let it show.

Mum and Dad came to the concert. The last time Dad was in the Albert Hall was when he fought 'The Dartford Destroyer' Dave Charnley in 1954. It was a proud moment for them.

It turned out to be an amazing night.

I got out there, did my thing, and not many people would have guessed that it was my first time with a full live band. I was what some would call in the boxing game *a natural*. Yes, I needed to work on it, but being onstage with a band of that calibre was where I belonged. Freddie Jackson came backstage and paid me a huge compliment, and that meant a lot to me and still does.

Steve was happy. Thrown in the deep end, I delivered. The boy did good.

A week before the Albert Hall show, 'Tender Love' was released. Trying to have a hit record in that formidable run-up to Christmas, when all the big guns are out, was not easy. A huge number of record sales was needed to make even the smallest dent in the charts. With its classy video shot in New Jersey, USA, and massive support on radio and TV, it only managed to get to Number 26 in the charts. Despite this, it was still a big record and all of our hard work had paid off.

Voices is a hit. It peaks at Number 3 in the UK album chart, going platinum in just a few days.

I am now in demand.

Other publishers and writers who would not have touched me before start coming out of the woodwork. That is how this works.

I am offered *If There's Any Justice* which goes on to be a hit for Lemar, but only in 2004. More than a decade on – in itself an insight into how this business operates with songs being touted around sometimes over a long period of time and record companies not fancying it at the time but then suddenly doing an about-turn when someone else comes into vogue. Often, if the artist is not the writer – and I was beginning to pen songs – then this decision can be taken out of your hands and sometimes only discovered sometime later.

You may recall Jimmy Nail – the actor who had one of the biggest hits in 1992 with 'Ain't No Doubt'.

I was offered that track! His big Number 1.

For some reason at the time we felt that it wasn't quite right for me.

You can't live life wondering what the impact of that might have been – but hey, I do wonder what the impact of that might have been!

In the moment and within the industry, it did not matter. The phone was ringing.

I get word Dannii Minogue wants to talk.

I think we first met at a Smash Hits Poll Winners Party, but you can never be quite certain. Events like that rolled into one another. Dannii, of course, is Kylie's sister. Dannii was trying a similar route, having begun in *Home and Away* and now was attempting an assault on the charts.

'She is going to ring you in the studio from New York,' Steve told me.

There was one particular track she thought was perfect for both of us. Steve played it to me and we both agreed that it wasn't right. It was too pop, not very soulful, and generally didn't sound like a hit record.

I wasn't fancying it as much as she was.

At this stage in your career, it would have been very easy to latch onto the Minogue name and think 'Why not?' It could take you to an audience you might not otherwise reach.

My gut was no.

'You are going to have to tell her; better if it came directly from you,' Steve said.

'Drop me right in it, why don't you?' I replied.

I would have to let her down gently.

'Have you heard the song?' she asked, bursting with enthusiasm.

'Yes, I have, and to be honest,' I began. 'it's not my kind of song.'

I could hear the deflation in her response.

'It's no bad reflection on you, Dannii, it's just that it really doesn't fit with the kind of music I'm making right now,' I followed up.

I wished her all the best with it, and we hung up.

The moment passed.

Until the next time I saw her at *Top of the Pops*.

She completely blanked me.

Kylie, however, *did not*.

I find myself doing a photo shoot in King's Cross with photographer Katerina Jebb who, a few days later, invited me over to her friend's apartment in Kensington so we could go through the shoot and choose the best pics. I had no idea who her friend was, but I soon found out when Kylie emerged from the bathroom, fresh out of the shower, wearing only a small towel.

'Would you like a coffee?' she purrs.

'YES. I WOULD,' I reply.

It beat Starbucks, any day of the week.

A few days later, the photographer sends the shots back to me. When they arrived, two of the pictures had *Kylie xx* written next to them. She had personally chosen her favourite pics.

101

Steve is urging me on.

'Get yourself back to that apartment. Get in there.'

'No can do… I am in a relationship,' I reply, smiling.

Was it the green light Steve thought it might be or did she simply just like those particular photographs? I think it was the latter, but we'll never really know!

At the same time, Steve is actually full on, busy working his BAMN Management company and the Fnoot production label. Looking back now, my deal may have seemed rushed, but he knew exactly what to exploit. I was signed to Fnoot, which gave us control over the making of the album. It was then licensed to Cooltempo. Fnoot therefore were the real owners of the album. It was then down to us to finish it and deliver it to Cooltempo. The contract Steve signed very cleverly did not include North America – the biggest pop music market in the world. This wise move meant a successful *Voices* album could then be signed to any label we wanted in the USA.

He invited Giant Records over to the UK to meet me and began to work his magic. Giant was created in 1990 as a joint venture between Warner Bros. and the record executive and music mogul Irving Azoff. Irving had managed the Eagles since the early 1970s and also looks after Steely Dan, Bon Jovi, Stevie Nicks, Christina Aguilera and Maroon 5, to name a few. A very powerful guy indeed!

Irving sent Cassandra Mills, head of Urban Music, and the president of the label, a well-respected PR guru Charlie Minor, to London for the meet. They were having massive worldwide success with Color Me Badd at the time. Knowing the right impression had to be made and being the master of closing a deal, Steve made sure the chauffeur took a deliberate detour from the airport to the meeting. They were driven down Oxford Street right past the huge posters of me that adorned at least three of those big windows in the HMV record store. Driving slowly enough so they didn't miss them, whilst subtly switching the radio station, every now and then, between Radio 1 and Capital, making sure they heard my song several times during that journey. Steve sold them star quality, subconsciously manipulated their perception, and probably added a couple of zeros to the deal.

However, there were tensions back at the UK label... and back at the ranch.

Though they take time to trickle in, I soon received some royalties and was able to buy a cottage in St Albans, Hertfordshire. I went from being deliberately cool and hanging out with Judy Blame, the British fashion stylist who worked with Neneh Cherry and Afrika Baby Bam of the Jungle Brothers, to disappearing into the countryside.

I had my wild days – *The Sun* newspaper, who seemed to know everything, reported that I had chinned someone in a nightclub in Oldham, which I had, but I was essentially still seen as the boy next door with a pretty squeaky clean image.

I was coming off-stage when this lairy drunk was muscling his way towards me. I knew what was going to happen. His body language could be summed up in an instant. He made a movement towards me and all I am thinking is, 'I don't wanna get glassed here.' The bouncers reacted too slowly, and I took him out with a corker of a punch. The boxer in me would always defend myself and do so before being aggressed. Dad always said, 'Be first, son,' meaning act quickly, and get in there before they get to you. It was only ever going to be me or him – self-defence in advance, if you like. Somehow the paper knew.

They were there when the police were called to control the fans at an album signing with Blur at HMV Manchester which turned out to be an absolute roadblock, and they were there again when I opened up the Nemesis ride at Alton Towers with Level 42 and Color Me Badd – bands and events of the moment and easy wins for me. I played that game and of course sooner or later the argument comes that if you court the press, you have no excuse when they turn you over.

That can be a very superficial line to trot out. It is not a one-size-fits-all argument.

But generally, the boy next door hung around with the right people and went to the places he was going to anyway.

Life was good. Sophie lived not too far away in Barnet, and we were holding it together despite my crazy schedule and the pressures. I didn't give a damn that some people at the label thought it was odd I had retreated out of the city when I had lived there all my life and that was where the party was deemed to be. Although there was no shortage of fun at my little cottage. Through Sophie, I had been introduced to new people and made some amazing friendships. Nick, Chad and Mason would now join James, Dave and Johnny Boy. This gang would further grow when I bumped into Steve Hart at a gig in Paradise Lost nightclub in Watford. I hadn't seen Steve in years, once a regular at my dad's boxing gym when he was younger. He was also in the boy band Worlds Apart who were just starting out and went on to have a hit here in the UK but far greater success in France. We all shared the same humour and a love of house music. We would go on to have some of the craziest and funniest moments of our lives... times which we will never forget.

So, I had a life outside of the music business and friends from all walks of life. I needed this. The record company, however, wanted me seen at everything. They soon realised that I would pick and choose the events I wanted to go to, more often *not* wanting to.

I preferred to remain grounded.

As ever, it could hit the buffers at any point.

The previous August on that helicopter swoop into the Radio 1 Roadshow, we had flown over Steve Finan's dad's house in Wentworth, Surrey, just taking it in on a leisurely run down to the West Country.

Steve even called his grandad on his mobile – just so we could wave from overhead. We were flying low enough to be seen and we were right over the garden of his house. His grandad was one of the loveliest people I have ever met. It would have been a treasured memory if we had got to wave to him from that chopper, but he never answered his phone and we had to move on.

We were playing at being popstars and I was to make the big entry when we landed. As we hit the ground, my phone rang. It was Sophie, bawling her eyes out. Front stage, the crowd is going mad.

Her grandfather had just passed away.

He lived in Bournemouth, the very place we had just flown over earlier.

There really was nothing I could do.

I had to perform in the next few minutes.

The show had to go on.

Not for the first time and not for the last.

Autopilot. Tunnel vision. The ability to flick a switch and deliver, and then come back out of that and face the reality ahead.

I don't know if this was the latest wake-up call that inspired me to get the cottage, or I had already seen enough of pop to know the move was sensible. There were times when I slipped into the lifestyle of being out all hours mixing with those whose best friend was of a white powdery nature but that was only because I was young and loved going out. For the most part I was trying to resist what others thought a popstar should be.

So, all roads led to Hertfordshire, and I blew £67k on this little, two-bedroomed Victorian cottage where you couldn't swing a cat, but I was fortunate that I could buy it outright. I should have held onto that one, though, as it is now worth a million!

Part of the process of pop is that the vultures swarm and you can't know who to trust. That meant I had people around me now telling me what to do with my money. Some of that advice was good for me, and some of it was good for the advisor who could take a slice of it. Simply, I didn't get the best information a boy from a council estate should have got at the time. But I chose to listen to that advice so that meant I was responsible for my own mistakes.

The finance, though, was all linked to the deal and the music. I was lucky in that Steve made sure I got what was due to me and no one was ever going to have him over. He was too sharp for that. Some of the stories that I heard of certain artists getting screwed were unbelievable, but sadly, very true. Yes, it was a dog-eat-dog world, but Steve had most of them on a leash and well muzzled.

That sphere of influence, therefore, steers you down certain roads. Steve, in particular, believed that I had to move back to London.

Play the game. Go to the next level. He was right.

The business was fickle. Steve knew how to play it as well as anyone. He could see the process from all angles. We had become good friends, but I was still a product. The moulding of that went hand in hand with what he was selling. But guess what? Whilst I understood this, that was not who I was. I was a singer and a musician – a music fan who got to live out his dream. Those hours staring out of a BT office window didn't include playing the game beyond singing on *Top of the Pops*, hearing my song on Capital, or performing live in front of huge crowds.

I had my dabbles of course with the scene. I played it for a while. Many people get lost in it and don't come out of it until they are *left* out of it. Whilst I indulged, I could see the dangers, too. But here's the point – Barrington Levy was right. I could get up caught up in the moment as much as anyone, but I did essentially know my own mind and my values weren't changing.

I had a very active social life outside of the industry and this was my escape from it. Trying to keep a balance between the two was not easy, and at times my socialising had got the upper hand. Steve Finan tried to rein me in, but he also knew that all work and no play made Kenny a dull boy. It can make anyone seem that, so I dragged him out clubbing with us more times than I can count!

So, me and the lads hit the nightclubs every weekend, even with the odd midweek outing to The Gardening Club in Covent Garden thrown in. Not much gardening, the odd bit of grass. We knew the music we liked, the DJs who played it, and the right places to hear it in. We often went to several clubs in the same night, but on a Saturday night we nearly always ended up at the Ministry of Sound. The nightlife scene in the 90s was exciting and very seductive. It had it all. From the glamour of designer-wearing champagne drinkers down to the serious house music devotees who just wanted to dance all night and didn't care if their Paul Smith shirt was soaked in sweat. On those nights we had some of the best and funniest times.

One evening, we were all going for it in the main room of the Ministry. We looked around and saw Nick bending over, his head down towards the floor with one arm sticking up in the air. For a minute we thought he was trying out some new dance move that none of us had seen before. He looked like someone attempting a half-swallow dive from the top board of Hornsey Road Baths. Chad bent down and asked him what was going on. Nick's back had gone and he was unable to stand upright. The Ministry wasn't the kind of place where you could shout out, 'Is there a physio in the house!?' and if you did you wouldn't be heard above the banging sound system anyway. Nick was stuck in that position, and we needed to get him out of there before the security removed him for what was beginning to look a lot like yoga on the dance floor. Carrying him out of the club like two labourers moving timber from a builders' merchants, we managed to get him onto the back seat of the car. All the while Nick maintained that shape. To this day Chad and I laugh about it, and we still wonder what that 'one arm up in the air' was all about.

Equally hysterical: we were staying at a boutique hotel after a long night of pounding the dance floor at the Southport Soul Weekender. James had a shower but became disoriented and wearing only a towel around his waist walked out of the room, down the stairs and exited the hotel, locking himself out in the process. When I realised that he had been missing for some time I went looking for him. Wearing just boxer shorts and a T-shirt, I did exactly the same thing. It was around 4am and now we are both locked out, standing in the street, in the cold, looking like a right pair of idiots. I had to wake up the hotel owner who was none too pleased, only letting me back in after a routine bollocking.

Yes, I was young and reckless at times, but I was trying to find my feet in a world that was shifting fast. Overwhelmed by it and unable to control those changes, I found my escape by exchanging one reality for another. Immersing myself into the feel-good house music scene, I negated all responsibilities and switched everything off for a few hours. Ultimately those escapes were short-lived, and the false sense of freedom it gave, impermanent. In the long term it destroys your will to win. Ian Green would often say, 'I am in it to win it,' and I had to be *in it to win it*, not out of it.

Then there were those other people around me – the types Barrington had warned about.

One particular encounter took place in Wormwood Scrubs prison in London. My friend Dave was visiting a friend of his who was doing time there. He looked across and saw another mate of ours from the old days on Stamford Hill. He was also doing a stretch. He was someone I used to knock about with in my more innocent times, but he now felt that I had sold out, by going on to be something of a success.

'You still see Kenny?' he asked Dave.

'Yeah of course, me and Kenny are still best mates,' Dave replied.

'Well, you tell Kenny, I am going to fix him when I get out of here. Now he's in the charts, he has forgotten about us,' he said angrily.

'Hold on,' said Dave. 'You ain't seen him in years, long before he became successful, and *now* you wanna sort him out?'

'Yeah, I do,' he concluded.

Imagine that – you have a hit record and somebody you haven't seen in ages tells someone in a chance encounter that they are out to get you.

Emotions and thoughts are bound to be all over the place when you are banged up in The Scrubs. Misdirected anger, focused on the wrong person. I got that.

Ironically, a few years later I ran into him at one of my gigs. I went up to him, put my arms out and gave him the biggest hug. He hugged me back, just like two mates who haven't seen each other in years *should* do. The things he said to Dave were so insignificant that I never even mentioned it. I was just happy to see him back on the outside and in a good place.

Growing up had been tough but I felt I had done OK. I sometimes felt guilty that I had survived it and prospered, but clearly this was nothing compared to some of the feelings others were harbouring towards me. Against that kind of childhood, your roots never leave you. It was still a part of me. Nothing was different. Others did not see it that way, without any real right to think like that.

I hadn't forgotten my origins at all. One Christmas Day, whilst driving back over to Hackney to see Mum and Dad, I stopped off at an off-licence to grab a bottle of wine for Dad. Outside the shop stood an old family friend whom I hadn't seen in a long time. Life had not been so kind to him, now down and out, clearly in the grip of addiction. His clothing was inadequate for that time of year, and he was generally not in good shape. I put my arm around him and asked if he was OK and if he had food and a place to stay. He told me things were not great, but he did at least have a room where he could get his head down. We spoke at length. I then reached into my pocket and gave him some money. He was so grateful that he began to cry. I did my best to fight back the tears, but once I got back to my car, I let it out. Seeing him like that hurt me a lot. Life is not fair sometimes.

I remember the days when he would be suited and booted, clean-shaven and off to work early every day. Just a normal guy grafting hard to feed his family. What happened? How did he go from that to this? Why did my life go in one direction and his another? This did not sit comfortably with me.

I cared very deeply about those people who had always been there and hadn't just temporarily come into my life to hang on for the ride. I wanted everyone to do well and be happy, to live a long and healthy life. The idealist in me was simply longing for the *Utopia* Thomas More had written about. Instead, I would have to accept reality; this world was in fact more of a *dystopia*.

I would also have to accept that, in my own life, I did not always live up to my own ideals. No one is perfect, for sure. Like so many, I experienced that intense struggle, a tug-of-war, between wanting to do good, to be good and the human tendency towards *getting up to no good*. Like a pendulum swinging from one extreme to the other, from the excessive popstar lifestyle to the complete rejection of it, I was engaged in my own spiritual battle, and I had to avoid the pitfalls or at least find a way to climb back out of them.

Boy George – who, let's face it, had seen it all – had warned me similarly one night at the Ministry of Sound.

'I can see what you have been doing,' he offered with the look of a man who had been there and done that – as he had. At his time, probably nobody had experienced more the prejudice of society, the pitfalls of the industry and the fickleness of the media.

I knew I was misbehaving a little, but I was also *just* out with my mates, enjoying the house scene, relieving that pressure. Having unrestricted access to the *in places* and knowing so many people in the scene made it easy to get lost in it, and at that moment lost I was.

'Be careful,' he simply said.

And he was right. The truth was my eyes were a dead giveaway. There was no hiding it: I looked like a rabbit caught in the headlights of a car.

I thought of the times I had seen those little packages of cocaine being passed around at music industry events. Being asked, 'Would you like a line?' became as normal as being asked, 'Would you like a cup of tea?' This was show business.

Having a 10am meeting with someone at a record company who was already off their nut was always interesting. The frequent trips they made to the toilet had nothing to do with a bladder problem. Always returning with such energy, vigour and enthusiasm. I once had such a meeting, only to realise that when I left the building, we had not even spoken about the very thing I came to talk about.

I witnessed one exec open up a birthday card to find a gram of coke in it. Happy Birthday, Best wishes from Pablo Escobar!

These people were just playing the game.

The 90s had big budgets, big dreams and big egos.

They worked hard and they played hard. Sometimes they just played hard and got lucky. For some, success came without working at all. All hidden beneath the veneer of *looking busy* and *doing a lot of meetings.*

'We're going to The Tunnel Club Glasgow for a night out,' someone at the label would ring. And I knew what that meant.

'Are you coming?'

Not one to miss a good night out. My answer was 'Yes'.

This was the fun side of the game. Going on a social with the guys and girls from the record company didn't happen that often, but when it did, we had good time.

Some of that, I began to fear, was coming out of artists' budgets in that invisible world of no receipts where it looks like the record company are treating you lavishly, but years later you begin to wonder if in fact you were paying all along.

Being ever the boy from Hackney and with old habits dying hard, I managed to find out the names, account numbers and passwords for the black taxi accounts the record company used. These I would use often when I was out on the town with my friends Chad, James and Johnny Boy. Admittedly there was the small problem of not looking like a *Jody* or a *Sarah* when the cab turned up, but some half-baked story soon sorted that out. Eventually the label rumbled me and I was caught bang to rights. It wasn't difficult to work out that Jody wasn't actually at the Emporium nightclub last Saturday night. It was good while it lasted.

Much was industry standard – at a Paul Weller album launch party at I was warned not to touch the punch. I didn't, but it was obvious who had, when they began to lose their inhibitions, adopted the standard euphoric grin, and lost the ability to talk with sentences that were joined in any way.

Father Hanshell kept me sane. I could tell him these stories and he would just say, 'Kenny, welcome to the human race.' He knew nobody was perfect but was the first to make me realise that creative people, especially musicians, often seek something that was out of the norm, the desire to experience altered states of consciousness, and that drugs can enhance the artistic process for some. This, he said, was a spiritual dilemma and what they are ultimately seeking can never be fulfilled this way. He brought me back to reality and made me understand that all things pass, and I would grow out of it. I would have to keep trying to do my best. The only real failure is failing to try.

On promo trips abroad, it could often be worse because your local hosts seemed to think 'excessive hospitality' was expected especially in Kuala Lumpur, and Bangkok in Thailand

and here, execs' behaviour was often worse than the popstars, letting themselves go even more because … what happens on the road stays on the road.

In Bangkok we went from bar to bar, and when we returned to the hotel, the partying would go on all night, from one room to another. I would often escape to my own, for a breather, a break from the noise, only to return and resume my rightful position next to the minibar. In truth, I was very much the party animal, so I was in good company.

The first night we were there, Steve and I were out having drinks with some of the label guys, and as the night went on our group got bigger and bigger as we were joined by girls, who I assumed were friends of the execs. Making our way back to the hotel to continue the soirée, we congregated into one of the suites. It was great to be in a new city, meeting new people. The group eventually became smaller as people retired to their own rooms, until this left only Steve and me in the room with two other young girls. They did not speak good English, in fact hardly any at all, and they didn't look like they were going anywhere fast. They looked nervous. Steve became highly suspicious.

In the best way he could Steve managed to communicate with them and very quickly worked out that they were prostitutes. Hired by one of the record company execs and given orders to stick close to Steve and me for the night. It was his way of saying, 'Welcome to Bangkok.' The girls gave us a very good description of who it was, but Steve had already worked out who had done this.

The following day Steve went mad, flying into the exec's office.

'Don't you ever disrespect a Western artist again!' he yelled.

'What about the money?' the exec replied. 'I paid for it.'

'That's your problem,' Steve replied.

'If an artist comes to your country and wants to do this kind of thing, they are more than capable of finding it for themselves. What you did is an insult,' Steve told him.

Of all the cities I had been to Bangkok was something else. I love Thailand and the Thai people, but that city is quite unique and not for the best of reasons. As with all my journeys, meeting people, seeing the culture and enjoying their food have become my predominant memories, more so than the gigs themselves. And sometimes unusual things happen in the most unsuspecting places.

Once again, the record company guys took it upon themselves and decided it would be a good idea to take us to a particular bar that specialised in exotic dancing, although they never told us where we were going, or even thought of asking us if we wanted to go. At first I thought it was a normal bar until several, what appeared to be, girls jumped onto the podium and began doing their thing. Sitting next to me was another young Thai guy from the label. He looked about as interested as I did in what was taking place on the podiums.

'I'm not really into this,' I turned to him and said.

'No, it's not my thing either,' he replied.

'I am into spirituality, and this place is *not* good for my soul,' I said in a random moment of honesty.

'Really? No way! Me, too,' he replied engagingly, looking like I had just switched a light bulb on in his head.

It turns out that he and I were very much on the same page, entering into a really deep conversation quite unbelievably, sitting there in a seedy Bangkok bar, discussing aspects of the *Summa Theologica* written by Thomas Aquinas in the 13th century. This was the kind of conversation Father Hanshell would have had in his younger years when he was teaching Theology at Campion Hall, Oxford University, but never in a place like this.

Oblivious to everything that was going on around us, we connected. What prompted me to say what I said to him? I wouldn't normally reveal my inner thoughts to someone I have only just met, but I did, and I found a kindred soul where I least expected it.

Everything happens for a reason.

We left the bar shortly after that. Steve and I headed down the road in pursuit of some Thai boxing. This was far more entertaining and definitely our thing. Once back at the hotel, I wasn't feeling particularly tired that night, so I made my way alone, back down to the main strip. It didn't take long before I bumped into an Irish guy in one of the bars and we had a couple of beers together. I just loved meeting people, normal everyday folk. I couldn't be around the music industry stuff all of the time. The one thing you can guarantee is that wherever you go in the world, whatever city, you will always bump into an Irish man, and there is no one better to have a beer and good old chinwag with than an Irish man.

So, my move out of town was my business to keep my *business* in perspective. And I knew my place at the label, too. I was somewhat behind Sinéad and Go West which was totally fine. And for a while they would switch their focus to their next hit record, as they did, when Chesney Hawkes rightfully occupied the Number 1 position in the charts with 'The One And Only' – a well-deserved hit for one of the industry's nicest guys.

My success did leave them caught slightly unawares by the time the *Voices* album came out.

Crucially, too, never mind whom I observed in the pecking order ahead of me, I had already seen several artists fall down the roster and off it altogether.

So, it was a ladder and every time you are told to be more like so-and-so, and to go to the next level, they are saying the same to someone else and citing you. Many of those do have investment but don't make it. By the time their song comes out for a second or third attempt, that can be it.

This will come as no surprise to you reading it. Your own record collection will be full of 'whatever happened to?' and the answer is more than likely in the previous paragraph. It is no wonder that even people outside the industry have heard the phrase 'second album syndrome' where the unexpected success of the first release placed huge pressure on the second and it often did not deliver. It has happened so many times that really you have to question if some of these people know what they are doing.

Of course, the songs may not be good enough, but apart from the singles that were played on the radio, the public wouldn't know how good the whole record might be until they bought the album, so logic would follow that actually you should struggle with the third album, not the second, because many would purchase that out of blind loyalty after their admiration for the first. The fact that this 'second album syndrome' is trotted out so often implies its truth, but also that something else went wrong – a deliberate change in sound and direction, a lack of continuity, or that race against time in which to write and record the album so as not to lose any career momentum.

That is why Steve was all over them to get the job done right and not lose any time. I might not have been the next Big Thing, but I did dominate that blue-eyed soul market at the time and the first album had more than delivered. He didn't miss a trick and was straight in there.

EMI had taken over Chrysalis and that left a trail of politics and a new set of internal dynamics. Steve was very unhappy with some of the promotional side of things from Chrysalis, and he wanted me to have the best shot possible with the second album. This often meant he had to outsource some of the work and put it into the hands of independent companies, as he did with Ferret and Spanner, who had done a great job for me at TV and national radio. This was always a bold statement. Public relations went to Chris Poole and Alan Edwards at Poole Edwards. These guys were at the top of their game. They could get the right press and finally place the correct stories. They didn't come cheap, and this would have to come out of my own pocket. I was willing to give it a try. Unfortunately, I felt that Poole Edwards turned out to be about as useful as an ashtray on a motorbike. As good as they were for some artists, it didn't work out for me.

So, we would say goodbye to naked Norwegian dancers or skipping on Motormouth, but crazy stories ending up in the tabloids were inescapable. Like the one where I had apparently driven my car into a shopfront window. My brother Steve phoned me to ask if I was alright. I didn't have the foggiest idea what he was going on about until he told me what was in the paper that day. Of course, I was alright, there had been no car accident. I didn't read 'red-top' newspapers. I have never had a need for sensationalism. If I want fiction, I'll read a John Grisham novel.

I recognise, of course, that publicity is oxygen, but when someone shows you a newspaper and you are wondering how a story got there, *and* your suspicion is that it is somebody in the music biz who you don't even know, then this is not a level playing field.

I was called to a photo shoot with Dina Carroll whose career was really running alongside mine. It was for *Harpers & Queen* magazine and penned by Alan Jackson, who has remained supportive throughout my career and later wrote a terrific piece for *The Sunday Times* in which he said that if I were American 'we would be taking him very seriously indeed'. I will always be grateful for that line.

Emerging in the early 90s, Dina was delivering quality pop soul music with hits like 'Escaping' and 'The Perfect Year'. Dina went on to have two platinum albums and won Best British Female Solo Artist at the 1994 BRIT Awards. In the moment, she was at the top of her game.

Perhaps we happened to complement each other musically in that we were both solo soul artists of the opposite sex, so I could see exactly why the magazine went for this piece.

During the photo shoot we had conversations about music and the industry. It was all really pleasant. I then had an idea that I wanted to put to her. I asked her if she was up for having some fun with the press, off the back of this. How about we play them at their own game and feed them a story for once? Circulate a little rumour, let them think that we might be seeing one another. The record companies are always banging on about getting more press, and this would certainly tick that box. Dina and I would undoubtedly get some mileage out of the story. She thought it was a mad idea, but she could see the upside of it and agreed. So, I set to work.

I had a chat with my press officer Jody at Chrysalis, who thought it was somewhat crazy and risky, but definitely worth pursuing. 'Any press is good press' is one of the sayings I often heard. I can't say that I always agreed with that statement, but on this occasion it was good and it was fairly harmless.

The rumour was promptly put out there, knowing that we could rely on people's natural inclination to gossip. It worked!

Dina and I also had some up-and-coming gigs together, such as radio roadshows, but that was the extent of the relationship in reality. However, as long as we played along with it and kept them thinking, the story was a goer.

At one of those gigs, I was approached backstage by a reporter for one of the main red-top newspapers.

'Is there anything going on with you and Dina?' he asked.

'Sorry, I am not prepared to talk about it,' I answered, knowing full well that I had just fuelled the fire.

We got on great the day of the photo shoot, but for goodness' sake, don't mistake two singers in the same genre on the front of *Harpers & Queen* for becoming an item, especially when both had partners.

Yes, of course, when the rumour began to grow legs, I did wind up the press a little, and I saw this as fun to do, but it was also complete nonsense.

This, in essence, is the game. It has nothing to do with music – and yes, I do get it. But it does become tiring, so concocting my own story injected a little excitement into the general monotony of things.

The following week, after appearing on the radio roadshow, the press were all over it, calling my record company and Dina's label, asking them to confirm the story. A simple confirmation from them was all it needed to go to press.

Jody at Chrysalis then received a very angry call from Dina's manager Oliver Smallman saying that he was not at all happy with this and wanted it to stop right now. He was sticking the boot in and pulling the plug on the non-story.

I admit that on this occasion I wasn't innocent. It was my idea, so it was my bad. But we almost pulled it off!

It was apparent to me that when some people in the music game say that 'any press is good press' or 'there's no such thing as bad publicity' they *don't* really mean it. This is usually what they come out with when they are being battered in the press by a story they have no *control* over.

Chrysalis Records were no angels either, and they tried their best to fabricate stories just to grab some space in the showbiz section of the papers.

'Kenny, I know it's short notice, but can you come in this afternoon?' they asked me one morning.

'What do you need me for?' I asked.

'We've got a journalist coming here from *The Sun* to do a piece on you, but you'll have to get here before he does, so we can first tell you what it's all about.'

I got onto the tube and made my way down to Chrysalis. When I arrived, there was a brand spanking new BMW parked right outside the front doors.

'Because of your success at the label, we have bought you this new BMW as a thankyou gift. However, there's no need to get too excited because it's not really a gift and you won't be driving home in it. It is just for the interview, it is an angle we have come up with to get you in the paper,' I was told.

'When the journalist arrives, he will ask you how you feel about being given the car. Act surprised, extremely happy, say great things about the label, have some pictures taken sitting in the car and then drive off into the sunset. Once we know the journalist has vacated the premises, drive it back, park up and return the keys.'

Sounds simple enough!

Now I wasn't a body language expert but during the interview I got a feeling that the journalist had a nose for bullshit. I played along with the whole thing, but I wasn't really comfortable with it, and I couldn't wait for it to be over. Some pictures were taken of me admiring the car, and a few fake grins from the driver's seat. I went for a spin around the block, handed the keys back, and then got on the tube and went home. I told the record company not to ask me to do anything like that again.

As I suspected, the journalist was no fool, because there was only a small piece in the paper the following day.

Kenny gets new car from record label as a gift for being a good boy.

The End!

The plan had failed, no big article, no pics of me trying to look well chuffed at the wheel, and most definitely no shiny new car. I was surprised that he even bothered to print anything at all. It was an ill-conceived, hastily manufactured story, and he knew it. We would have had more success if they asked me to streak naked up Ladbroke Grove.

'How's your new car, bruv?' my brother Steve asked me on the phone.

'It's great, Steve, got it parked up in my garage,' I replied.

'Oh right! What garage? You don't have a garage at your house,' Steve said in a confused tone.

'You're right, bro, I don't have a garage and I don't have a new BMW. It's all record company nonsense,' I told him.

They were all at it. On ITV's *The Chart Show,* a Saturday morning syndicated music video programme, these little text boxes would appear next to the video of your hit and its chart position. I would get a call from the record label to say that my video was going to be on the show and did I have any interesting information for them to put in the space? If it was just an average week and all I was doing was recording in the studio, that was seen as 'not juicy enough', so the label would come up with something. I have to confess that apart from those early *Top of the Pops* broadcasts, I never watched myself on TV or listened back to interviews. After all, I was there so I knew what happened and what was said. I would, however, watch *The Chart Show* just to see what would come up in the boxes and have a chuckle at the stuff I was supposed to have done, or all the exciting things I was about to do. Most of it was just made up. This didn't bother me. I secretly enjoyed watching the illusion play out. As long as I could differentiate between what was real and what was not, I could navigate my way through the smoke and mirrors and not buy into it.

A fake BMW-driving actor by day, a singer by night – somewhere in the middle, a superimposed character in someone else's fantasy land. Somebody whose job it was to feed every aspect of my life, whether true or otherwise, significant, or less so, to a friend of theirs at the showbiz columns.

Steve Finan knew the music business better than anyone else and exactly how to play it. He made me realise very early on that all of this is a process; keep your eye on the endgame. Any negative press, or fabricated stories were just a storm in a teacup, quickly read and soon forgotten. He was always focused on the bigger picture, in search of what could become possibly the defining moment of my career, beyond those first hits.

Steve cleverly left the American option wide open, and he had a deal on the table. He was already managing Monie Love, who had moved to the States, along with the Jungle Brothers and the rapper Ice-T. So, he knew the moves we had to make. It's a leap of faith, but if we don't have a go we would never know.

America was calling!

We had already gone a bit rock'n'roll by shooting the video for 'Tender Love' in New Jersey, but Steve's seduction of Giant Records meant that trips to the States were now becoming a regular thing.

I wandered round Times Square thinking, 'This is cool.' It's just like I had seen it in the movies. I loved New York! It was like London on steroids.

Steve gave me strict instructions on how to behave there.

'Talk to no one, do not make eye contact with anyone, and act a little bit crazy. You'll fit right in,' he told me on my first night in the city.

'Oh and take that gold chain off, you can't have that hanging around your neck out there,' he said, as I made my way out of his apartment.

Wearing a three-quarter-length leather coat, bright red Nike trainers, an oversized Stüssy T-shirt and a Chicago Bulls basketball cap, I went out for one of my late-night walks around Manhattan. I looked like a cross between a pimp out of *Starsky & Hutch* and one of the Beastie Boys. As long as no one got wind of my cockney accent I did indeed *fit right in*. In a city filled with eccentrics, I felt extremely comfortable, and as far as acting *a bit crazy* goes, well, that was my usual modus operandi in the 90s.

We hung out in New York for a few days, checked in with our lawyer to go over the new record deal, and then made our way to Los Angeles. Before going to the airport, I took a cab to America's iconic store Macy's and decided to buy a Game Boy for the plane ride. It came with a RoboCop game, where you had to make your way through each level avoiding missiles coming up out of the ground.

For most of the journey, I am dodging those silo missiles, occasionally taking a break to read a book entitled *No One Here Gets Out Alive*, a biography of Jim Morrison, the lead singer of The Doors. I wanted to find out more about the 60s, the decade of my birth and the counter-culture that changed the world, or where it all went pear-shaped, depending on how you looked at it.

I was going to LA, the place where all of this went down.

Welcome to Hollywood, baby!

Problem is, Los Angeles needed a health warning that we were coming.

On a warm, sunny day in January 1992, we arrive in LA. Steve and I head straight to the Hollywood Hills to drop in on a mate of his named Benny. He was one of his music industry friends, very successful and seriously connected. It just so happened to be the day of Benny's birthday. Coincidence? I think not. Steve's perfect timing? Absolutely.

We knock on the door.

Benny greets us with a huge smile.

'It's so good to see you, Steve,' he says.

'We just got into LA and I thought we would swing by your place first,' replied Steve.

He introduces me to Benny.

'Kenny, welcome to LA.' He said, 'I heard you signed a new deal... Man, that's awesome.'

Benny has got a good vibe about him: I like him immediately.

'Hey, guys, it's my birthday today. I'm having a party and you gotta stay for it,' he insisted.

'Guys, this is my friend, Lenny, he's just flown in from San Francisco for the party,' says Benny.

Lenny was cool, a laid-back dude, and up for a party, big time!

'Lenny, Benny and Kenny...' and we all laughed. This could get confusing and maybe a bit messy.

As with every day in LA, the sun was shining and the vibe was perfect. A party by the pool, looking down as the city sprawled out below us sounded good to me. Steve and I were right up for it. What could possibly go wrong?

We still had our luggage in the car. We hadn't even been to the hotel to check in. We landed only an hour ago and here we are getting bang into the LA scene.

People were yet to arrive, so we really were in early doors.

'Come on, guys, let's go for it… let's get started,' said Lenny, as he invited me into the kitchen and poured me a large alcoholic drink.

Let's go for it. He was not kidding.

'You want some of this, Kenny?' said Lenny, as he presented me with a tub of crystal-looking white powder.

'You ever tried this before?' he said with a cheeky smile. 'It's pure MDMA, straight out the lab.'

'Yeah, I've had a dabble before, back in the UK,' I replied.

'Not like this you ain't. This is the best there is,' he said as he tipped a small amount of it onto a Rizla paper and began to make an ingestible bomb.

'In for a penny, in for a pound,' I thought. So, in one of my many impulsive and irrational moments I reach out, grab the bomb from Lenny and wash it down quick with the nearest drink. No time to discuss what I was to expect from this chemical compound, or its possible side effects… it was gone. Down the hatch. Too late now.

Judging from Lenny's constant smile and his euphoric glow, I figured the side effects looked pretty good, and hopefully that will be me in an hour or so.

Steve suggests that we get in the car and head to the hotel to check in and freshen up. It seems people did that. They would turn up for a bit, go home, then return later on.

The drive back to the hotel is very pleasant. I feel extremely relaxed, chilled out and in a good space. The plan is to go to the room, have a quick shower, a change of clothes and then head straight back up to the party.

123

Standing in the shower… Wooosh! It starts to hit me. This is something else.

I have absolutely no intention of going anywhere right now. The water feels so good as it cascades down onto me. My whole body is buzzing like I've been wired to the mains.

I am not sure how long I stood there in the shower, but my experience was interrupted by the phone ringing. In slow motion I pulled back the shower curtain and saw a phone hanging there on the wall by the toilet. I am thinking, 'Strange place to stick a phone.'

'I know, let's go,' I say to Steve.

'Yeah, let's go…' he replies.

That is all we said to each other. I have got to get out of this hotel and back to Benny's as soon as possible before all normal human function disintegrates.

This is an Ali v Frazier 'Thrilla in Manila' moment. I am on the ropes.

And being hit hard.

I manage to pull myself together, get dressed and make it down to the hotel reception. The receptionist is glowing like the Ready Brek kid; the world outside is super bright and vibrating, as if someone has switched on the LEDs with a few lasers thrown in for good measure.

We head back to the party.

Lenny and Benny greet me with a big hug.

'How you feeling?' Lenny asks me.

'Completely off my trolley, Lenny… but in a good way,' I reply, with words that become slightly more slurred as my heart rate and breathing ramp up.

'Cool, man! Enjoy it!' he says, putting his reassuring arm around me.

Everything has a dreamlike quality to it, and despite the intense but ever-increasing euphoric rushes coming up through my body I am still very lucid.

Lenny was right. This is nothing like I have ever experienced before.

Then came the real test.

'We are gonna need some bedclothes!' Benny shouted.

124

Someone was staying the night.

'Oh, I'll go and get them for you,' said Lenny.

'What car do you want me to take?' he asked Benny.

'Take the convertible Mercedes,' he replied.

'Hey, Kenny, you wanna come?' he asked.

'Yeah, why not?' I responded, following Lenny to the car.

What happened next is unparalleled.

With the hood down, Lenny and I took a drive to the shopping mall.

'Lenny, watch out for those missiles!' I screamed.

'What missiles?' he replied.

'If we get hit by one of those we're finished,' I pleaded.

'Don't worry, Kenny, there ain't no missiles, we'll be fine,' Lenny promised.

I shouldn't have bought that Game Boy.

Or perhaps touched Lenny's party powder.

All I know is that for the entire drive I am trapped in the RoboCop game and missiles are coming up out of the road in front of us. They are huge and I watch them thunder past us and into the sky. This is a whole new level of interactive gaming. Lenny and I laugh our heads off while I keep a vigilant eye on those silos.

I have no idea how we got to the mall.

The whole sequence is dreamlike and disconnected.

We're standing in a massive store, in the bedding department. From there I am able to look over a barrier to the landing below us.

'Lenny, we're in the Stock Exchange!' I now shouted.

I could clearly see everyone below wearing bowler hats, vigorously trading.

'Don't worry about them,' Lenny replied. 'Come with me and you wait here, and I'll get the bedding.'

He positioned me right next to a king-size bed, complete with duvet and pillows.

The next thing I know... there is a tap on my shoulder.

'Excuse me, sir, you can't do that in here,' said a member of staff.

I am lying down in the bed, fully clothed, having a quick siesta while Lenny is deciding what colour to go for. I don't remember climbing into it, but it was very comfy.

'Don't worry, he's with me. Come on, Kenny, you'd better get out of there...' Lenny urged.

Clearly, I was out of my depth, out of my mind, and it was definitely time to get out of bed.

We get back to the party and things are in full swing. I am having a great time... allegedly!

Later I am chilling out on the sofa having a chat with Steve when suddenly there is the most amazing, luminescent dragonfly hovering to the side of his head. I am watching it for quite some time, then Steve suddenly moves his head to one side, opens his mouth and eats it.

'Do that again,' I tell him.

'Do what again?' he said, looking slightly bemused...

'Eat the dragonfly,' I reminded him.

'What dragonfly?'

'The one that was next to your head, the one you just swallowed.'

'I never ate a dragonfly,' he replied, beginning to laugh.

That in turn set me off, along with Benny and Lenny... The four of us were rolling about.

'He's trippin', man,' said Lenny.

'It looked real to me, man,' I replied, as I sank back into the sofa and went for another tour of La-La Land.

It is like that moment when a hypnotist clicks his fingers and says, 'You're back in the room... No, sorry! You're not back in the room, you're off again.'

Dragonfly or no dragonfly, I know I was flying that day as my senses crossed one another and opened up a Pandora's box in my mind.

Meanwhile, back *in* the room I find myself sitting next to a married couple, two of Benny's friends. Really nice people. We're having a drink, listening to the tunes, and talking about soul music. They ask me what I am up to, about the new record deal and stuff like that. We were chatting for ages, when in one

126

of my more with-it moments, when my eyes were able to focus, I looked at the guy and said, 'Hold on, are you Ronald Isley?'

'Yes, I am,' he replied with a smile.

'So that means you must be Angela Winbush?' I said, looking at his wife.

'Yes, baby, that's me,' she replied.

'Oh, my goodness, I've been sitting here for ages talking to you both without realising who you are. I'm so sorry' – I confessed embarrassingly.

'Don't worry, baby, that's OK,' said Angela. 'We're all good.'

It was an awesome moment for me because I am a big fan of both The Isley Brothers and Angela Winbush. Two soul music legends right there!

They were more interested in asking little old insignificant me about my fledging music career than talking about themselves. No self-interest there, nothing to prove, just a level of humility that spoke volumes. Ego has left the building!

Of course, I switched the conversation and revealed that I have all of their albums on vinyl. Being a soul music fan, that was a given. Ronald then told me about the early days of The Isley Brothers and the making of those iconic records. Thankfully no dragonflies got in the way this time. Clearly Steve was the only one with an appetite for insects that day.

Eventually we made it back to the hotel in the early hours. Again, I don't remember getting there, but I know that's where I woke up the following morning feeling as right as rain. Like nothing had happened, but it did happen. It was a totally mad experience and not forgotten in a hurry. Whatever that was, it is probably best confined to the lab.

Don't try this at home, folks!

Unless you're accompanied by an adult called Lenny.

A couple of nights later after too many beers, and a bit of coercion from me, Steve and I decided that we would find the house that Jim Morrison lived in during the 60s. I wanted to see the very place that I was reading about in his biography. All I knew was that it was in the Laurel Canyon Hills. Not exactly a precise location but it was a start. No Google Maps back then.

If Steve and I had some survival gear and were prepared to navigate through those hills, I reckon we would have found it within a week or so. But luckily for us, Cassandra Mills said she knew where it was. So, with Steve in the front, and me crammed into the back, Cassandra drove us there in her Porsche 911.

'It's over there, you can't miss it,' she said, as she pointed into the darkness.

Making our way up the lane we found a big house. Climbing over a small fence, Steve and I made our way into the garden. Suddenly! Bosh! On came a very bright security light followed by some noise from the house.

'Oh shit! It's the wrong house,' said Steve. 'Run!'

I am thinking – no one here gets out alive.

In a trigger-happy US where intruders are definitely not welcome, we ran for our lives, scrambled over the fence, sprinted down the lane, and lay low for a few minutes before we continued our search for Jim's gaff.

Then we find it. It was empty, derelict, boarded up, with a tall wire fence surrounding it. Yes, you couldn't miss it, unless you were drunk.

Like two naughty kids we climbed the wire fence and made our way inside. We were clearly not the first to do so, because there was some graffiti on one of the walls, no doubt from fans and ageing hippies to one of rock'n'roll's most controversial figures.

I wasn't even a massive Doors fan.

Most importantly amidst all this nonsense, we had done the deal. We were there to work (sort of), get to know the team at Giant and prepare to release the adapted version of the *Voices* album. Constant socialising was all part of it. Whether it be the Boyz II Men record launch party, hearing CeCe Peniston sing at LA Live, or attending the American Music Awards where C+C Music Factory stole the night, this had to be done and it was expected.

The most insane gig I went to over there was when Steve took me to see Ice-T performing with Jane's Addiction. Ice-T rapping over the funk metal-psychedelic rock music, while the audience go completely nuts, occasionally taking a break from rocking out to engage in some much-needed violence, knocking ten barrels of crap out of one another in an area called the 'Pit'. Utter madness!

The following night Steve and I found ourselves with $500 a-piece front-row tickets to see the LA Lakers, sitting just a few seats away from Jack Nicholson. Crazy really.

They know exactly how to work it over there, and they do it better than anyone else. I am sure many young artists buy right into it and get swept up into the spectacular nature of it all. Don't get me wrong, I enjoyed it, but this was far removed from the lives of most people I knew, and ultimately I couldn't help but feel that the whole thing was about as real as the dragonfly.

'Kenny, I want to make you into the new Boz Scaggs,' Irving Azoff promised.

Boz Scaggs, originally managed by Irving, was famous for the hit 'Lowdown' and for forming the band Toto.

Once again, somebody always wanted to make you into the new so-and-so. But at least they identified something.

I'm sure they had the best of intentions, but in reality, the *Voices* album never made it out of the starting gates over there. It didn't succeed, because it wasn't given the chance to succeed, or fail.

I cut two additional songs for the album with Giant, did a photo shoot at Venice Beach, had dinner at Irving's house. The rest of the time Steve and I had as much fun as possible.

In effect, all I did on my various trips over there was work a little and misbehave a lot.

In effect they paid me a lot of money to do nothing much at all.

But it was one hell of a trip… in every sense.

EMI wanted us back in the UK and nothing was happening with Giant.

We could remain in the USA and see, but it would probably take a long time. Sales had been flying at home and across Europe, but we could lose it all if we stayed. Steve decided that we should return to the UK and consolidate what we had there.

The trip was over.

129

17 Home and… Away

Equally, the move to St Albans was not working out – I was recording the second album in Islington. Leaving there at 3am and driving home to the cottage every night was hard work. I needed to be back in North London nearer the studio.

Sadly, the relationship with Sophie had run its course. My life had changed, and I with it. She wanted something else, greater commitment, those next steps, and I couldn't give it. I admit, I was going through one of the more selfish phases of my life, self-absorbed and focused on what to do next with my career.

The pressure was on to deliver music and be available 24/7. I knew, too, that I might not get another shot at it so that demand was from both the label and myself.

My gut feeling to move out of town, though, had been correct at the time. Sophie and I were now worlds apart – and young – but she was absolutely right about a couple things. That sixth sense, which sometimes guys do not have, put her on guard against 'the circus', and she warned me that there were two or three individuals out there whom I could not trust.

Call it what you like, from back-stabbers to disloyal to never being there when you actually needed them, she was spot on. It was in my mindset not to judge these people because you do not know how they walk through life, but it was clear that they definitely existed.

Though we were drifting and inevitably parted, I was grateful for that insight, but the fact that I did not detect it myself is perhaps a marker that I was sufficiently in the bubble as much as I tried to remove myself from it.

I took a timeout and went back to basics. I would call Norman, hang out with Dave, Chad and Mason, often checking in with Father Hanshell and Fr O'Reilly. They were solid and knew me mentally and spiritually. We could be honest without pretence. They would listen and nobody would condemn.

I told Mum I was feeling lost and needed to get off the treadmill. She, like any mum, could see that her boy was struggling.

'Don't worry, things will be OK, you will get through it,' she would say in such a serene and reassuring way.

She was simply a rock and my best friend.

I decided to move to Finchley. I bought a house just around the corner from where my nan and grandad's house stood. Familiar surroundings, filled with memories, and in this I found comfort.

Within 24 hours of breaking up with Sophie, the press were at the house.

In fact, it was a journo on a motorbike banging down the front door.

I do not know how they had got wind of the 'story'. It wasn't Sophie, for sure. I had confided in very few people, but they knew alright. Maybe there was a snitch in my circle. Years later, after phone-hacking etc, the only thing I can conclude is that the tabloids were keeping *tabs* on a hell of a lot of people, as though moles were just sleeping for years waiting to pounce at the moment something would go wrong – which, let's face it, it does at some point.

I did not like this one bit because – aside from the moments when I had got caught up in rock'n'roll craziness, some of which you can just put down to a young man at that stage in life – my whole ethos had been about staying grounded and continuing to do the things that made me 'Me' and not Kenny Thomas the industry product. Person versus popstar. I was always the person.

This, too, though, was part of the game. When a relationship breaks down the tabloids expect you to open up in public about it. Why would you do that?

So, I have music to promote, and a newspaper rings up Jody my press officer and says they want to do an interview about its release. Normally, the record company would beg, steal or borrow to get you an interview in a major newspaper, as you saw with the BMW malarkey. Very rarely do they ever call asking for an interview. Jody's alarm bells are ringing and I can smell a rat: a curve ball is coming.

Equally, I have no choice but to do it. The label will insist and if I know what is good for me, I have to promote the music. However, Jody warns me that this might be a ploy to pull me into a conversation about my split with Sophie. She gives me strict instructions to say nothing, not even 'No comment'. Stay silent the moment the journalist attempts to go there.

I try to remain focused during the chat. It is all very upbeat and friendly but with little or no substance to his questions. It felt odd and unlike any other interview I had done before. Something is not right here. All the time I am thinking, 'I am waiting… it is coming.' I know they are trying to lull me into a false sense of security and wait for my guard to be down. I can talk until the cows come home about music without blinking an eye. Of course, I love music. Then on the blind side from nowhere, even though you know it is coming…

'So, what about Sophia…?'

I'm thinking, 'You plonker! You can't even get her name right.'

The journo leans across the table.

I stare back.

I don't say a word.

He resets the scene, reminding me how long we have been together and that we are now no more.

'You don't want to add to it?'

I just smiled back.

This was the game.

And I was playing it.

The interview ended abruptly, and nothing was ever printed in the paper. He was hoping that I had some kind of axe to grind or looking for some dirt. The only dirt he found that day was right there in the gutter that he had crawled out of.

18 The Brits

It is February 1992. I have technically been in the biz for just over a year and the industry's showpiece event sees me nominated for Best Newcomer and Best Male Vocalist.

The label tells me in advance that I am very unlikely to win.

I am up against artists like Van Morrison, Elton John, George Michael and Seal. Seal had had a terrific year masterminded by the legendary Trevor Horn and I had always been a fan since the hit 'Killer'. It had also been a huge year for Simply Red.

For many, this is one of the great honours in the music biz to even attend. It looks big on the telly. Essentially it is the music industry giving itself a pat on the back and placed at a time of year when sales are at their lowest with everybody having thrown everything at the Christmas market. Generally, you could expect your numbers to pick up after the event.

I had been to similar events in the States – like the American Music Awards – and they do things off the scale. Obviously, the Grammys are the big one.

But this was the main event in the UK – one of those events where the record company would ring and say, 'You have to be there,' and it was true: the good, the bad and the ugly were all in town. You never knew whom you might bump into especially at the after-party.

I only went once.

Proud to be nominated because *Voices* had done so well, I sort of felt I was there remotely. I wasn't really into all the back-slapping industry nonsense, but I played along with it. Equally, you do have to pinch yourself a little. I got to meet George Michael, for example, which for me was an honour, because I loved his voice.

I turn up in one of Mark Powell's suits. I end the night at the roller skating rink and funfair provided. It's not every day

133

that you get to ram your bumper car into Dave Stewart from Eurythmics.

I take it seriously in my career because it has been mentioned so many times over the years. It is one of those tags that people like to place in front of your name... 'BRIT-nominated Kenny Thomas', but what I do know is that this was a completely different era of pop and awards ceremonies where the gongs reflected sales, and even average acts were churning a lot more units than today.

Of course, if you wander into any record company building, you will expect to find gold discs adorning the walls and trophy cabinets housing many of these accolades. They were the promised land.

Some people in the industry, however, did not treat them with the same respect.

I arrived for one meeting where the office door would not stay open.

A BRIT Award was propping it ajar.

It was for Betty Boo – that year's Best British Breakthrough Act.

As the year was almost over and the 1992 BRIT Awards were fast approaching, space was needed on the shelf to receive the latest trophy.

On the shelf this year, next year you are the door wedge.

Noted.

This was the most transient game in the world.

I didn't win of course but I knew I was in a really good place and had developed a following to approach that second album with confidence. I was also well aware – doorstop or not – that acts who had been bigger than me had already fallen by the wayside. I looked at George Michael and was acutely aware that to replicate what he had achieved, you had to have incredible staying power.

I needed to invest in me.

I began to see the vocal coach Glynn Jones. You might well think, 'Hang on a minute, you are on a roll: why do you need to go and get trained?' It was more complicated than that and this guy was the best. From Olivia Newton-John to Engelbert

Humperdinck, from Annie Lennox to Tom Jones, he had worked with them all.

You would arrive and see all sorts of people going in – even the comedian Lenny Henry... and politicians. I began visiting every week.

'I've been following you and waiting to see you.'

I was flattered to be greeted with these words.

I knew I had to take care of my vocals, iron out bad habits and be able to sustain myself night after night. Like a kid falling off a bike smashing their knees on the pavement, suddenly something clicks, and you don't do that anymore.

You begin to ride with greater ease.

This is the process.

And as well as keeping yourself fit – so to speak – there was also the question of tone. I do not necessarily mean the notes you were hitting but the feeling you were radiating. Soul music's biggest strength was that emotional sensation and that warm connection. Despite the success of *Voices,* I could always get better at that.

So, he didn't change the way I sounded specifically but increased my range, made me breathe correctly, gave more power to my falsetto, made my notes fuller and showed me the way to create that deeper connection.

At the same time, I started to be styled by Judy Blame who did all that work shaping the singer Neneh Cherry. I began experimenting with photo shoots.

Or perhaps *they did.* Ahead of the second album, there was a definite sense that the label was trying to mould me and rightly so.

They could never have anticipated the success of the first album despite having that gut feeling to persevere with me. Now they had sat down and thought about it. Damn – they had a product on their hands. This was the record company desperately trying to get me to the next level.

Whatever that illusive next level *is* I was also becoming aware that within the music industry itself there are tiers and some of them quite deep and dark.

EMI invited me to one of their 'let's give ourselves a pat on the back' dinner events. They suggested that it would be nice for me to bring my parents along, too. Mum wasn't one for huge social gatherings, so she declined the offer (wise move), but Dad was up for it. It was a swanky black-tie event and in attendance were all of the usual execs along with artists like Cliff Richard, Kate Bush and the lesser mortals like myself.

It was actually quite a good night and the alcohol flowed steadily in all directions which made Dad happy. Dad was introduced to all of the most important people there and, being a very social creature, he enjoyed meeting them all.

At the end of the night when it was time to go, Dad had clearly had a lot to drink, and he took me to one side. He did something he had never done before. He opened up to me on a subject we only ever argued about.

'Son, there's a lot of Freemasons in your game,' he confided to me.

'What do you mean, Dad? Have you been passing yourselves off to each other here tonight?' I asked him.

'Yes, son, your game is full of them.'

To pass oneself off is the term used when a Freemason secretly reveals his identity to another Freemason. So, it was dodgy handshakes galore that night. This was the first and last time Dad ever revealed something like that to me. Maybe he was giving me the heads-up on the music game, that all is not as it seems. I would love to have known exactly who was in the *one trouser leg up* brigade, but he would never have told me, and I knew not to ask.

I had a lot to learn but was getting wise quickly.

I noticed, too, that before interviews, I was being primed, almost coerced into adopting an alter ego. I was being cleverly nudged into steering chats in a certain direction. I was not comfortable with this. It must have happened countless times before. The first album was born out of an age of innocence with no massive pressure – remember the original deal was just for the single 'Outstanding' with an optional album, and then 'Thinking About Your Love' went massive. From that moment, we were all playing catch-up.

136

This was different – from being called back from the States to getting in the studio on New Year's Day. In reality, the USA jaunt should have been encouraged apart from the fact that nothing was happening, *and* it was a different label. Success there would have meant so on a global level.

Now that was dead, and Ian Green and I barely saw a soul, bar the odd session musician. The contrast could not have been greater between the hope in between albums one and two, and the reality of making the latter.

That aside, a couple of key elements were missing. We were lacking the A&R input and nobody at the record company threw us a 'Thinking About Your Love'. They didn't owe us that, of course, but that key ingredient was missing. Simon Dunmore did suggest we record 'Stay', which was quite a risky song to cover but we went with it, and I felt it was a hit.

I was writing as well – I never wanted to be totally dependent on songs coming in, but I was still inexperienced.

But I had lived a little, and that sense of feeling from the vocal coach and my own sense of loss paved the way to pen 'Garden of Pain' which started as a piece of poetry about the death of my late grandmother and concluded with us contacting the estate of Richard Burton to 'borrow' his voice for the recording.

We got lucky – they gave us permission.

I discovered 'Separate Lives' by Randy Crawford and wrote a new section for it. I tampered with a classic artist's material!

I loved both songs, but I was still short of a commercial hit. Equally I did not have the best advice. I was persuaded at the last minute – with time running out – to cover 'I Keep Forgetting' by Michael McDonald.

I shouldn't have touched it. Ian and I felt forced into it. I didn't like what we did with it, and I have never sung it since. I loved his original. This was bad territory, in effect trashing your heroes.

I have never met him. If that should happen, I will apologise. I feel that bad about it. It really represented the speed to get that album out. We recorded it as quickly as we could.

Despite that haste, the truth is that the process dragged. I was on a completely different racetrack of emotions to *Voices*. That feeling of coming from nowhere, building to something and the excitement of seeing it climb the charts and doing your first round of interviews and *Top of the Pops* was not matched second time around where expectation was now high, investment greater, speed was the order of the day and, whilst I believed in huge amounts of the album, I didn't quite believe as much as I should.

Part of me wanted to escape. I knew I was starting to self-destruct. You spend so long trying to get a foot in and then it can all be over in an instant.

Steve Finan sat me down at his house:

'I don't want to carry on if this is the noose that hangs you,' he said.

Wise as ever, he knew. He just knew.

'Of course I want to carry on,' I half-bluffed.

I did and I didn't.

I just needed to sort myself out.

People knew I liked to party. I needed to stop waking up in places I didn't recognise – including my own home!

But it was bigger than that. Nan's death in 1990 only really took hold of me in delay in 1992. As you may well have experienced in your own life, suppressing that emotion can be damaging. Some sort of safety mechanism in my mind hadn't allowed me to go there when, really, I needed to grieve properly. I only began to address it when I started writing 'Garden of Pain'.

It was the bereavement counselling I didn't get, alongside the self-medicating I was doing in nightclubs.

Overall, though, I am detached and acting single.

I am following the music remembering what it is like to be a fan. I am surrounded by lots of attractive women. The clichés and the temptations are there. But I am also in the gym most days and running 30–40 miles per week.

Order and chaos.

The more the label seemed to be moulding me, the more I wanted to be the antithesis of the previous year.

I grew a crazy beard before it was fashionable to do so. To my pleasure, nobody recognised me. I was at a function with the legend Lulu, whom I knew, and about halfway through a brief chat she suddenly blurted out, 'Kenny, it's you'... so concealed was I.

The only other person to recognise me was the British reggae singer Bitty McLean who had a few hits in the 90s with tracks like 'It Keeps Rainin''. He spotted me as he was driving down the street and rolled down the window curiously.

'Is that you, Kenny?' He laughed.

The garden of pain was also growing on my face. I was under the radar at a time when I needed to be flashing up as incoming.

The pressure was growing musically. They were looking for an even bigger hit and they wanted me much more involved in the process. I enjoyed co-writing but I also loved it when someone said, 'Here's a great song for you.' In reality, America had been a distraction. Meanwhile, other territories were catching up, so as I was moving on in the UK the process was once again just beginning elsewhere. The treadmill never stopped.

Nor had I really had that time to grieve. Added to that, Dad fell ill with a blocked carotid artery. These issues were becoming more important.

By 1992 he was suffering really bad headaches, numbness in his fingers and then one day went temporarily blind in one eye going round the South Mimms roundabout in London.

He went to see our family GP.

They ran all the usual tests – checking his blood pressure etc – but could find nothing wrong. It had been a blip, they concluded. Except none of us believed that – especially Dad.

So, we had no choice but to carry on.

Only a random stroke of luck changed things.

Dad's sister Marie was reading the *Reader's Digest*. There was a story of a man with exactly the same symptoms who had a blocked carotid artery.

Dad went back to the GP and showed him the article.

'This might be what it is,' he suggested.

More tests followed.

This time they kept him in.

The medics discovered that there was just one millimetre of blood going through into his artery. This was potentially critical and that chance discovery clearly life-defining.

There was only one surgeon in the UK at the time who was capable of performing the necessary operation with any success.

We therefore moved Dad to St Mary's Hospital.

The facts were simple. There was a 50:50 chance of a massive stroke.

He was under the knife. We were on a knife-edge.

After the operation, he did recover but was never truly the same again.

He could no longer do physical work. I employed him as my driver.

I also began to notice subtle changes in his personality.

Nowadays, many hospitals can perform that operation, and some studies have indicated that it could possibly be a trigger for the onset of dementia.

I was in the summer of my life; Dad was in the winter of his. He was now in that final season of life, and like he told me so many times before, the seasons pass by very quickly. It was not easy seeing him grow old, and of course it brought my own mortality into focus.

The whole episode filled me with enormous sadness, not just because of the inevitable conclusion to which it was heading, but also because of the small number of people who came to see him in hospital. Dad had helped and given hope to so many people – generally, and through the boxing – yet of course it was not returned.

'Always factor in betrayal,' my good friend Michael Moore once warned me. 'You will be prepared for it and not surprised by it.'

This turned out to be true in pop and in real life.

I knew after this album I could technically walk. Equally, expectations were enormous after shifting 600,000 of the first one. This is what we had abandoned America for when EMI called us back. We were massively rushed and short of time. The pressure was on.

By 1993, the debut single 'Stay' peaks at 22. It is not the most encouraging start. The next release, however, 'Trippin' On Your Love', is the highest new entry in the charts the week it comes out. This cover version was Steve's idea, the record company were running out of theirs.

Our big hope was that gospel song originally by the Staple Singers. It had been a club hit for a band called A Way of Life, released on the Eternal label in 1990. My friend Joe Beckett, a percussionist, was actually in the band, so I asked him if he minded me covering it. Perhaps I should have done the same to Michael McDonald.

'I don't need no speed or weed to groove me.' These are the opening lyrics to the original song. Couldn't see Saturday morning children's TV supporting that, or even radio stations playing it. We had to change it.

As I said, speed was of the essence! And at the time, the lyrics certainly rang true.

But it was the video that was the killer.

It is possibly the world's worst – an early experiment with green screen doing me no favours, coupled with a bad plot, out-of-depth effects, an overdose of make-up and models who had been hanging around all day, way past their agency hours. We waited forever while the director and his team fiddled around with the equipment. By the time we actually came to film it we were exhausted and out of all patience.

It proved to be a pivotal moment.

That video killed that song.

'You are the highest new entry in the chart,' Steve had told me midweek. 'This is gonna be a big one.'

141

And we were up against some pretty good acts at the time.

The next week it stayed exactly where it was – at 17.

The reason was the video.

Nobody would touch it. *The Chart Show* declined. *Top of the Pops* said no. Normally you would be on with the highest new entry, and a clip of the video would pretty much guarantee you sales and an appearance the following week. It had that amount of power.

They couldn't even find 30 good seconds to show – the video was that awful.

After stalling, the song plummeted to 46 and then down to 63. It was gone.

When you are successful, there is always more than one person at the record company who will tell you how they did it, as if part of some master plan. They can walk you through it step by step. When the reverse happens, you will be unsurprised to know that nobody holds their hands up.

Someone concluded that someone working on the video must have spent most of the money on drugs, and the video for 'Trippin' On Your Love' remains one of the worst videos I have ever seen. They were out of ideas and possibly out of their heads.

It took the whole momentum out of the album, even though other singles would follow – and I did love parts of it, especially the personal songs.

I was wise enough to realise, though, that it was not *Voices 2*.

Another single, 'Piece by Piece', barely scrapes the Top 40 in November 1993. Despite not being a hit, I am very proud of this record. Once again, it was Steve who introduced me to this song originally recorded by the Scottish singer John Martyn. It was the title track from an album he released in 1986. Not exactly a soul record, but with Ian Green's production it was creatively transformed into one.

Six months later we released the final single from that album, 'Destiny', a great song written by Eliot Kennedy and remixed by Danny D, accompanied by a very colourful video shot in Amsterdam.

There was no momentum to the campaign, and that gap of six months from the last single showed that. This was one last attempt at raising the dead.

Destiny didn't even make a dent in the Top 40.

If only we had got the guys in Amsterdam to make the video for 'Trippin' On Your Love', I am sure we would have been in a much better position.

Whatever the merits of the music, I am certainly not repeating the success of *Voices* with 'Wait For Me'. Even though it sold over 200,000 copies, which by today's standards is not to be sniffed at, and it still made it into the Top 10 of the album chart, it was seen as somewhat of a failure.

For me, the fact that by the age of 26, I had eight UK Top 40 songs under my belt was a pretty good achievement, and it was a far cry from the days of traipsing up and down the country singing in clubs so minging that you had to wipe your feet on the way out of them.

It is not good to solely focus on where you want to get to: sometimes you have to look at where you are at, and how far you have come. It was all good, and I was ready to make more music.

Steve's negotiations with the label had meant that much of the focus was on the finances and that did afford a greater budget for productions and video shoots.

He felt that the songs had legs, and I think we now both agree that for whatever reason the album should have been bigger. I am bound to say that of course, but after the success of the first one, I had returned their investment and that meant more was coming my way. I was established and a success at that moment in time. It should have been seized upon.

Steve, to his credit, was always months ahead of real time. He could see what was coming and harshly or wisely took me aside one evening at a gig.

'Listen, Kenny, I am going to give you a prediction,' he began.

'Next year, and for some time after that, it's going to be about manufactured bands. It is going to go extremely pop and be really hard for solo acts like you to cut through it.'

When he said this, many of these bands did not exist. They were not around yet. He was right, of course. We were about to enter a huge pop period.

Somebody at the label had decided they knew how to dictate to the public what the people wanted. The whole market pointed in the direction of Take That, Boyzone and then Westlife, the Spice Girls, A1, Five etc... the seeds were being sown and over the next few years these would dominate.

This should come as no surprise to you. We have all by now had enough experience of reality pop shows where it is clear there is an agenda, and at some point along the way somebody behind the scenes is working their magic. Sometimes a runner-up has done better than the winner. On others, a cobbled-together group of wannabes from previous auditions end up stealing the show. The record companies' fingerprints are all over it. The level of predetermination precedes its traditional autumn unravelling on British television.

Back then we did not have the juggernaut of talent shows but we did have that mindset. In a year's time, it will be boy bands. We will go and find those acts. And they did!

This, of course, both subscribes to that 'you need to be more like so-and-so' ethos and goes some way to destroying the evolution of pop. We can make anything work with the right image and marketing is very different from 'Wow, you have got to hear this new soul singer's voice.'

One is product, the other is a person.

All they wanted to do then and now is make money before music.

I do not criticise them for that and Steve's words left me scratching my head wondering how something so prealigned could be so clear as their vision, when on a day-to-day basis, I would often see them change their minds on a flick of a coin. I took everything Steve said with the wisdom that his experience merited.

Points noted.

To keep going forward with even greater determination is very much in my genes. This was not the time to throw the towel in. I had music to make and a fan base to perform to. Steve

144

always told me that you just keep going through the ups and downs and changing trends, and if you're still around 20 years on you will be perceived as a success.

He decided that it was time for me to go out on tour.

Steve decided that I would gig across the UK with three other acts, Monie Love, Sinclair and EYC. Mike Sinclair, a good R&B singer, had a chart hit with 'Ain't No Casanova' in 1993. EYC were a short-lived trio from the USA. The four of us with a full live band embarked on the 'You Can't Say Fairer Than That' joint headline tour. This title reflected the value-for-money aspect of the concert.

Four acts, one cheap ticket and no profit.

Yes, those were the days when you worked your butt off on tour, came away with naff all – but it was all done in the name of 'promoting the album' and generating record sales.

The show started off with DJ Pogo on the turntables warming up the crowd. He was one of the UK's top hip hop spinners who made his name through the World DJ Championships. He was then followed by each act in no particular order.

A few days into the tour it became apparent that a lot of the audience were there to see me, so Steve decided to move me into the final slot, and I closed the show from there onwards.

It was a great tour, and it gave me the experience and confidence to then move on to my own headline tour.

Putting together an awesome band we rehearsed for several days, making sure the show was seamless and as punchy as Roberto Durán.

With the record company's financial support and the ITB agency at the helm I was ready to go solo for the first time. You would naturally think there was enough of a budget to splash out and make it the best show it could be? Wrong! With Chrysalis Records I always felt it was like trying to drink champagne but on a Lambrini budget.

The band had two backing vocalists who were very good, but I really needed three backing vocalists to re-create the sound of the records. The money wasn't there to afford three BVs.

146

On the first rehearsal day a singer called Rita Campbell came down to the studio. She was close friends with the guitarist Mark Jaimes who was in the band. She could see there was clearly a need for one more voice and she did something that not many people do in this game. She joined the tour and gave her time and services without getting paid a penny for doing so. No one else apart from Mark knew she was doing this for me. It made a massive difference to the sound of the BVs and I made yet another friend for life. Being half-Spanish like me, and half-mad like me, we formed a solid brother-and-sister kind of friendship. I don't think there is anyone else in the music business that I have socialised with more than Rita. She has been there for me through some dark times, and I have been there for her. We have shared some of the craziest moments, and some of the funniest.

If I put music, success and all material things to one side it is the friendships that matter. This is the thread that runs through my life. It is a journey, and it is not about what I achieved or the things I own, but who I connected with along the way.

On that tour we did connect and found something greater than music. Rita would throughout the 1990s join me in later bands and on further concerts – but being paid this time. I made sure of that. It was she who later introduced me to record producers like Nicolas Bulostin and Mark Wilkinson. These random and unexpected connections with people are what makes the music business exciting and of course the songs that flow from those new relationships.

Steve, not allowing any dust to settle, began to negotiate a deal with Chrysalis/EMI for a third album. We were free to go anywhere we liked, but knowing that they would still want to capitalise on their investment, he hit them hard. A much bigger spend on recording, videos and marketing was factored into the deal. This time, I signed directly to them and not as part of a production deal. This meant they had to come up with the album content and the recording of it, whereas before we made the album and then licensed it to them. They now had greater control over me, the album, the songs and the planning thereof.

The first mistake that they made was to remove Ian Green from the picture. They wanted a different sound. They put me in the studio with loads of other writers and producers, eventually settling on Simon Law and Dancin' Danny D. Two very good producers in their own right, but two very different sounds.

I began writing with a lot of songwriters, Jonathan Butler, with whom I wrote the title track 'Him' and one other track, 'Given You All'. I also wrote songs with Danny D, coming up with the first single, 'When I Think Of You', and another song with Simon Law.

I spent a number of days with Bluey from Incognito, writing three songs which I thought were great. Ken Grunbaum thought otherwise and chose not to use them. I think this was another mistake. Bluey and I became great friends, and our musical collaboration did not stop there with Ken's decision. We would go on to make records again much later in time when I was able to choose for myself what I could and couldn't do.

Steve put me together with Paul Moessl, a great keyboard player and producer. We wrote one of the songs on the album which I ended up co-producing with Richard Bull who works with Bluey. I managed to sneak that one in there.

Paul Moessl arranged for Skip Scarborough to come over to the UK to write with me. Skip wrote 'Lovely Day' for Bill Withers and he also penned 'You Can't Hide Love' for Earth, Wind & Fire. He heard my version of that song on the 'Wait For Me' album and thought it would be good for us to do something original together. Skip, Paul and I wrote two songs, but these, too, were rejected by the record label.

No songs were put forward by the record company; more songs were rejected than suggested. No cover versions: this would be an album without cover versions, they decided. Somehow forgetting that my career was founded on a remake. If I was not being given any songs then the only way they would come would be through the co-writes, and that at times can be more or less experimental. Some days you come up with something good, other days you don't. You just have to keep churning out the ideas.

This can be a tiring process and one that doesn't go well with a record company cracking the whip every few days.

They were frustrated and so was I.

'I can't work miracles,' I told them.

'If you want a miracle give Moses a shout.'

Steve became extremely busy with other aspects of his business. I was not the only artist he represented, and music was not the only business he was involved with. So, my day-to-day contact with him became less and less. The record company also did a pretty good job of keeping him out of the loop creatively, and they dealt with me directly in regard to songwriting and the studio sessions. This was another mistake. Without Steve and Ian Green there would have been no *Voices* album. Trying to replicate that level of success is what we should have been aiming at.

I'm not sure what they were aiming at. I don't think they even had a target in their sights.

Why didn't they approach some music publishers asking for songs from some of their top songwriters? That would have been a good idea and a great starting point.

Without Steve rummaging through their waste-paper baskets and finding a discarded hit record this was going to be an uphill struggle.

21 Him

The best song on that third album was undoubtedly the title track 'Him'. Simon Law did an excellent job in the production of that track. Over seven minutes of pure retro soulfulness. Mostly recorded live at Metropolis Studios London, and then a 30-piece orchestra, with arrangement by Gavin Wright recorded at Angel Studios, Islington.

Working with Simon was such a pleasure. A true professional, who understood this genre and instinctively knew exactly how this song needed to sound. He totally got the vibe of the lyrics and what Jonathan Butler and I intended when we wrote it. He wanted to make a timeless record that would be around long after we had left this planet, and that is what he did.

I felt that I was finally making the kind of soul record I always wanted, and in all honesty, I wish that I had made the whole album with him.

Steve warned me that things were not good back at camp. There were political rumblings within EMI, and this was not going to bode well for Cooltempo. He knew what was coming down the pike. He did warn some people within the label, advising them on how they might avoid the inevitable, but his advice was ignored.

We had to get this album done and out there before all hell broke loose. Maybe this is why there was so much pressure being levied on me by the label to get this record over the finish line. My gut feeling told me that things were not going to go well, and the overexaggerated optimism at the record company made me wonder who they were trying to convince.

The Simon Law tracks were the most expensive to record, but the budget *was* there this time for it. On the day we recorded the orchestra at Angel Studios I called my friend James.

'James, meet me down at Angel Studios,' I urged. 'I want you to see the orchestra play on my tracks. It's the first time I have ever had this on one of my records, and to be honest with you, mate, it may be the last time we ever see this.'

I was right!

Working with Danny D was fun, but it was very different from the way Simon worked. Danny and I got on really well, worked hard but we also had a laugh in the studio. This took my mind away from the pressure being exerted by the record company and I was able to escape into that creative space.

Because his sound was very different from Simon's, the album was already beginning to sound disconnected. His production was more R&B-flavoured and the beats were more street. Danny called on the services of some of my favourite singers to do some backing vocals in Juliet Roberts, Steven Dante and Paul Johnson. Their voices added a new dimension to the tracks and I think it could have been a potential single, but once more its sound was even further removed from Simon's.

Danny D liked to work in what I would call *the old-school way*. Getting in the studio, creating the rhythm track, trying out chords, beats, sounds, and seeing where the wind takes us. Often we would hit upon a groove and some magic would happen.

This can be a drawn-out process with no guarantees at the end of the day. You need a lot of patience and stamina for this way of working. I used to fall out of the studio with Ian Green at silly o'clock in the morning when we were making the first two albums. I would go home, grab some sleep, and then repeat this the next day. It becomes so exhausting that the productivity suffers in the long run. I didn't want to work that way anymore. I wanted to get into the studio early, get the job done, go home, get a proper night's sleep, and have a life.

With Danny we would start at 11am, work late into the evening and then both agree it was time to go home. Cool!

When I get back there the next day around 11am it was like a ghost town. The studio was empty, looking like it had been abandoned mid-session. Only to be told by the studio owners that Danny had carried on working through the night. I would often wait around for hours until he turned up later that afternoon. Not cool!

Maybe a text to say 'don't come in at 11am, we won't be there' would have been good!

I am not saying it was wrong, it was just a different way of operating and not one that worked for me. He got the job done, but our body clocks were not in sync.

I reached a point where I had had enough of this time frame.

It was a Sunday evening, and I was due to be back in Swanyard Studios with Danny the following morning. Paul Moessl was over at my house, just chilling out, having a chat and listening to some music.

'Come on, let's go clubbing,' I said in a moment of spontaneity.

'What!? On a Sunday night?' he replied.

'Yeah! The Gas Club is open tonight. Let's do it.'

'You're completely mad, Kenny.'

'I know I am,' I said as I went upstairs to get some glad rags on.

We went, we saw, we conquered – or should I say we went, we misbehaved, we came home and conked out.

I am woken up by my mobile phone ringing.

'Where the bloody hell are you?' said an angry Ken Grunbaum down the line.

'I'm at home,' I replied.

'Well, you're meant to be in the f***ing studio right now. What's going on?!' he yelled.

'It's all gone pear-shaped, Ken,' I told him straight.

'What do you mean it's all gone f***ing pear-shaped?!' he shouted.

'Look, Ken, calm down! I am not really needed there today.'

'That studio is costing us a bloody fortune, and you are supposed to be there,' he countered.

'No, they don't need any vocals from me today,' I reassured him.

'Danny is waiting there for you right now.'

'Well, this makes up for all those times I am hanging around like a fart in spacesuit waiting for Danny to turn up. I'll be there tomorrow.'

I put the phone down.

I turned up to the studio the next day and Danny was cool. He didn't have a problem with any of it. I needed some time out and he understood that. Plus, I wanted to make a point, and my actions, albeit not entirely good, did send a message.

There was really no need for such drama, but no doubt Ken was under his own pressure at the label. It was a Monday, and Mondays are never really that nice. Equally, the Chrysalis ship was sinking. The iceberg had hit, it was going down, and taking most of the passengers with it. Ken simply wanted the band to play on. I got that! It could not have been an easy time for him, and the last thing he needed was for me to be throwing my toys out of the pram.

Despite the uncertainty surrounding the future we carried on and finished the album. It was what it was. There were some great tracks on it, but it felt more like a compilation than one seamless piece of work. This album should have had one record producer and one sound. The songs *were* good, but they did not go together no matter what order you put them in. It was too late to fix it and time was not on our side.

'When I Think Of You', written by Danny and myself, was chosen as the first single. It was the best choice, but 'Outstanding' it was not.

We headed down to Cornwall to make a video for the single with a brief that it should be a mini-replica of the Hollywood movie *From Here to Eternity*, arranging the set and drafting in extras to play American GIs, along with a hired American Jeep from the period. They promoted it like the movie! They were chucking serious amounts of money at it.

We managed to pull off just one significant TV performance of the track on GMTV. At the time they were broadcasting live from various holiday locations in Europe, and we were invited to perform on the beach in Benidorm.

I flew over to Spain with the band the day before the scheduled appearance, and we were under strict instructions from the record label to behave ourselves and give a stellar performance.

It was going to be a very early start down at the beach, so the evening before we all went for a meal and agreed to have just

153

one beer at the hotel bar afterwards. After my single beer allowance, I went to my hotel room and got my head down.

The following morning, I went down to reception to meet the band as arranged. There were only a couple there and they looked very hungover. The others were nowhere to be found.

When I left them at the bar the previous evening, they all had more than one beer, followed by several more, and then stampeded down to the main strip in Benidorm town centre and went for it... all night. Good at the time, but not good when you have a live TV show to do in an hour's time.

We managed to wake up the other band members and drag them down to reception, but one of the backing vocalists was still missing and not responding to the loud knocking on his room door. The hotel manager was summoned and decided to go in and check if he was there and still alive. When the door was opened, we were unsurprised to find an unconscious and completely butt-naked backing vocalist sprawled out across the bed. He was alive (barely) and in no state to sing. Somehow we managed to get him standing upright, dressed and onto the tour bus.

When we got to the beach the sun was banging hot, and it hammered the band on top of the self-inflicted hammering they had received the night before. Looking fresh and awake on breakfast TV is not always an easy thing to do but, on this occasion, it was not happening – for the band at least.

We took up our positions on the stage in that blazing heat and then it was time for... camera, lights, action. It was a long three and a half minutes for me, but an eternity for the band. We got through it and celebrated the fact that we had pulled off a minor miracle considering the state of play only an hour earlier.

Then my mobile rings... It is Ken Grunbaum back in the UK.

'What the bloody hell happened over there?'

'You looked great, Kenny, but your band looked terrible,' he said.

'Ken, it has been an interesting morning; they all went out last night and got totally smashed,' I confided.

'To be honest with you, the fact that they managed to get onto the stage today was an achievement,' I told him.

'All they had to do was behave themselves for one night and they managed to screw that up. They looked half-asleep, no energy, and their performance was unexciting… it was shit,' he said disappointedly.

'I'm so sorry, Ken… Next time I think they will need a good babysitter,' I apologised.

There was no next time.

The single was released in September 1995. With a reasonable amount of support at radio, some airtime for the video and the hungover GMTV appearance, it failed to make it into the Top 20, peaking at Number 27.

I think Steve was right (as usual). As he predicted, this massive pop band culture that dominated the charts, radio and TV was almost impossible to circumnavigate. There was no getting around it or cutting through it. Blue-eyed soul boys, or brown-eyed in my case, were not the flavour of the month.

Ken Grunbaum set his sights on the next single and his intention was to keep going, as any label would. But what you want and what you get are often two very different things.

The powers that be in EMI, the higher-ups, thought otherwise and in one fell swoop Chrysalis Records ground to a halt as they brought out the guillotine and began to give everyone the chop, bar a couple of people who found safety at EMI head office and escaped sudden death. In corporate business terms, it was brutal.

The second single, the third album and my career were left hanging in limbo while their desks were emptied and the offices dismantled, clearing the building of all evidence of the successes it had achieved over the years.

Ken Grunbaum and the team I had worked with since 1990 were gone.

OK folks, the show is over, there is nothing to see here… Move along, move along!

155

22 Bye Bye, EMI

In 1996, I left EMI Records. I had to spend a lot of money fighting my way out of the deal. Normally you fight hard to get a deal. This was the reverse.

It was a car crash. EMI had come in and did what they did to Chrysalis Records. The *Him* album was now in the hands of Jean-François Cecillon, the A&R man behind groups like Eternal.

There was no way that they were about to endorse and release an album made by the very people they had just sacked. He wanted me to rerecord the whole thing, and knowing his history, it would have no doubt gone down a far more pop route.

As if there wasn't enough pop out there already.

I wasn't surprised that he never liked the album I had recorded. After all, it had two distinct but separate sounds. But scrapping the whole thing and starting again was not something I could have endured.

'You can jump into bed with J-F Cecillon,' Steve warned. 'But you'll have to record a whole new album. On top of what has been spent already, that will put you in the hole. You'll never make any money out of this deal because you'll never recoup that kind of debt.'

I didn't lie awake at night praying for the music to come out, but equally I had invested (or wasted) a lot of time and energy in its writing, production and recording. Picking yourself up and going again should you sign for another label with a blank canvas to create a 'fourth album' would be really tough mentally.

Again – J-F Cecillon thinking it should *go* to the imaginary next level… you had to *be* more like such and such…

In my mind that was not going to any new level other than one below. When I emerged on the scene, the market was clear ahead. Nobody was doing my kind of music. That remained – in the UK soul bracket – pretty much the same. I knew I had to do what I was good at. It was clear it was a mistake to lose control. I resented this idea that someone can just rip up the

156

album, the identity, and therefore the career just on a whim because he had different ideas.

So, I said no.

The label went quiet. A classic stonewall. It had happened to many artists many times. Nothing was happening, no communication. Nada!

They had one big problem, though. The album had a planned release date, and the single had already come out, so the wheels were in motion. Ignoring this and leaving it all in limbo meant they ran over that time and failed to put the album out on schedule. They still didn't seem much bothered by this, and the silence continued as they hung me out to dry.

My lawyer jumped straight onto this and began the process of suing them for failing to release the album, and the resulting damage to my career.

But then *Music Week,* the trade paper for the UK record industry, got wind of it. Both Steve and the label knew that they had me on a pay-or-play deal, which means: release the album or let me go, but either way, you pay for the privilege.

Nobody wanted to litigate in public.

This was the last thing EMI needed at the time, so they asked us to withdraw the writ and then settled out of court.

I only got the money that was due to me as advances, as per the recording contract, the costs would be the same to them either way. It was really out of my hands.

That was all very well, and I am sure that most people would take it, but of course it left you nowhere. Your third album was stuck on the shelf, and you had no access or rights to it. At the outset it really could have been the one to cement me as an adult artist. Perhaps now I think it was a cool, self-indulgent album with the chance to see a 30-piece orchestra play on 'Him' and 'Let It Rain'.

When I asked my friend James to come and see the orchestra being recorded on those tracks, saying that, 'It may be the last time we ever see this.' I uttered those words in the moment. Later, I reflected on their prophetic nature.

All of this came as no surprise. I had been warned and prepped for it.

Before we even released a single from that doomed third album, a conversation with Steve outside Chrysalis Records stayed in my mind.

'Whatever happens with the record company, even if it all ended today, you've done alright... you've had hits and you've made some money,' he said, leaning against his car.

'Steve, it has never been about the money. It has always been about the music,' I replied, perhaps failing to grasp commodity over calling.

'You'll never be out of work. You can just go out there and gig non-stop like Edwin Starr does,' he advised.

'Yes, that is true. I can do that, and I probably will,' I responded.

The conversation did leave me feeling sad. He was still looking out for me, but I felt in some way that maybe he was moving on, too. His life was heading in multiple directions and, fair play to him, but he had ceased to be my main point of contact on a daily basis during the recording of the album. The dynamic had changed between us and it is fair to say that I had been drifting anyway.

So suddenly I had no deal.

In short, it was all over.

I really was having serious doubts if I was on the right path at all.

I was still young enough to do something else.

Was this meant to be my vocation in life?

I can write now that my days were numbered. They weren't of course and they are not. I continued to write and gig as I do today, *but* that fifteen minutes of fame that commands *Top of the Pops* appearances or *Smash Hits* covers did end there.

I drove to Stamford Hill and sat on the end of the bed of my oldest friend Dave Sassoon.

'Dave, mate, it's all over with EMI,' I told him.

I *did* need to get off the treadmill. In all honesty I did want out. Too many factors had always been on a collision course – let alone without having to second-guess the two faces that many individuals wore in the industry, or having to succumb to conforming to either 'go to the next level' or attend the opening of an envelope.

'It will be good for you to be there' was a phrase I would be happy not to hear again – as fun as some of that was when you actually showed up.

Did I have a good laugh getting into trouble at Planet Hollywood in London in the company of Steve Hart for chucking popcorn at each other during a VIP film premiere? Yes.

Unfortunately, the popcorn I threw at Richie from the boy band Let Loose missed him and hit Tim Vincent, the *Blue Peter* presenter, who happened to be sitting next to Lionel Blair's daughter Lucy, who happened to be sitting next to one of TV's biggest agents. All of this of course was not helped by the copious amounts of alcohol they plied us with prior to the screening of the movie.

All of this was forgivable, I am sure, if it were not for what happened next.

Steve Hart and I were standing outside the venue at the end of the night, along with Richie and Fish from Marillion. We were signing autographs for some fans who had been waiting patiently for us to stumble out, when three random blokes decided that they would start giving us some grief. I told them to leave it out, but the bigger one of the three decided to shape up to me and came towards me with his fists up. He wasn't fast enough and I landed, what they call in boxing, the perfect right cross, straight on his chin. He fell back and was caught by the other two, who then dragged him away, clearly not wanting any more of that pugilist activity.

It was this incident that got me barred for life from Planet Hollywood. The popcorn thing was just an added extra. What was I supposed to do? Declare that I was 'a lover not a fighter' and let three blokes pummel me? I defended myself, just the way Dad taught me.

So, would I miss the record company phoning me up the next day telling me I had to write a letter of apology as though I was at school?

No.

It was never just the laying down of ten tracks for an album. Music was medicinal and, in that zone, I could cope and flourish.

All the bullshit wore you down.

Yet I had been in it and reaped some reward. It did also attract some huge negatives. I had begun drifting into a world that was just not me. My faith and spiritually just about dragged me back every time, but I nearly had enough rope to hang myself.

I got to meet and know a vast number of people from all walks of life. Often being booked to sing at private events, from wealthy city bankers to the highly successful gangsters who spent a lifetime robbing the banks. The world of entertainment, just like the boxing game, has always rubbed shoulders with those less desirable worlds.

One of those events was a lavish birthday party; it was also a 'Who's Who' in organised crime like a gangster convention. I love performing onstage, but the night should always end with that final applause and then me going home. But as you have probably gathered by now, I like people, I enjoy meeting them, I try my best to see the good in them, and I love making new friends. So, I became acquainted with a few of them, some of the most charming people I have ever met. This is fine as long as you are not in the same business as them and you know your place.

This was all good until one night in a London club or, to be more precise, it was in the toilet of the club whilst I was standing at the urinal. A guy standing over by the sink turned to me.

'I know you,' he said. 'It'll come to me.'

I thought he was about to say, 'You're that singer bloke,' as has happened many times before.

'You're with the ********,' he said, pointing at me, dropping in the name of a serious London mob.

'No, mate, not me,' I replied.

This was not good. I am that 'singer bloke' and that is all I've ever wanted to be. I don't want to be associated with some underworld thing, unless I am being paid to sing a few numbers.

On another occasion, one of my dad's friends pulled me to one side at the boxing gym. He just happened to be in a branch of the Serious and Organised Crime Command, also known as The Flying Squad.

'You've been knocking around London with the ******,' he said, dropping the name of another very serious firm.

'You've been to (such and such) nightclub with them.'

'How do you know that? Who told you that?' I replied with utter surprise.

'Don't worry about that, you just be careful, OK?' he warned me.

How did he know that? I never spoke to my dad about these things. Wherever he was getting his intel from, it was spot on.

This was yet another sign that I might have drifted in the wrong direction and needed to do a 180-degree turn, sharpish.

I hadn't *just* begun to think this was not where I wanted to be. I was, I admit, at times a bit of a nut and didn't really give a second thought to my actions or the consequences. Personal grief had met artist pressure head on at the making of the first album, and I had felt I was on that relentless treadmill from that point. Getting slightly out of control or finding myself in situations that were beyond my control had become quite normal.

I needed to revert to the environment I grew up in.

So, I was relieved and resigned to it, but for now, the recording career had definitely gone.

Over.

Yet, you also do feel that sense of betrayal. It was the nature of the industry. I was sad for all the good people at Chrysalis. Lines through names regardless of who you were or what you did.

I did begin to achieve some clarity and a sense of release. At the time, events like this can look like disasters. They are often not. I did sense that in life nothing happens without it being allowed to happen. There is always some higher plan.

For the rest of 1996 and through 1997 I did exactly what Steve said I would do… I gigged like Edwin Starr, non-stop. I hit the road, being driven by my tour manager Tom O'Regan. I played in every First Leisure, Rank or Luminar Leisure Nightclub up and down the country… so much so that I picked up the PA of the Year Award, which I am sure had nothing to do with my singing, but more to do with the sheer volume of gigs.

I now had a trophy to use as a door wedge.

One night it almost came to a complete and very real end, when Tom nodded off at the wheel on the M6. He momentarily had a kip, the MPV swerved and I grabbed the steering wheel. We managed to get the car over to the hard shoulder; I took over and continued from that point onwards. Now you know why I drive myself to gigs. It is good being alive!

So, unless you saw me in one of those nightclubs, to the general public it just looked as though I had disappeared. Fallen straight off the edge of a flat Earth. One minute I am on Radio 1 pushing the first single from the album and then there is no album. I had an official fan club, too – mostly of women – and that just ended.

Many careers tail away because the last release does not cut it. I simply vanished. I might have got the pay-off that was owed to me, but egos stopped that album coming out because, after all, the people now making the decisions had nothing to do with that record which was already in the can. You *couldn't* let someone else take the credit and, in this business, you are only as good as your last or next release.

I was almost in the unique position of having neither.

It remains an unsatisfactory ending.

It can be hard to switch off that lifestyle, though. The appetite to carry on always seemed to meet tragedy head on.

My dear friend Norman passed away in 1996 aged 47. Perspective.

I stayed by his bedside day and night in intensive care, at Homerton Hospital, Monday to Friday until he left us. The paramedics found him lying in the street not far from his stomping ground of Stoke Newington. The clothes were cut off his body, and the Timberland boots I gave him were removed. These were handed to me, along with some other personal items found in his pockets, in a plastic bag when I arrived at the hospital. We had the same shoe size, so I often gave him some decent footwear. Those boots now sit in a cupboard at my house, and my family know that when it is my time, I want to be buried in them! I purchased a burial plot, organised his funeral at St Ignatius Church (or Iggy Pop's, as he used to call it) and we laid him to rest in the clothes I had bought him the previous Christmas. A year later I purchased the two empty burial plots next to his… Always thinking ahead.

Articulate, a huge reader and a great letter-writer, we connected spiritually. To this day, I can still hear his laughter in my mind, and I often reread the many words he wrote to me. They make me laugh and, in some way, make him present.

It was Norman who deepened my own faith when we spoke for hours about dogmas and doctrines. His tremendous knowledge and insight into lofty theological concepts were the kind of ideas a fully fledged theologian would tackle.

In my late-teens when I became totally uninspired by the banal liturgical innovations that had hung around since the 60s like an ageing hippie, it was Norman who opened my eyes to a whole other side of things. He took me very early one Sunday morning to the Brompton Oratory in Knightsbridge where I attended my first Tridentine Mass. This is an ancient Latin rite that goes back hundreds of years and remains unchanged. It was suppressed and run underground by modernists who turned the church on its head following the Second Vatican Council, but it is now enjoying a worldwide renaissance. This floated my boat because I was seeking something deeper and more beautiful, and I found it there that day. I continued going there for many years, long after Norman had passed away.

At the age of sixteen I asked him, 'Is this life, and our existence here, some kind of giant cosmic joke? A short experience of joy, with large measures of sorrow and chaos thrown in, right up until the day we kick the bucket?'

'No, Kenny, it's not a cosmic joke. God is a god of order not chaos, and God is love... it's all about love. Don't worry: *All shall be well, all manner of things shall be well,* he said, often quoting the medieval mystic, Julian of Norwich.

The night he died, around 3am, and as always happens, I am booked to do a gig later that evening. I could have pulled out of the show, but I really do not like letting people down, and I knew Norman well enough to know that he would want me to soldier on. So, I decided that I would do this one for him.

I take my friend Nick Holmes along with me for support.

In time, Nick and I would lose touch and I would lose him, too. The effects of some of that partying in the 90s either ended there and then or it stayed with you, and sadly for Nick, it was the latter. Things went from bad to worse, including a terrible mental breakdown and paranoid psychosis. The lowest moment was when we were clubbing at the Ministry of Sound and nobody could get hold of us for 24 hours as we did not have our phones. When we rejoined the land of the living, we found it had one less soul in it. Nobody had been able to contact us, and in the missing hours Nick's dad, to his devastation, had passed away. It was moments like this along with the breakdown of his relationship with his girlfriend, the loss of his home, and the continued escapes into excess that tipped this deep, sensitive and beautiful soul over the edge.

As things spiralled, he moved in with his sister for a while, was broke and at times he just walked the streets of East London. Chad reached out to Nick several times but there was nothing he could do to save him. For years we all wondered as to his whereabouts or if he was even still alive. Then one night whilst I was gigging in Essex, I spotted a young lad in the audience who was the spit of him. It turned out to be his nephew Liam, who confirmed that Nick was still alive but he was in a bad way, now living with his brother in Bristol, where he did ultimately die – a tragic end for one of the funniest people I knew and a decent musician, too. Very few people attended his funeral. I was grateful to have the opportunity to pay my last respects.

On that night, it was a long and lonely journey to Leicester. I had hardly eaten or slept all week as I prayed constantly by Norman's bedside. Backstage I put on my clothes for the gig, noticing that my belt went up two extra notches.

I looked thin and unwell. My heart was broken.

It was one of the toughest gigs of my life.

'Why don't you smile?' a woman heckled from the crowd.

If she only knew what kind of week it had been, and what had happened in the early hours of that very day.

And I did my best to offer a false smile. But it did break me.

One good thing that came from his death was meeting his dad, Norman Senior. He had an up-and-down, on-and-off relationship with him over the years after his divorce from Norman's mum. I became very close friends with him and I took care of his mum who was suffering from senile dementia and who eventually needed a nursing home. I felt it my responsibility. I never ever considered it anything other than the natural thing to do.

One very unusual responsibility was laid on my shoulders by Norman Senior when he was in his last days at a nursing home in Pimlico, London.

'The black box, Kenny, you need to sort out the black box in the flat,' he said to me from his bed.

He was dying and at times not making much sense, so I didn't know what to make of his words, but he kept coming back to it.

165

'Get the key and make sure you dispose of the contents of the black box,' he told me.

I wondered what could be inside this mysterious black box.

His partner Cissy filled me in on the details. Hidden away at their flat in Chelsea was a locked metal box. Inside, I would find a gun that he had confiscated from a German officer in the Second World War. The gun originally belonged to an American soldier who was taken as a prisoner of war, so it was not the standard-issue Luger you would expect a German officer to have.

I opened the box and sure enough there was the gun surrounded by dozens of bullets. It was loaded with a magazine full of rounds, so it was ready for action. I removed the clip and made it safe. Did it still work? Yes, it did, and the reason I know this is because Cissy told me that one firework night Norman went up onto the roof of his block of flats to check it out by firing a round into the sky.

There was no way I was walking down to the local nick with this box under my arm. So, I called one of my dad's police friends and made arrangements for it to be collected from the flat. The first policeman came but he was not authorised to handle it. Then came the firearms men in the red police car who were able to bag it up and take it away. Norman Senior passed away just a few days later and Cissy let me keep the black box.

You never can be quite sure what is going on in a human being. Norman Junior meant the world to me. The only thing I did know was that I seemed to have had a fair share of bereavement and that, on each occasion, the circumstances felt unjust. I realise that many people feel that way and it is cliché to say that he was taken too early, but if Father Hanshell's passing in 1994 had left a huge spiritual abyss then Norman's young death represented a similar void – the pair were my kindred spirits. If I had questions – spiritual or otherwise – then these two often had the answers.

And now they were both gone.

One look inside myself warned me that bereavement was a process that troubled me and did not leave me at speed. There was always a delayed reaction. A period of both reflection and craziness was potentially on the cards.

And so, it transpired.

I had met Luciano, or Louie as we call him, dancing around my living room one night as the sun came up. It had been one of those sessions. We had been introduced to each other earlier that day at the wedding of a mutual friend, Tony Maffeo. Tony is Italian and he married Samantha, of Irish descent. The one thing about Italians and the Irish is that they like to celebrate, especially weddings. When the reception was coming to an end, I had no intention of stopping. When I got into that party animal mode, anything could happen.

'When this ends, you're all invited back to my house, we'll continue the celebration there!' I shouted to the guests.

There was a huge cheer from the crowd, everyone scrambled to their cars and a massive convoy made its way to my house in Finchley, or 'Casa Loca' as I called it.

They all knew where the party was at.

The music was thumping and the house was rockin' big-style. I only knew about half of the people there that night, but by the following morning I knew them all and made friends that now 25 years on are like family to me. Everything happens for a reason, even the crazy stuff.

Tony's brother Giulio lived over in Boston in the States so next thing I find myself on a plane with Louie and Chris Kelley heading out to see him, then driving together with Jonathan from the international boy band New Kids on the Block to go skiing in Vermont.

I honestly don't know how it happened.

But I have a pretty good idea of *what* happened.

We began racing Jonathan, who was in his own car, up the highway, across state, drinking beer and throwing the empties in amongst our skiing gear. Let's just say this – we were travelling well prepared for a lot of après-ski, too!

You can guess the next bit. The cops pull us over.

'We're British, we can drink in the car back in the UK,' I protest.

'Well, you can't do that here in the USA, sir,' he corrected me.

He has heard it all before and wants to see my passport.

I have to think where I have put it, whilst trying to act as normal as possible – whatever normal is.

I locate my ID in a pocket. There is a massive whiff of – let's just say – something herbal when I open it up.

I am thinking, 'If he gets a load of this stink, I am nicked and on a plane, straight back to Old Blighty faster than you can say "Pass the Dutchie".'

I gave him my passport. He must have had a blocked nose that day.

Giulio, who was driving and hadn't been drinking, had to get out of the car and perform all sorts of strange sobriety tests. Walking in a straight line, standing on one leg, putting one hand out and then bringing it back to touch the end of his nose with his forefinger. The cop intimidatingly stuck his nose deep into Giulio's mouth to have a right old sniff… Good luck with that one!

This was like something from a bygone age. Why didn't he just get him to blow into a breathalyser? Job done!

Another police car then pulled up. This guy had a massive cowboy-type hat on and a big, gold star-shaped badge. He must have been the sheriff.

'I want you to get all of the empty beer cans out of your car and put them on the roof of the car, so I can count them,' he ordered.

'How many beers have you all had?' he asked us.

'About three each, so nine in total,' lied Chris.

'OK, there had better not be any more than that or we are gonna run you in,' said the sheriff.

We pulled out nine cans and placed them on top of the car for all the passing traffic to see that we had been very naughty boys.

'You got any more in there?' he asked.

'No, that's the lot,' I said, knowing full well that there was probably at least another five tucked under the bags.

'Right, gentlemen, I'm gonna radio ahead to the next two states,' he said. 'You can expect to be stopped again.'

We weren't. Nor were we his responsibility once we crossed the county line. I am sure that he had trotted this out before.

We pulled into the first service station we could find and discarded the remaining evidence. We arrived without further scrutiny but when we got there we went nuts, smashed off our heads hitting the notorious elite double black diamond runs on Killington Mountain.

We were absolute lunatics on those slopes. I came unstuck quite a few times, learning the hard way by earning myself a nice double inguinal hernia.

Living dangerously. In every sense.

Boys just having fun.

Looking back now on all of my escapades, I think about the words of George Bernard Shaw: '*Youth is wasted on the young*'. He wasn't wrong.

The holiday in Boston was cut short when I received a call to say that Norman's mother, Winnie, had passed away. I held the deeds to the plot Norman was buried in, so I had to fly back to London to organise her funeral, and give the permission needed for her to be buried in the same plot with her son.

As much as I enjoyed my time in Boston and as crazy as it was there, it is a moment like this that brings things to a halt and brings a person back to their senses.

Being free from EMI and only having gigs to contend with gave me a newfound freedom to do what I wanted and to go wherever I chose. I was for the first time in ages relieved of the pressure that comes with a record deal. I liked this freedom, and it made me wonder even more if I should retreat altogether from the music business.

I then made a very difficult decision and one that I had to think long and hard about before doing it.

I split from Steve Finan.

He had been brilliant and remains a friend. Simply, I would definitely not be here without him. But I needed to cut loose and find myself again. My gut was telling me to do it. Most people around me thought I was mad, and they were probably right at the time. It was a tough thing to do, and I knew it would leave me unrepresented, exposed and on my own in an industry where a good manager is very much needed, and Steve was the best.

I had big questions about the path I had been on and what route I now needed to take. I had to throw myself out there into the desert so to speak, exchanging the safety of the known for the uncertainties of the unknown. Sometimes you have to run the risk of losing everything in order to gain something greater. Whatever was going on inside of me, it was far deeper than music. It transcended all of those things.

Later that year I went on a pilgrimage with Mum to Fátima in Portugal. It is one of the most important Marian shrines in the world. This had been on our bucket list for some time, and now I had time to do these things. On 13 October 1997 we joined over 100,000 other pilgrims at the shrine on the Cova da Iria. We had such a wonderful time together, and it had a positive and lasting effect on me.

As you will appreciate, a 'bucket list' is often for people who have a sense that time is running out. Time is always running out.

But for Mum sadly this was true. Although we didn't know it at the time.

Going to Fátima was, without a doubt, a spiritual preparation for what was to come.

24 Date: 29 June 1998

Soon everything came crashing down.

Dad's birthday. Restaurant booked.

Mum is diagnosed with cancer.

29 June 1998. I will never forget it.

One minute I'm on the phone to Johnny Boy, laughing ourselves to tears, the next minute I get a phone call from Mum.

I dropped to my knees when she began to speak. I knew, just from the tone of her voice.

'Kenny, I have got bad news. The results came back. I've got stomach cancer.'

'Oh Mama, oh Mama, it will be alright,' I replied as many do in this situation.

We both cried.

'It's in God's hands, Mum,' I tried to reassure her.

Unfortunately, it was also in the hands of the doctors – despite my faith.

It was so not going to be alright.

I cancelled the restaurant.

Mum had been indicating, rather than complaining, that she was having a few problems with her stomach but believed it to be the ulcer that she was previously diagnosed with. When I went with her for the endoscopy, they let me into the room with her. What I saw on the monitor when the camera went down, I honestly thought was the ulcer, so naturally I assured her it would be fine.

It wasn't an ulcer and things would not be fine.

All the gigs, every moment of politics, the excesses, the money, the 'fame'… none of it meant anything now. Mum came first.

I tried my best to keep gigging but I knew I would be taking a lot of time out to be there for Mum. The road ahead was not going to be an easy one.

Dad was also in the early stages of dementia – except nobody agreed. At that time I didn't know enough about the

171

illness to formulate an opinion, but I learned quickly, and that medical explanation which I had for some reason instinctively been challenging for so many years kicked in again.

Now it would never leave me. It became a constant.

Dad did not have dementia.

Because he took the dementia questionnaire with his GP and could answer details like who the Prime Minister was or what year it was. That was the benchmark. Therefore, according to them he didn't have it!

I knew what I was seeing, though, and now I was on a collision course with that doctor.

Dad did in fact have dementia and we knew it, because we knew him better than any GP ever could. We observed those subtle changes in his personality, those micro-indicators that tell you something is just not right. For now, we would have to deal with it ourselves and go it alone.

My friend Phil came by. His mum had been diagnosed two weeks before.

'I am so sorry...' I had told him just recently with as much empathy as you think you possess.

Now I *really* knew how he felt – not through imagination but experience.

The next week evaporated into consoling and praying. I did not know how long we had. Who does? I had no idea what the doctors planned to do next. But I knew one thing: Mum was very ill.

At the first oncology meeting, we took Dave's Auntie Freda with us for support. She has a wealth of medical knowledge, and will help us understand the jargon and make sense of it all.

They told us systematically, 'This is what we plan to do.'

In essence, it was to remove Mum's stomach. She would not be able to eat normally again, but she would get used to this, and chemo would follow.

On 14 July they took her down.

Your life is in their hands, and you hope they know what they are doing.

Like most people we believed this was the only option, and to not take it was not an option.

Mum was scared. Very scared. But resigned.

I waited alone the whole day. Saw every minute of it. That clock stood still.

Mum was in the operating theatre for hours; much longer than they said she would be. Something must have gone wrong, I thought.

I walked around the hospital slowly going out of my mind. At one of my lowest points, I called Myra. I was like a grandson to her, and she knew how I ticked. With words that came from a lifetime of adversities, she kept me sane.

I then saw them hurriedly wheeling a bed through the corridor. I looked at the person in the bed, and for a second, I didn't recognise who it was. Then I realised it was Mum. She looked a greyish-white colour, like a corpse. My heart jumped out of my chest. It was so shocking. I followed her as she was taken straight into intensive care – one blood transfusion quickly following another.

'It's 50:50,' the surgeon told me. 'The next 48 hours are critical.'

'We found more cancer than expected. I had to make an on-the-table decision. Do I close your mum up and tell you she has fourteen months to live, or do I go in and get it all out?'

'We have removed the tip of the pancreas, her spleen, her stomach and the surrounding lymph nodes. She lost a lot of blood during the operation, so she is in an extremely unstable and critical condition right now.'

Mum was fighting for her life.

She was in and out of consciousness and in so much pain.

Seeing her like this, I think I would have preferred the fourteen months option.

I know I would have.

Time no longer stood still. It was racing.

This is it.

I ask the nurse to call the priest. Not out of desperation or false hope or drama. When this is your upbringing, this is what you do. Mum might not make it through the night, so instinctively I wanted her to be given the last rites or the Sacrament of Extreme Unction, as I was taught to call it.

Mum put up the fight of her life and over the next 48 hours she pulled through.

Three days later the surgeon came to see her:

'Mrs Thomas, we got it all out.'

'I'm glad to see you're recovering from the surgery. We hope to get you onto a general ward very soon.'

When a surgeon says, 'We got it all out,' these words need to be taken with a huge bag of salt. What they mean to say is: 'We got out what we could see but we didn't get out all of the other millions of microscopic cancer cells left behind, especially the ones we cut into that are now coursing through your bloodstream.'

Telling my mum that he 'got it all out' built our hopes up and was simply not true. But we believed him.

She remained in the ICU for a number of days until she was strong enough to be transferred.

She had no stomach, so she couldn't eat as she did prior to the operation, she kept vomiting and her weight just plummeted.

Eventually she came home and began to eat small amounts of food, mainly soups, and built up a little strength. But she soon deteriorated again and had to be readmitted to the hospital.

It was my 30th birthday. I went to the hospital.

'Kenny, I'm dying,' she said to me.

'Mum please don't say that. You're not dying. We're gonna get you well and get you out of here,' I replied, trying to be positive, but breaking inside.

These were the last words I wanted to hear Mum say. For her to say that she must have really felt like she was short of time, because she would normally never let anyone know how she was feeling.

I went for a little walk with Jan, my sister-in-law. She had been there before and instinctively knew that I needed a few minutes to get my head around what I was seeing and hearing.

174

Mum *did* slowly recover and we did get her out of there.

Mum's sister, Auntie Lala, flew over from Las Palmas to be with her. She stayed with her at my house and at my sister Sandra's. Together we all took care of Mum, getting her as well as possible in preparation for the immanent first round of chemotherapy.

In reality Mum was not well enough or strong enough to begin chemo but the doctors said it was important to get it started. They told us that she might be lucky like some people who seem to tolerate it well and don't experience too many side effects. Sounds good!

They never seem to tell you how bad it can be, or how horrendous it often is for most people. They also never told us exactly why she had to have chemo. After all, the surgeon 'got it all out', right? We were never given a true and proper prognosis. Or how much time Mum had left with or without the chemo? It was all so vague and ambiguous.

But like most people we put our faith in them. They know best and they have all the answers, or so we think. So, you blindly go where so many have gone before hoping they will cure this dreadful disease and not kill you in the process.

She was sent to St Bartholomew's Hospital, London, or St Barts as we call it, to start the treatment. Mum seemed fine during that first course of chemo but as the days went on, she began to experience more and more of the adverse effects, such as the hair loss, the nausea and the mouth ulcers. She was deteriorating again.

Nevertheless, they still continued with their poisonous protocol, giving it to her in a small container connected to an intravenous port. This meant she was able to come home and the chemotherapy could continue uninterrupted.

It was at my house that things just got worse.

She was – to put it bluntly – going downhill fast. But to her credit and true to the woman she was, she never told you the level of pain that she was in, or complained. You could gauge it of course but probably always massively underestimated it.

She was thin and frail, her hair was gone, her fingertips began to turn black, her gums bled, the skin on her hands and feet was inflamed and painful. She was in a terrible state. Her food and fluid intake had dropped to a minimum.

I kept asking her each day, 'Are you alright, Mum?'

'I'm fine,' she would reply.

'I don't think you are, Mum; I think we should go to the hospital,' I insisted.

'No, I'm OK, I'm fine.'

By the third day of my scepticism, she confessed that she was not.

'Kenny, you had better take me back to hospital,' she confessed.

I gently pinched the skin on her forearm to see if it had lost its elasticity. It stayed up and didn't spring back into place, a sure sign of dehydration. This was something I had seen the doctor do once before.

'Come on, let's go... We need to get there fast. Why didn't you listen to me, Mum? I could see you were not right,' I said as I helped her to the car.

I felt so angry, not at Mum, but at the situation, and at myself for not going with my gut instinct and taking her to the hospital three days before.

And I know that she was beyond pain at this point. For her to ask meant that she was several stages past the point where she should have demanded.

After bombing it in the car to Barts Hospital, the doctor gave me an answer which was both satisfactory and nowhere near so:

'Mr Thomas, I am so glad you have brought her here,' she said. 'She is not in a good way. She is severely dehydrated, and we need to get a drip into her arm immediately.'

They needed to do a blood transfusion, too.

Mum was in the right place.

Chemo at home supervised by your non-medical son was a bad shout.

The following day I met with the doctor.

'We need to stop the chemo,' she said. 'It's not working. It has made her very ill.'

'In fact, if we continue it will probably kill her,' she told me in no uncertain terms.

'We suspect that your mother lacks a particular enzyme which has made the chemotherapy far more toxic for her.'

'I agree, I think it's the right thing to do. I don't want to see her suffer like this anymore,' I replied.

It is not like we weren't warned. A family friend, Irena, had been diagnosed with cancer a few months before Mum and decided to refuse the treatment being offered to her. Instead, she went down a completely natural, holistic and alternative route. She allowed the hospital to scan her, but nothing more than that.

When Mum was first diagnosed, Irena handed me a letter at church advising my mum against surgery and chemotherapy, saying it would only spread the cancer and wipe out her immune system, the very thing needed to fight the disease. Instead, she recommended a list of things to take, such as vitamins, minerals and herbal formulas, along with strict dietary changes which included superfoods and an organic green leaf juicing regime. She also advised that we go to see a doctor in Bristol who has many cancer patients who are all using this kind of protocol with some amazing results.

Honestly, I thought this was complete madness, and that Irena had effectively just signed her own death certificate. How could this combat cancer? Surely the oncologists know best, and they have the medicine for the job. If people were having success in treating their cancer this way, we would know about it. It would be headline news, right?

So, we chose our path and Irena continued along hers. Every now and then I would reread her letter and seriously wonder if we might have got it wrong. I was hoping and praying that we hadn't. Whatever route Irena or my mum had chosen, I just wanted to see them both healed and well. The problem I now had was that Irena had given me a small glimpse of the truth. Closing my eyes to it only worked for a time. It kept coming back at me until I was forced to open them and look at it head on. Ignorance is bliss, so they say, but for my family, ignorance was deadly.

Auntie Lala returned home to Las Palmas. Her being there for Mum was much needed and definitely helped her recover from what she had been through.

Of course, she never fully recovered.

But she just about survived.

By Christmas 1998, I moved her in with me.

In reality, the separation from EMI was now a blessing. Getting off that treadmill was a relief and absolutely providential. Everything happens for a reason. We often don't understand why until the next bit of our life journey comes along. Now I knew why.

I still did the odd gig, which for me was a release from reality and my own form of therapy. It was nice to escape for an hour onstage, but once the show was over, I would emotionally crash back down only to face reality once again.

25 Viva Las Palmas

The chemo was stopped.

It had nearly killed her.

Mum miraculously – or not, depending on what you believe – begins to recover. She is doing really well. Her hair begins to grow back. She is in a good place. There is hope.

She decided that she wanted to spend some time in Gran Canaria with her sister Lala. Dad would go with her for a couple of weeks and then return home, leaving her there to convalesce.

She was also joined out there by her very close Spanish friend Emily, who was originally from Las Palmas but now lived not far from her on Stamford Hill. Once Dad and Emily had returned home, I would then go out there for a few weeks.

Barts Hospital were slightly reluctant about her holiday plans as they still thought they might have one more treatment up their sleeves. However, they agreed with me, that after the last chemo disaster she was better off getting herself really well before that could be considered.

Being with Mum in Las Palmas was just the medicine she and I needed. This was a place full of childhood memories for her, and a few for me, too. We would make some new ones, too.

At the same time, my friend Tony Ayers was staying down the south of the island in Maspalomas. I met Tony some years earlier when he was working backstage at a Soul Weekender and we have remained tight mates ever since.

Mum said I should go down there, take a couple of days out to have some fun. She was always thinking about others and never about herself. Part of me wanted to go, but another part of me felt that I should stay with her.

So, with her blessing, I went to see Tony.

Back in 1990, I had wanted to go and live in Gran Canaria but never did because I got the record deal. Now, through Tony I got to know all the faces on the island, the DJs and the club owners. It became my home from home. Once again I made some enduring friendships, Dodgy Dave, Shakey

(Paul), Dawn, Rocky, Dawnie and Mo (RIP), to name a few from that GC Crew. I would return there many times after that, also joining them on a crazy skiing holiday in Livigno, Italy. No double hernia this time.

I left that mad lot in Maspalomas and returned to be with Mum.

She celebrated her 56th birthday with the Spanish side of the family – something that she had not done in years. They made a real fuss of her. It created a special memory.

She looked better than ever. Her hair had fully grown back, she had a nice tan, and her energy levels were amazing. She would take really long walks along Las Canteras Beach and beyond into the heart of the city.

If you didn't know it, you would never have guessed what she had been through. But she was not out of the woods, and this was hammered home by the call I got from Barts asking when she would be coming back.

They wanted to give her a scan and discuss further treatment.

Discuss further treatment? They never discussed it much before. They just steamed in and it nearly killed her.

My trust now is limited. There is an inner circle.

I speak with my cousin José. Mum's nephew is a radiologist.

He agrees to scan her, write up a report and I can then give this to Barts. This will speed up the process massively.

It will also give me for the first time a complete, unambiguous and clear picture of what is going on with the cancer. That way, I could be sure there was no concealment or half-truths. I knew the health services in the UK did the best job they could to the summit of their abilities with the narrative they were prescribed, but a different viewpoint from a trained family member was an option that everyone would take in this situation if they could.

It was not good news. José told me there were lesions on her liver and provided me with their exact measurements. The prognosis was very poor.

'Maybe chemo can shrink these a little, but you will not cure them, she only has a few months to live at best,' he told me.

José did not deal in half-truths. This could not have been easy for him to have to see that and tell me. This was no ordinary patient this time, it was his auntie, *Tia Lita* as they called her. It was heartbreaking.

We chose not to tell Mum at that point in time.

But we didn't have to.

I think she knew.

I obviously had no choice but to take the report back to Barts. I recognise that I was in a unique position where I was doing the work for them. This data was very important. Most people in hospitals are told. Few can question. Having that second opinion gives you a voice. I was never *not* going to trust my cousin. He had no reason to conceal things – he is a professional.

Mum took one last stroll along Las Canteras Beach, revealing to my sister that she realised it was her last view of that place and she was saying goodbye to her childhood home. Mum never told me these things, knowing it would hurt, so sparing me that pain.

Barts saw the scans and told me, 'If we do this it will buy her more time.'

'We have got the chemo right this time,' they said convincingly.

She came back from the Canaries looking well. I know we should have left the treatment at this point, but her will to live and her willingness to do whatever it took, or go through anything to achieve that, were deeply rooted in her personality. When she was born, the doctor said she was very weak and would last only a few hours, but she survived. She had had a hard life. It was always a fight, so why stop fighting now?

At this point, I am really succumbing to suspicion. Mindful of the excellent work performed under duress, I knew that I had to challenge the medical narrative. I was in possession of fresh eyes and the knowledge that there could be a different opinion.

This was an ethos now embedded in me forever.

'From my cousin's scans and his detailed report we know there is nothing more we can do, so why should we go for more chemo?' I said to the oncologist.

'This time it will be different, and we have a very good chance of shrinking the tumours and giving her much more time,' she said in that *trust me I'm a doctor* tone.

Denial is a strange thing. Knowing what I knew from José's scans, I still so desperately wanted to believe the oncologist was right and somehow that my cousin might be wrong on this occasion. The pressure we got from the hospital to make a decision didn't help us think straight. Plus, it wasn't my decision to make. What did Mum want?

'I want to do it. Let's see if it will work this time,' was her answer.

We had to respect her free will.

Although I am now finally looking heavily into the alternative option. Irena's letter and the fact that she seemed to be doing very well were not something I could ignore any longer. I made contact with the doctor in Bristol and was ready to take Mum there to see if they could help her in any way.

Meanwhile, Barts began a new round of chemo. This was the one thing that they said they had got right this time. Our hopes were raised and we hung onto that little bit of hope with all we had.

At first it seemed to be going well, but its toxic accumulative effects soon took hold. Mum once again lost all that lovely hair she had grown in Las Palmas, and her tan faded, only to be replaced with that off-white colour I now associate with chemo. It robbed her of all the vitality she had acquired on those long walks down Las Canteras Beach. She was back where she started. No, she was worse than before. It was killing her. They knew it and that is why they had to stop it again. But it was too late. The damage was done.

Mum was the sweetest, most beautiful person and now, she bore no resemblance, in her body weight and frailty. It was terrible.

There really was no need for her to have gone through this. She could have carried on feeling as well as possible until things naturally took their course. And who really knows how long that could have been. I couldn't help but think that this final round of chemo was simply one last opportunity for them to tick a few boxes. It was nothing short of experimentation.

I did take Mum to Bristol, and we began the natural, alternative protocol. It was our last and only hope, but, like so many people, this is often done far too late. It is a much harder battle to win after the so-called standard cancer treatment has damaged and weakened the body. With her immune system now completely annihilated we needed more time to undo it, and time is the one thing we didn't have. We should have taken this alternative route from the beginning, but we didn't know enough to make an informed choice. You can only go with what you know. There was one thing I now definitely was certain of. I was never going to allow this to happen again to a member of my family.

My eyes were now wide open, but too little, too late. I realised why the war on cancer will never be won with the current treatments on offer, such as surgery, radiation and chemotherapy – cutting, burning and poisoning. I absorbed one key piece of information whose truth I could not confirm but resonated loudly when I read it: chemo with its 97% failure rate in adults worldwide. Largely unchanged since the 1970s and largely ineffective unless you're in that 3%. But it remains a multibillion-dollar industry, and they are not going to give that up anytime soon. It may work for the few, but for millions of others it is nothing but a source of immeasurable suffering.

Now I understood why I personally only knew of three people who had come through that treatment and survived. All the others were dead. The three who did make it were cured through surgery. The chemo almost killed them, but not quite.

Primum non nocere. 'First, do no harm' from the original Hippocratic oath is not something that was first and foremost on the minds of the doctors when they administered that carcinogenic substance to my mum, especially when they knew full well what it had previously done to her. Shame on them!

It did her *great harm*, and it was far worse than the symptoms of disease itself. Whatever time Mum had left was now greatly reduced thanks to chemo.

It was never the cure they made it out to be when they first gave it to her. Although they never actually used that word. It is simply what is cleverly implied when they convinced her to have it. Later the narrative changed, saying it would at best give her more time. What would her survival rate have been without it? What purpose did it serve? Other than to make her so dreadfully ill.

Time no longer stood still for me as it did that day in Homerton Hospital; it was now racing. It was unstoppable.

26 Lourdes

In October 1999, I asked Mum if she wanted to go to Lourdes in France, a famous Catholic shrine visited by millions of people each year, especially by those who are sick and in the last stages of life. We had been there together once before in 1994. Now we would return under very different circumstances.

The doctors at Barts Hospital were not keen on the idea and thought she was too unwell to travel. They knew death was not far away, but they never quite found those exact words. We were very much kept in the dark. If death was *not* far away, then all the more reason to go to Lourdes. They tried their hardest to dissuade, but Mum was determined and nothing was going to stop her.

She refused to complain. She did not want to inflict suffering on myself. She told me little, but always a little bit more to Sandra. We would of course check in with each other. To the end, Mum *was* a mum. She worried more about us than she did about herself.

'Spend some money on yourself,' I said to her in those final months.

'Go out and treat yourself, Mum,' I insisted.

'Kenny keeps telling me to go out and spend some money on myself,' she told Sandra. 'But I can't do that because you will need that money for my funeral.'

She was the only person who was thinking like that.

Dad was also starting to be more affected by dementia.

How was *he* taking the decline?

Well – his condition meant that nobody could really know. He *didn't* really know.

Sandra kept an eye on him, while Mum and I flew to Lourdes.

With Mum wrapped up warm and in a wheelchair, we joined thousands of other pilgrims from all over the world. Each evening, I would wheel her down to the grotto to spend time in that special place where peace and tranquillity permeate the very air you breathe. It is like nowhere else on this earth.

Time was not racing in that grotto. In silence, comfortable in each other's presence, we experienced an inner peace that was other-worldly.

Mum was in the last days of her life.

Really things should be falling apart right now. I should be falling apart. Instead, we enjoyed a profound spiritual peace that descended upon us and penetrated the deepest part of the soul. Even these very words are insufficient and incapable of explaining it.

We never went to Lourdes expecting a physical miracle, even though many well-documented ones have occurred there. Moments that defy all modern scientific explanation. No, we went there because this was Mum's last wish. But we did experience *something*. In many ways, it was far greater than a physical healing. It took place deep in our very being, a foretaste of something beyond this world. Paradoxically, it came through, and out of, the very suffering we were experiencing. We understood that, and above all we accepted it. This would not have happened unless we had made the journey there.

It was also – coincidentally – the anniversary of *Voices* being released. At this point, I have no record deal, but I couldn't be further from it all. In fact, it feels like a previous life to me now. None of it mattered anymore. I am at peace with it. More than ever.

I realise that there is the real risk that I could be coming home with her body. It is that close. But I live in the moment, grateful for what I still have, and trusting that *All will be well*, as Norman used to say.

Then one evening, Mum did become quite unwell. She was sleeping a lot and she was in a great deal of discomfort.

I called Amy, a member of the palliative care team at St. Joseph's Hospice in Hackney, and told her about Mum's condition.

After explaining what I was observing and the fact that Mum was slightly more jaundiced, especially her eyes, she made it clear to me that these were signs that she had moved into the final stages of her illness. She suggested that we make our way back to London as soon as possible.

I then called the pilgrimage representative, explaining the situation, and asked her how we could get back to London. She told me there were no flights out of Lourdes for the next few days. The only way back was to make a journey down to Toulouse and fly from there. That journey would have been too much for Mum.

Thankfully, Mum became more comfortable as the night went on.

Tomorrow I would see how she was and take things from there.

Can she handle travelling to Toulouse and flying from there?

Can I maybe find a doctor out here who can deal with this?

How much time do we really have?

A lot of questions were racing through my mind.

Then I had an overwhelming feeling that things would be OK. Don't ask me how I knew, but I felt sure that we would complete our time there and go home as planned. It was all in God's hands: He will provide. Mum was not about to die here in Lourdes.

The following morning, she *did* feel a lot better. This was a huge relief.

She wanted to go down to the grotto to attend Mass.

It was a beautiful day and the shrine was very busy with pilgrims.

Afterwards, I decided to take a picture of Mum by the grotto. I then looked around to see if I could get someone to take one of us together.

I was approached by a man who speaks almost no English who kindly took the camera off me.

What happened next is the very reason I do not believe in coincidence.

'Can I have a chat with you?' he managed to express. 'I am a doctor. I saw you yesterday at the grotto... Do you need any help from me?'

He was there on a private pilgrimage from Italy.

I was speechless, thinking that he must be an angel and he has been sent to us.

He asks me which hotel we are in, and he promises to come and see us later that afternoon.

He was true to his word. He examined Mum and gave me specific instructions on the pain control medicine. He slightly reduced the dose. The amount recommended by Barts was too much, making her too sleepy.

What he suggested worked. Mum was more alert, comfortable and able to enjoy the rest of her time there. He enabled us to get her home.

I remain truly grateful.

True to his character, he continued to write to me long after that.

On our last night in Lourdes, Mum and I decided to go down and join the huge, candlelit procession that takes place there. Tens of thousands of pilgrims, holding candles in the dark, make their way around the Sanctuary, ending in front of the Basilica. It is one of the most beautiful things that happens there and is quite a sight to behold.

'I would like to get to the front of the procession,' said Mum.

'Mum, there's hundreds of people in front of us,' I attempted to dissuade her.

'I'll try, but I don't think we'll be able to push through to the front,' I said as I attempted to shove the wheelchair through the crowd.

Then suddenly out of nowhere came a guy dressed in the official garments of the shrine. He pushed his way through the crowd, came up to us and gestured that we follow him. He then led us all the way through the throng of pilgrims right up to the very front of the procession.

'Someone up there must have heard your prayer, Mum,' I said in amazement.

Later I took one last picture beneath the central statue of Our Lady where it is customary to pray that one day you will safely return to Lourdes.

Mum would never return and that was the last picture I ever took of her.

When we got back home, she was admitted to Barts Hospital where they did more blood transfusions and kept her as comfortable as possible.

Auntie Lala flew over again from Las Palmas to be there for Mum and for us. Her face lit up with joy when she saw her sister walk into the ward with me. We couldn't have got through those final two weeks without her.

The doctors suggested one last procedure – a stent in the liver. When Mum returned from the operating theatre, she was in so much pain. For the first time she told the doctors to leave her alone. She didn't want them to do anything more. She had had enough of it all.

I am wondering what the hell is going on. So, I went into the office where the doctor was.

'Can you tell me what is going on?' I asked him.

'What do you mean?' he replied.

'Why is my mum still being prodded and poked when all it is doing is causing her more pain?'

'From the very beginning, you've never been straight with us about her condition, the treatments, or how much time she had left.'

He nervously backed away to a corner of the room and began shuffling some papers, unable to look me in the eye.

I moved forward, pretty much trapping him in that corner.

'So go on, tell me, how much time does she have now?' I demanded.

'Your mum has done very well already,' he replied, still not wanting to give me a direct answer.

I thought, what a crap answer that is!

'So, what you're saying is, my mum has been on borrowed time for quite some time?'

'Yes,' he admitted.

'We already knew that, but it would have been better if you were more truthful from the start,' I said as I turned and walked out.

189

It was, to me, trial and error medicine.

Mum asked me what happened in that office. If there was anything she needed to know. There was nothing to say. If I told her, it wouldn't help. The look on my face said it all. The process was not now reversible.

'I want to go home,' she pleaded.

I spoke to the doctors and told them just that. They were totally against it. They knew she had days or maybe just hours left, but still they never said it.

'Look, you can do no more for her and she wants to go home. We don't want her to die here in this place,' I firmly told them.

I spoke to my cousin José and explained the symptoms to him. He knew straight away and told us that the time was very near. I got more truth from him, 2000 miles away in Las Palmas than I did from the doctors right there by Mum's bedside. He said it was better for Mum to go home.

This was her last and final wish and we had to do it.

The doctors finally capitulated and agreed to let her go the following morning.

I spent that day by her bedside having what can only be called final conversations. Things I will never get to say again.

'Mum, I'm sorry for anything I've ever done wrong over the years,' I said with tears in my eyes.

'If you said sorry a million times,' she replied, 'I forgive you a million times.'

'I thank God for giving me a son like you,' she said.

'Don't worry about Sandra and the kids, I will take care of them,' I told her, knowing that she worried about them a great deal.

'I know you will, you're a good boy.'

I remained by her bed late into that Sunday night.

The following morning, we packed up her things, and we got her out of there.

I called the palliative care team and told them to meet us at Mum and Dad's house. They made her comfortable in what used to be my old bedroom. A room filled with so many memories for me growing up there, but now to be forever overshadowed by a memory so sad.

Dad was not fully aware of what was unfolding. He knew, but his cognitive decline made it difficult for him to process everything. It was happening so fast, and it was too much to bear.

I realised it was coming:

9 November.

The long night.

Mum received one last visit from her dear friend Emily, and later from Dave Sassoon. She was still able to have some conversations but was increasingly becoming more tired. Surrounded by Lala, Sandra, Dad and myself we kept vigil and prayed the Rosary, Mum's favourite devotional prayer.

In these final hours she stopped talking English and reverted to her native Spanish. The closest person to Mum had always been her sister Auntie Sole. Now in her fading moments, she kept thinking Lala was Sole.

She was drifting in and out. That unconscious phase of being between two places did give you insight. Or rather confirmed it. The subconscious calling for her sister Sole reflected a loss she had never overcome and displayed the knowledge that she was joining her.

Of course, you try to rush in everything you ever wanted to say. Time allows you to reflect that the course of life had already allowed you this opportunity.

I knew there was nothing more to add. I spent the whole night in prayer.

10 November.

Just after nine that morning, Amy from the palliative care team arrived and could clearly see it had been a rough night.

Mum had been in great discomfort in those last hours. All we could do was helplessly watch and pray.

Amy gave her an injection that would assist her breathing and make her more comfortable.

Unable to contain her sadness, she stayed for a while and wept with us.

'I can give your mum one more injection before I leave. It will probably ease things even more,' she consoled.

'Will it hasten death?' I asked.

'That is not its purpose, but yes, it sometimes can do that,' she replied.

'No thank you, let's not do that one,' I said.

Euthanasia was the furthest thing from Amy's mind, but any hint of it betrayed my principles and Mum's also. It would have probably prevented the ending which every Catholic Christian sought, surrounded by their family, and receiving that final blessing, even though I was clearly delaying the inevitable. All I knew and still firmly believe is that all human life, *from the moment of conception to natural death,* is sacred, in God's hands and in His plan. I was not going to interfere with that.

I called St Ignatius Church to see if one of the priests was able to come to the house. I knew it was her last hour.

By 10.45 Mum was in the final stages. Her breathing was shallow.

The doorbell rang.

It was Father William Pearsall. I had known him since my days of being an altar boy at St Ignatius.

'She is going now, Father,' I told him – that same phrase Uncle Leslie had used to me before.

He rushed to her bedside, gave her the Apostolic Blessing, and placed a very small piece of the Blessed Sacrament on her tongue. Mum's mouth gently closed after receiving that Holy Communion and she breathed her final breath.

She was gone.

Then something happened that we all experienced but have no explanation for.

The room filled with the sweetest smell of perfume. It lasted for quite some time, possibly an hour, and then vanished.

It was the kind of death few Catholics actually get to have, and it was the one Mum wanted. To use Fr Pearsall's words, 'It was a classic Christian death.'

I was completely heartbroken, deeply wounded, but still in possession of that inner peace I found with her in Lourdes.

My sister took Mum's death very badly. They were extremely close. Mum spent a lot of time with her and the kids, doting on those children. It has taken Sandra years to come to terms with it.

The priest mentioned that mysterious perfume at the funeral which became an amazing tribute. There were so many flowers left that we required another hearse.

We laid her beside Norman in one of the burial plots I had so wisely and fortunately bought in 1997. Never in a million years did I think that plot would be used two years later for Mum.

Like anyone in this position, the first time you circumnavigate the calendar it kills you – Christmas, for example, had always been at Mum's. The Christmas of 1999 was at my house. We all came together and did our best to make it a happy occasion. My cooking was good, but nowhere near as good as Mum's. Without Mum being around, it was really tough. There was now a massive void in our lives that nothing could ever fill.

When the surgeon said that day in Homerton Hospital, 'Do I close your mum up and tell you she has fourteen months to live, or do I go in and get it all out?'

How I wish he would have closed her up and let her be, because from diagnosis to death it was still fourteen months. All that she went through at their hands proved to be unnecessary and only greatly increased her suffering.

Our friend Irena, who refused all treatment, is alive and well today.

After her death, Mum's best friend Emily sold up and left the UK to head back home to Las Palmas to live out her final years there. Eventually she, too, passed away, and quite unbelievably, she died on Mum's anniversary, 10 November. Yet another sign to me of that spiritual connectedness of everything. They were close friends in this life and now they are friends in eternity.

Rest In Eternal Peace, Mama and Emily.

A cup of tea at the clinic in Cologne

Brothers, sister and dad

Christina's First Holy Communion Day September 2021

195

Smells and Bells at St Ignatius Church, Stamford Hill

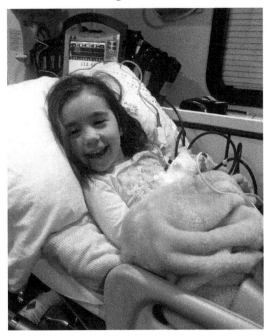

The ambulance journey to Addenbrooke's – I Love You Big Much

196

An evening with Quincy Jones at the Royal College of Music 2014

Jocelyn Brown, Bigger and me

Army Barmy 1988

My driving was that good

Dad getting ready to rumble

ABA London Finals 1983

David Sassoon 2011

Francisca and me – wedding day

Hanging out with the soul legend Bobby Womack

Backstage with Edwin Starr and Freddie Jackson – Albert Hall 1991

Ian Green making music at the flat in Brixton 1990

James and me – The Terrible Twins

A Night 4 Christina

Kim and Ricky Wilde rockin' out at a Night 4 Christina

Midge Ure – Night 4 Christina

Marcus Vere and me backstage – Night 4 Christina

Mum and Dad at a 1960s hippie party

Mum and Dad backstage at the Royal Albert Hall 1991

On tour with the band 1993

Signing my life away with Ken Grunbaum

Steve Finan and me in a meeting in Thailand

The front of Jim Morrison's old house

The Greatest: Muhammad Ali 2009

Me and Tyson

208

Jude, Angela, Christina and Joe

Auntie Sole and me 1969

The last picture ever taken of Mum – Lourdes October 1999

At the turn of the millennium, my dad, my brother Steve and his wife Debbie came round. Supposedly a brand-new era for the world – or just another day. I know this much. I can't tell you an awful lot about the years 2000 and 2001. I have very few memories of that time. I was in some kind of autopilot mode.

I did gigs but I remained in shock – with a downheartedness nobody would normally associate with me. Money was coming in and I had a nice house, so they were not concerns. Somehow, through this haze, I did manage to work, live and I was able to stay fit. The gym had always been a big part of my life. My body still responded but my mind was somewhere else.

I deliberately went back to Fátima and Lourdes. I knew I had to. If you like, I was making the pilgrimage to the pilgrimage, honouring Mum by retracing our steps. Also spending quiet time in the room she had died in. I had two choices: I could run away from the places that brought up painful memories, or I could face them. For me to heal properly I knew I had to face them.

Once again I crossed over the bridge next to the grotto and remembered the sunny day Mum started quoting from the prayer known as the Salve Regina. Catholics, of course, will know this prayer as it concludes the Rosary. Generally, it was said by us in happier times. We had prayed this all of our lives together. It was an aspect of our world that we were familiar with but now found new context.

'This is a valley of tears,' she spoke softly with a knowing realisation.

'Yes, Mum, it is a valley of tears.'

I will never forget that moment and now here I was seeing it again as though in the moment. With the passage of time I was able to reflect that she clearly understood what she was saying when she made that statement. That was her way of telling me that she knew, and my way of acknowledging that I did, too.

It brought a lot of memories, some of which hadn't really registered at the time. This is clearly part of grief.

I turned to bereavement counselling for help, a therapist recommended by a priest friend. Those specialist sessions were invaluable in helping me navigate my way back out of the darkness.

Next, as a result of a lifetime of curiosity and an attempt to understand, I began exploring alternative medicines. I knew there was a Plan B. It was clear that there were other narratives and different solutions and approaches to medicine around the world. Of course, not being a doctor, your desire to discover this is prompted by loss or impending grief, something which is then too late to reverse as your journey of discovery unravels.

But the course of life so far had made one thing clear – this would come again. I had questioned almost every death and every process of treatment I had witnessed – from Auntie Sole's passing to Mum's, and that whole suspicion of conventional treatment. My radar was now fully up and running.

Whether it was a conscious thought or not, perhaps something told me that I was arming myself with knowledge for the future.

In time this would prove to be correct.

Yet at home in the immediate aftermath, the pain continued in a process that was going to be difficult to avoid. I realised now that we were entering a different stage of life.

Dad was now really starting to become unwell.

Then he, too, fell really ill, suffering a heart attack resulting in an urgent triple bypass. He had been alone in his house at the time. He managed to call 999 and very wisely opened the front door and then lay back down on the sofa. The paramedics were able to walk straight in and get him off to the hospital.

His bypass operation was carried out at the London Chest Hospital in Bethnal Green. It was here, though, that a truth emerged which backed up my previous concerns that I wasn't always getting the right answers from Dad's GP either.

'Mr Thomas, have there been any problems with your dad's behaviour?' a doctor rang to ask.

'Yes, of course, he has not been right for quite some time,' I replied.

'We suspect that he has a cognitive problem. We're going to keep him in to assess him further.'

I had seen it first-hand – simple things like Dad losing his way on the smallest of car journeys.

Three days later, I was called into the hospital.

The doctor said, 'We're so sorry, Mr Thomas. We are certain that your father has dementia or possibly Alzheimer's. Mr Thomas, it must have been very frustrating for you all these years seeing him slowly deteriorate, and nobody taking it seriously. I'm sorry that has happened to you,' she said.

This, of course, was a reference to the previous GP visits and that dementia test. We had been to his GP at least four times.

'He will have to undergo a brain scan at another hospital to determine the extent of it,' she concluded.

It had taken a heart attack for this acknowledgement to come. The irony, of course, is that he would survive the heart attack, but dementia would start to see the end of him as a person.

And yes, his heart was broken at Mum's passing. It had been less than a year. I can only guess at how much that accelerates the process.

Dad eventually went home, but as time went on, his decline became more apparent. My sister Sandra and I visited him most days and I would bring him over to stay at my house.

One day I went to visit him, and he asked me for the first time, 'Where's your mum?'

'She passed away, Dad,' I replied.

'Where was I when she died?' he asked.

This really took me back. What do I say? Does he not remember her death, or the funeral? I reminded him about all that had happened, Mum's illness and those final days. Then he did recall that time. It all came back to him and he simply relived it again, along with all the painful emotions.

213

I took him to the cemetery a couple of times. It began to break him and in turn me watching him unstable with the realisation. He had always said that meeting Mum had made him.

In short and in delay, Dad was picking up the pieces without knowing where they were.

He was a clever, funny guy who inspired so many people through the boxing gym. It was scary to see his mind go. One social worker said to me that I was facing losing both parents in the worst ways possible – cancer and dementia.

The only difference was that I had a little more time with Dad but that also made the pain worse because he was still here, but having lost so much understanding of the world he must have felt abandoned in.

More and more he kept returning to this point, asking me where Mum was and then going through the grief. It was as if every time I told him what had happened he was hearing it for the first time. We were going around in circles. I couldn't do this anymore. I had no training whatsoever in how to deal with a person who has dementia. I was learning as I went along.

Then one day he asked me, 'When is she coming back from the Canary Islands?'

This was a very different question than before; he must have remembered her being over there when she was convalescing.

This time, I changed my response.

'Yes, Dad, she is still on holiday,' I replied with a lump in my throat.

'Is she coming back soon?' he quizzed me.

'Yeah, she'll be back soon enough, Dad,' I replied, trying to not let him see the sadness on my face.

This was so difficult to do, but I soon realised that if I went along with the holiday story, it gave him peace of mind and he would then move on to something else. Of course, he would ask me again the next time I saw him, and in his mind the narrative was evolving with even newer questions.

'When you speak to your mum, please say hello from me,' he said once.

'Why did your mum leave me and go to the Canaries? Will she ever come back to me?' he asked another time.

This was killing me, but I had to give him the answers that stilled his mind which was slowly fading.

I lost count of the number of times I left his house and wept in my car on the way home. Dementia, often called the long goodbye, was beginning.

One day I went to see him and the police were everywhere.

I didn't have clue what was going on. I feared the worst.

This is 2001.

At the time, Britain was on anthrax attack alert.

'Your dad's OK but he has been sent a package, and he called the emergency services,' the officer told me.

'My dad is in the early stages of dementia,' I advised.

Out of another vehicle came some people dressed in white hazmat suits and wearing masks. They then entered the house.

'You can't go in there, just wait in your car until we have inspected the package,' the cop replied, which I understood.

I think we all knew that if my father was being targeted for anthrax – as random as terrorism is – then they probably weren't really doing their research!

The problem was, Dad like so many others sat there each day watching the news, getting his daily dose of fear. That coupled with the dementia resulted in bizarre moments like this.

I suspected that I knew what was happening and was proved right.

Dad had ordered some jewellery from one of those shopping channels on the TV. These were items he had no use for and, more importantly, couldn't remember purchasing.

He really was not coping well at all on his own. He began making strange financial decisions such as withdrawing large sums of money from the cashpoint which then went missing. His dementia was really not good at this point but not bad enough to 'move him on'. He was hanging onto his last moments of freedom. He just didn't know it.

'This is not working,' I said to myself.

215

This was the point. I need to change my outlook on what was the next step.

By late 2001, my mind was made up. That nagging voice was telling me, even though I saw him regularly, to pop in. I found him in a state, clearly unable to cope or function in that house any longer. I knew I needed to take swift action. If there were any lessons from Mum, it was to be decisive and seize control.

'Dad, you are going to leave this house,' I told him bluntly. 'Trust me, I am getting you out of this house and moving you nearer to me.'

I was fortunate enough to have saved some money, and had recently sold a property, so I thought now is the time to use those funds. This is what it is there for. I went straight back to Finchley that same day and found a one-bedroomed flat. It was the first property I viewed; it was perfect for him.

'I am buying this off you now,' I told the agent and moved like lightning.

I knew I had to act.

It was in the adjacent street which obviously was practical but would also give him the familiarity he needed. It was on the same road where his grandmother and his mum and dad lived out their final years, so he knew it well.

Saying goodbye to the old house which had been our life was the hardest thing. I made a final visit to my old bedroom where Mum had passed away.

But it was time.

For nearly a week, I slept on the floor in the lounge to check Dad was OK. I did not want him to wake up and feel disoriented. Slowly, he began to get used to it and carve out a new life for himself.

My sister and I were now able to see him every day and take care of him. I did his shopping, washing and cleaning, and just checking. Constantly checking.

I did not want to take away his dignity or freedom. I knew the point was coming where I would have to take over power of attorney, but also that I had to hang on. He wasn't slipping away as obviously as Mum, but it was a battle to deal with the constant demands of the illness. On the one hand we would stay up late and watch Lennox Lewis fight with all the lads at my house or I would take him to see George Benson at the Royal Albert Hall; on the other he would still ask when Mum was coming back from the Canaries.

We had quite a few months of what you could call normality. Things were manageable and Dad still enjoyed some freedom.

Then my old concerns resurfaced.

His level of awareness was zero. There were no physical signs of his decline. The only clues he could hold were a terrible anxiety, paranoia and occasional aggression, plus that confusion. He just couldn't make sense of it all.

I came back from a gig at 4am, drove past his flat and saw all his lights on. I went in and asked him what he was doing, he simply replied, 'Watching television.' He had no idea what time of day or night it was.

At times it was like dealing with a child. I had to cut off the gas to the cooker hob for fear of what might happen, but I needed to give him a certain level of independence, so he didn't resent my level of intrusion and control.

'Please, Dad, let me do what I have got to do,' I would plead with him. 'I need to keep you safe here or won't be able to stop you going into a residential home.'

I was very uncomfortable with this role reversal in life – that I was now being father to my dad. That is not an evasion of responsibility, more a sadness at the turn of events.

He lasted some time (until 2007) before I concluded that he was no longer safe on his own. Obviously, I had thought this many times before finally deciding once and for all.

I gave him a mobile, but he never turned it on.

One night he just did not come home.

I began driving around all the places I suspected I might find him, then, drawing a blank, knew I had to call the police. My brother Gary was so concerned that he drove to London from Suffolk.

I spent hours going down street after street, literally around in circles and getting nowhere.

Sandra thought to phone the number at his old house.

That is where we found him. He had walked all the way from Finchley to Lower Clapton, East London. I wouldn't even go that far if it was a sponsored event, but he had made his way through even the dodgy bits. Again, it is almost impossible to fathom the contrast between such a detailed knowledge and memory and almost none at all. It was as though a magnet had lured him back to the place he called 'home'.

I spoke to his social worker. She had seen this kind of thing many times before. She was very supportive and implemented a care plan. Dad now had a home help person who would come in to see him every day. Going forward, we could all keep an eye on him and hopefully he could remain in the flat for as long as possible.

'Is Joe Louis still the World Champion?' he asked me one morning.

'I don't think so, Dad. There have been a few world champions since then, like Muhammad Ali and Mike Tyson,' I replied.

Joe Louis had finished boxing by 1951.

Dad was going further back in time. Hanging onto those bedrock memories from his youth. The recollections of the last 20 to 30 years were now gone or maybe locked away somewhere… access denied.

It could be more disturbing at times, like the morning he phoned my house.

'Kenny, come and get me,' he said in a distressed and confused way.

'What's the matter, Dad? Are you OK?'

'No, I'm stuck on this building site. The other guys went off and left me here on my own all night,' he responded.

I shot straight up there. It took me two minutes to get to his flat and an hour to get his thinking back on track. Slowly but surely, he realised he was in his own home.

I was always on high alert, waiting for the next thing to happen. Continually living in 'fight or flight' mode for months. It takes its toll.

His social worker warned me one day:

218

'Kenny, be careful, make sure you look after yourself,' she said.

'I've seen so many carers go downhill and end up being more ill than the person they are caring for.'

She was so right. I took her advice on-board and made sure I got to the gym and did all the things necessary to keep myself well. After all, Dad needed me and his situation was not improving. It was only going to get much harder. I was also beginning to get heavily into complementary medicine, reading a vast amount of books on so many different aspects of human health and healing. I was becoming far more informed and equipped for the battle in hand and the ones that might lie ahead.

As long as I could keep Dad as well as possible and prevent him going walkabout, I knew that I had to stop that happening again.

Sure enough, it did.

The second time, it took longer than before.

It was clear that we were now in a repeat cycle.

My brother Gary once again came over from Suffolk.

I got in my car and began to drive around searching for him. I drove down all the roads through Wood Green and on towards Hackney, hoping I would find him. No luck!

Sandra joined in the effort.

We called the old house in Lower Clapton but he wasn't there.

The hours passed by slowly as we all became more and more worried about his safety.

'Mr Thomas, if this goes on much longer, we will have to get the helicopter out and start searching the parks,' a police officer warned me.

It almost got to the point of choppers and night vision cameras, when we get a call from the lady who lives in the old house. Dad has turned up there, exhausted and confused. The relief we felt was immense.

Gary and Sandra drove over there and picked him up. It was 4.45am.

There was no obvious way to give Dad his freedom and stop this happening again. The social worker clearly agreed:

'Let me step in and get him somewhere that he can have some respite,' I was urged.

'Kenny, this will give you some much-needed respite, too.'

As much as I wanted to keep going, this situation could not continue and she was right: we all needed a break.

It was hard to let go.

He needed to be safe, to be fed and to be looked after 24 hours a day.

We found a care home in Edgware.

I did not want him to lose his environment, but it had to be done. It was getting too late. It broke my heart, but for the first time in nearly a decade I was able to breathe a sigh of relief. Dad was safe there.

Somehow I had still been managing to write in the studio and perform onstage.

Dad stayed in Edgware for a few weeks until we found him a care home in New Southgate. This was not far from my house so I could continue to have close contact with him and keep checking in… always checking.

Dad was in a better place. Or so I thought. I had a previous run-in with the people who looked after Norman's mum, when I questioned them about some bruising on her arms one day, only for the truth to emerge that they were from her being grabbed very hard by a member of staff. I removed her from that home and found her another one. So of course I had a built-in suspicion of these places.

At first they did a fairly good job of looking after Dad. They had to, because I kept them on their toes by being super vigilant. My visits were very regular, but the timing was random. They never knew when I would bounce through the door. Early mornings, mid-afternoons and many late-night appearances. They were unable to set their clocks by me. If they sensed that they were being policed, then those feelings were correct. I was not going to miss a trick.

I was on 24-hour standby, back into fight or flight mode again. The phone would ring often to tell me Dad had had a slight fall, or he was not feeling so good that day. But they had their work cut out with him. His dementia was slowly worsening, and this meant that in his mind he was not in his seventies, he was still in the 1950s and ready to take on his next opponent in the ring.

One day I took a call:

'Mr Thomas, don't worry, your father is OK but there has been an incident,' the nurse called to say.

'A new resident came here for some respite, a Spanish man, who was in the lounge with your father. The man would not stop crying and moaning.'

'Your father yelled at him to stop moaning and then walked over to him and hit him. He was knocked out cold and has been taken to Barnet Hospital.'

I went to the care home straight away. Dad had little or no memory of delivering that knockout punch. This was not a situation where you could tell someone off and ask them to not do it again. This was the world of dementia, where anything can happen from one minute to the next. And then happen again.

'Which member of staff was in the room with them when it happened?' I asked the care home manager.

'I will check to see who was in there at the time,' was her response. 'We think it might have been Ruben.'

'No, you should know who was in there, not think who might have been,' I told her.

Nobody was in there at the time. For around ten minutes, the lounge was unsupervised. This was when Dad seized the opportunity to go toe-to-toe with the Spanish guy. Thank goodness that his victim ended up alright in the end. Nothing broken other than my trust with the care home.

I spent a lot of time there and got to know quite a few of the other residents. All from different walks of life, with varying past careers. One of them was a decorated police officer, another a school headmaster. From housewives to housebuilders like Dad, now all in the same place waiting for the sun to set on their lives.

Some days, they remembered a lot more things than they did on others. So having a conversation on those occasions could be more revealing about their history. I had one such chat with the ex-police officer. It was all going well until he told me he had to go now because he was off to see his mum and dad. He was in his late-eighties; his mum and dad were long gone. This made my heart sink into my boots.

But I loved talking to these old folk. Their minds and bodies might be failing yet there was still a person somewhere inside that deserved to be treated with respect and dignity. Like Norman used to say, 'It's all about love'.

Dad was soon ready for his next contest.

222

In the red corner we have Ken Thomas weighing in at around 69 kg (122 fights, 90 wins).

And in the blue corner we have Ruben (Dad's personal nurse), weighing in at around 80 kg. Zero fights.

Seconds out... Round one.

Ken was sitting down in the chair in his room as Ruben approached to start dressing him. As he bent down to put on his socks, Ken took him out with a flawless uppercut from the seated position. Ruben sprawled out across the floor unable to call for help. The severity of that punch delivered with such precision to his solar plexus left him completely winded. After a good few minutes Ruben managed to regain his composure and help was summoned. Ken was declared the winner by KO and then it was time for lunch.

In all seriousness this was not good, but Ruben and I did have a good laugh about it. I did recommend he wear a good head guard and a quality gumshield, and I gave him some tips on how to box clever in the future.

It is unbelievable the way the mind can betray people with this condition, somehow convincing Dad that he is that 30-year-old fighter again with no self-awareness of his current surroundings.

This would be his last and final contest. There were no more boxing incidents after that legendary KO. He had hung up his gloves!

The phone rings (again). It is late in the evening.

'Mr Thomas, we have a problem, can you come to the home?' the care home manager said.

'What problem? Is my dad OK?'

'He has managed to get out of the building and he is now missing,' was the nervous reply.

'You have got to be kidding me. How the hell did that happen?'

'We're not sure,' was the next response, 'but the police are on their way here now.'

So, Dad had escaped. You can't blame him for doing that, but you can the care home for allowing it to happen. I was fuming.

It was a cold night, and they were not exactly sure what he was wearing when he did his great escape. The police were on the case, but as before I knew that on this occasion I had to move much faster and find him before he succumbed to hypothermia.

I drove every conceivable route from the care home to Lower Clapton, knowing full well that the old house would be his destination. I was getting nowhere, and it was getting later and much colder outside. I took the main route one more time, down into Wood Green and then taking some of the back doubles that he would have known quite well. Still no Dad.

Then on the way back out of Wood Green as I headed towards Bounds Green I saw him walking in the distance towards me dressed in just a thin, white T-shirt. I pulled the car over, got out and ran to him and put my arms around him. He was freezing cold and completely confused. He had been out for hours. I got him back to the care home. The police were still there so I held it down but as soon as they left, I kicked off big time.

'I'm not in the game of making you like me. In fact I don't care if you hate me. If you can just do as half a good a job of looking after my dad as I have, then we will be fine,' I told them.

'What happened tonight is unacceptable and downright dangerous. Sort yourselves out.'

It was an epic fail.

If you can't trust those you assign to look after those who can't be trusted themselves anymore through age and dementia, then what hope do you have?

Within 48 hours an 'all-singing all-dancing' electronic intercom system was fitted to their front doors. This replaced the manual locks that only stopped potential escapees when someone was guarding the door, which they were clearly not doing the night my dad walked out of there.

With the new intercom system Dad was now safe. Sort of.

The phone rings. Once more.

'Mr Thomas, your dad has fallen out of the bed and hit his head on the bedside cabinet. It is quite bad but does not require a visit to A&E,' the nurse informed me.

'OK, I am coming there now.'

Dad had a massive lump on his head which probably looked a whole lot worse than it actually was, but still this was not a good look.

'What can we do to prevent this from happening again?' I asked his care team.

'We can put some crash mats down by the side of his bed,' was the pathetic reply.

'Are you serious? If he falls onto a crash mat, he can still hurt himself. He could break an arm or his hip. I can't believe you just said that.'

My anger was rising.

'How about we get him one of those beds with the side guards that come up, like they use in hospitals?' I suggested.

'No, we can't use one of those because he might get caught up and trapped in the guard.'

'Are you just saying that to get out of buying one? If it's a problem financially then I will buy it,' I offered.

'No, it is the policy of the home. His illness is not at the stage where we could safely use it with him,' I was told.

'That is complete nonsense,' I fumed. 'So, you're saying that it is safer to let him land on a crash mat? Really? I've heard it all now.'

Rules and regulations replaced common sense. There was always a battle to be had.

While Dad was still physically able to get out of the care home and had his long-term memories intact I did things to help him stay connected with his past. I took him to the Imperial War Museum in South London. He told me how he could vividly remember hearing the doodlebugs in the sky. He described the loud humming sound of their engines and then the sudden silence followed by the ominous whistling noise as they hurtled towards the ground, never knowing where they would hit.

He often spoke about 5 November 1944 when Archway, Islington, was hit by its first German long-range V2 rocket, and the morning he woke up to find most of the area flattened by number of V1 rockets. Sure enough, there were pictures of this at the museum.

I took him for a long drive around Archway one day. This was in many ways more for me than it was for him. I needed to have one last chance of gathering as much information as possible about his childhood before it faded away. Amazingly, he was able to take me to every inch of Islington where he grew up and narrate its history. He pointed out all the different houses where his relatives used to live, his old primary school along with stories about his classmates. He knew the name of every road before we even turned into it. I was totally dumbfounded. His narrative was as clear as yesterday to you and me, except to him there was now no immediate yesterday.

But Dad's time in this care home was about to end. Unsurprisingly. In fact, if I didn't visit him on this particular day his life would have ended right there and then. I found him sitting in a chair in the communal lounge placed in front of the TV as many of the residents are for hours on end. He looked terrible, half-conscious and clearly dehydrated.

'How much fluid has he had?' I asked one of the on-duty care workers.

'I don't know,' she replied.

'What do you mean you don't know? Do you not have any record of what he has eaten or drunk in the last 24 hours?'

I stormed downstairs to the manager's office.

Within 48 hours since I had last seen him, he had gone from being fine to being on his knees.

'Would you like to have a dead man in a chair here today?' I raged.

'No, that's the last thing we want,' the boss replied. 'Why do you say that?'

'Well, if you don't want that then get an ambulance for my dad right now,' I ordered.

He had drunk next to nothing.

They took him straight to Barnet Hospital. The dehydration was severe.

'Mr Thomas, his condition is very poor. He is very weak. It could go either way,' the doctor told me.

After 24 hours on a saline drip, he began to recover. Every day I went to the hospital and fed him with food I had cooked myself at home. I gave him vitamins and minerals, especially vitamin D3 and green superfood juices. Between the nurses and me, we turned things around.

The residential care home had done a reasonably good job of looking after Dad for the first few years. So I can't bash them on every front. Where they had failed miserably was in not recognising those clear signs that his illness had progressed, and he was in need of more specialised care. They were not equipped or capable of giving him the attention he needed. This almost cost him his life.

I spoke to the manager of the nursing home who simply told me off the record and in a sorry indictment of where the whole 'industry' seemed to be:

'If you want your dad to live a lot longer, get him out of here and into a good nursing home.'

I admired her honesty and the risk she was taking in telling me this, but it should have been said at least a year earlier.

I transferred him into a new home in High Barnet, who did an amazing job of looking after him, and there he stayed until the end.

At the same time I began to manage my own dementia – trying to understand it before it might kick in a generation on from here – and generally taking a good look at the illness, and therefore Dad, made me take a good look at myself.

Despite his thinning hair and weight loss, I could see the physical similarities. These are cosmetic thoughts, though. The reflection in the mirror pointed inwards and I realised much of what I didn't like about myself through any of those frustrations I might have had with Dad.

We locked horns during my teens like many fathers and sons do, but I was a 'chip off the old block' and we were very much of the same temperament and mindset. The things I disliked in him in my earlier years are the very things I am today, and I now very much like these characteristics.

227

But he was straight and honest, and I knew I was that, too. I never doubted how proud he was, and he *did* make sure he said it. It was his devotion of course that persuaded Steve Finan round for Sunday lunch to listen to my demos. Only that paternal glow could have driven that invitation, so I knew it anyway whether he said it or not.

Another thing that happened during those final years was a moment I thought I would never live to see. Dad decided to convert and was received into the Catholic Church. On the anniversary of Mum's 70th birthday, he was baptised by a priest friend of mine. Finally hammering a big nail into the coffin of his Masonic past. I can't begin to tell you the joy this gave me. How I hated his Freemasonry.

Brought in at the 'eleventh hour', or to use a boxing phrase he was 'saved by the bell'...

Even though he would live on for another two years, I was acutely aware that we were in the end zone.

We had time to prepare but, as ever, death has no concept of timing.

When Mum was ill, I really started to cherish the time away from the limelight – even though it had been some *considerable* time. After she passed away, I began penning songs, perhaps more prolifically than when I was recording.

I was on a mission to write pop. Those boy bands which Steve Finan warned me were on the way needed hits writing for them. I was introduced to Kim Wilde's brother Ricky, such a good songwriter and one of the nicest guys I have ever met in the music biz.

Day after day I would drive over to his studio and we would just write pop. Ricky and his wife Mandy made me feel like part of the family. This was just what I needed, having gone through such a tough time. Working with him taught me so much, plus we formed a friendship that I consider to be one of my closest in the industry.

Through the contacts we both had combined with Ricky's production skills we got artists like Antony Costa from Blue and Ritchie Neville from *Five* into the studio writing potential songs for their albums. I really enjoyed that time, even though I wasn't making songs for myself per se, I was still doing what I loved – music. Plus, I was learning, always learning.

Gary Howard, a music agent at Mission Control Agency at the time, had an idea to put me on the road with Errol Reid the lead singer from the group *China Black*, who had a massive hit with the song 'Searching' in 1994. This was a great idea and it worked. We went out as 'The Brothers of Soul' and performed all around the UK. I do not have a clue how many venues we sang at because I lost count, but we were out on the road for months. Not only was it a good earner, but by the end of it, Errol and I also were, as the show title suggests, *brothers*.

At one of our gigs in Romford I bumped into an old acquaintance, Bradley Wicks. He used to DJ at Hollywood's nightclub in that same town. Every artist who had hits in the 90s played that venue at some point, booked by the immensely likeable Gordon Phillips, who went on to manage the famous BCM super-nightclub in Majorca, where I performed, too. Bradley and I exchanged numbers that night and little did I know at the time, but we would also become 'besties'. He is now my right-hand man at gigs, making sure the sound is always spot on, and the resident DJ for my garden parties.

Dad made a lot of friends during his lifetime, too, so it is no surprise that I am the same way inclined. If I meet someone, and I like them, get along with them and connect with them, why leave it there?

Like the time I was booked to perform at Kings nightclub on Canvey Island by DJ Ian Reading in the early 90s. We became mates straight away. I sang at his 40th birthday party, I sang at his 50th and 60th, and I'm often seen hanging around at the many BBQ parties he has at his house. He can't get rid of me.

Another very fortunate friendship has its origins at the Southport Weekender. Whilst enjoying an amazing set being delivered by Masters At Work I was introduced to the DJ and record producer Piers Penfold aka Sir Piers. We would go on to make some great music together with songwriter Mike Diaz and one of the industry's best studio mix-down engineers and production geniuses, Toni Economides.

But way above and beyond the music, Piers and I made a spiritual connection. A fellow truth seeker who looks at the world through a very similar lens as myself. Many a night we sat down together like two universe-probing philosophers and got into some heavy, mind-bending conversations. I don't think we found all the answers we were looking for but it sure felt good stretching the grey matter.

Even on holiday in Fuerteventura where I would often go to get away from everything, I bumped into Duncan Coles – The Duke Of Soul. Yes, you guessed it, that is his DJ name and soul music is his thing. Of course, at this point it goes without saying, we became great friends and my holidays became an education in Northern Soul which he happens to know inside out. There was no getting away from music or accumulating more amigos.

If I keep collecting friends like this, one thing is for sure: if the wife were to ever give me the elbow, I've got a lot of couches I can sleep on.

In the Noughties I had some flirtations with the production company Metrophonic which took me to places that hindsight may reflect on better than in the actual moment. For example, I heard the early demo of Cher's classic 'Believe' way before it was a hit. Equally, the manager of Natalie Imbruglia, a pop unknown who achieved fame through the Australian TV show *Neighbours*, played me 'Torn' long before it went on to be a worldwide hit that is still played on the radio today.

There was some good talent around and some class songs passed by my ears. Yet, there was also some industry bullshit.

'Get yourself back here… the deal is done… I've nailed it,' I was told whilst looking after Mum in the Canaries at a time when she had shown great signs of improvement.

'You need to come back and record the next record… the conversations with the majors are going really well.'

So, I told Mum I would see her when she gets back and headed home for these meetings and studio sessions.

They never happened.

I was hurt by that. Beyond the timing, I thought I had done enough in the game to be treated a little better.

I could have stayed longer in Las Palmas with Mum, made some more memories at a time when time was running out. But I was denied that, and that moment was lost because lies came so easily to lips of certain people in the music game.

But, despite the let-downs and the amount of effort I put into things that do not materialise, good things still managed to find a way of coming through. One of those was the song 'Don't Come Around Here', which I wrote with the songwriter Paul Barry, part of the Metrophonic camp. He wrote 'Believe' for Cher and 'Bailamos' for Enrique Iglesias. My intention was to keep this song for myself, but as I was not in a record deal, I had no way of releasing it. It just sat there in the studio, and I had almost forgotten about it when I got a call to say that it had been played to Rod Stewart and he wanted to record it for his new album. Of course, my response to that was a resounding 'Yes, he can have it.'

The song became a duet with Helicopter Girl and was released as the first single from the album called 'Human'. Seeing Rod Stewart singing my song on TV was a real privilege and definitely one for the CV. Unfortunately, the song was not a big hit and the album not very successful. Helicopter Girl flew off to some undisclosed destination never to be heard of again, whilst Rod moved on to record an infinite number of American Songbook albums.

Another song I wrote with Bluey from Incognito back in the 90s which was unwisely rejected by Cooltempo made a surprise comeback.

It is 4am and I'm tucked up nicely in bed dreaming about the good old days when the phone rings.

'Hi, Kenny, it's Bluey. Sorry to wake you up, brother,' he began.

'What's up, Bluey, everything OK?'

'Yeah, everything's great. I'm in America right now and I'm here at George Benson's house. I just played him our song 'River to the Sea', he loves it and wants to cut it. Just wanted to check if you're OK with that.'

'Wow, man, that is cool. Of course I'm OK with that.'

'Bluey, you don't ever need to call me to ask a question like that, you know it's gonna be yes, but I'm glad you did because it's always good talking to you whatever time it is.'

George Benson did record the song and asked me to do the backing vocals. Another one for the CV.

I wasn't obsessed by being back *in* the business. If you were gigging and writing, which I was, then you were always in it. It was not an inability to get before the senior execs to cut a new album that irritated me. It was more people who promised false dawns. But any faith I lost in those people who promised and then failed to deliver was made up for by the Ricky Wildes and Blueys of this world.

Steve had been right again. I could always gig – and first and foremost I had wanted to be a singer, so that ambition was realised and prevailed. But seeing the record industry from just outside it while caring for Mum and Dad and starting to unpick medicine meant that it was not a priority.

If it happened, it happened. The truth was a few incidents in my own life meant that my focus was starting to lean elsewhere.

A seed had been planted in 1998 when Mum fell ill, and we got the letter from our friend Irena strongly advising us to 'go alternative'. That lingered in my mind.

I also had a very rare type of conversation one late night with a record producer. In between the beats we got talking.

About quantum physics.

'Do yourself a favour,' he said. 'Go and read *In Search of Schrödinger's Cat.*'

I will leave you to choose whether you Google it, but for me, that was it! A new viewpoint to explore.

After that I literally blew my own mind reading every quantum physics book I could lay my hands on. I had done a pretty good job of blowing my mind in the past and altering my reality in every way possible, but now I was beginning to understand that the world as we know it and perceive it is nothing like we think it is. Alternative medicine and quantum physics were shifting my paradigm in a big way.

In 1999 I became ill – which was rare. I had been on the way to a gig in Essex when I had to pull over and ask my road manager to drive me straight to hospital.

It was a Friday night. I sat there in Basildon Hospital alongside all of the walking wounded who had punched the living daylights out of one another after the pubs had shut. I was in excruciating pain. They couldn't do much for me there. Somehow I still managed to leave the hospital that night, get to the club and do the gig.

My GP suspected IBS: irritable bowel syndrome. This was later confirmed by two specialists who told me there wasn't really a cure for it other than some medication to ease the symptoms. They both told me that it was quite likely that I would have this for life. I started to get very familiar with medicine.

'You need to go and see Rosalind,' my friend Sue suggested. 'Let her do some herbs and acupuncture.'

I kept hearing this over a sustained period of time. Sue was also a practitioner of alternative medicine and a big advocate of Chinese medicine.

I thought it was nonsense. What could herbs and needles possibly do for this? But I agreed to go. For one reason.

Me – with the open mind and always in search of truth. I went to write it off.

I would go there, try it out, and when it didn't work, tell Sue it was a waste of time and that would be the end of it.

I did not enjoy the needles and I really didn't believe in the herbs, but she was a fully qualified practitioner of traditional Chinese medicine. She went to China originally as an English teacher, but ended up staying there to study TCM. Her entire house stank of herbs and they tasted awful.

She diagnosed me with damp-heat in the lower jiao and kidney yin deficiency. Damp-heat? What is that? Sounds like I need to call my mate Johnny Boy. He is the best when it comes to building work and damp courses.

She gave me several bags of herbs that looked like something she had raked up in the local park and told me to boil and prepare them at home. My house stank for days. That made me even more certain not to go back.

Soon I started to feel energised. I really did not want this to succeed but I began to feel a lot less sluggish. The IBS symptoms were lessening.

I went back for more and within a few weeks I had little or no signs of the IBS. I was converted. Totally hooked.

I began to buy up books on Chinese medicine, some of which were so old and mysterious but yet here they were, still in print and clearly perceived to be of value.

My adventure had begun.

Bradley Wicks knew two doctors with PhDs in Chinese Medicine, Dr Graham Chandler and Dr Philip Lawes. Assisted by the expertise of Professor Jiao originally from Beijing, China, they ran the Academy of Oriental Medicine in Essex. I went there to get a treatment, and afterwards I got chatting to Dr Phil. He spoke to me about the Bachelor of Science course they taught there in conjunction with Liberty University in the US. I knew one thing. I was never going to understand this subject unless I took the plunge. So, after some serious thinking and few more conversations with Phil, I did.

Some of my friends were surprised that I decided to embark on such a difficult and unusual course, but those who knew me well enough understood that I did nothing by halves. I was either all in or all out with most things in life. Dad was the same. When he took up photography in the late-1960s, he was not satisfied with a few snaps developed at the local pharmacy. No, he went the whole hog and ended up having a darkroom with all the gear to process his photographs, even going as far as experimenting with trick photography.

So, this is all rumbling within me. From what I can remember from the early Noughties, I know that I slowly began to emerge from a tunnel after losing Mum and with Dad deteriorating. But the truth is that by 2004, I was not well at all – at best in a deep clinical depression.

For someone who had always explored the body through gym, boxing and the Territorial Army and the mind through the Church, libraries and the exploration of philosophy, this was an incredible shock. I did not see it in those terms at the time because I didn't see anything clearly. It wasn't me at all and it just shows how paralysing grief can be.

Yet, I was possibly doing better than I imagined. I was able to put a smile on for a gig. Any performer has to do this at some point, and it does provide temporary solace for you to get lost in the performance. Anticipation of the gig and the comedown after can provide further dark moments, but *in the moment* you can do it. Time and emotion become suspended.

'You've done some of your own work here,' the bereavement counsellor recognised. 'But you do have clinical depression.'

You never saw it in those terms. You only viewed it as doing what anyone would do when faced with a dying mother and a dad in decline. But my energy levels were zapped, and I did not have the strength to realise that now I was suffering from much of what I had read about.

235

I understood a lot more when I saw it from the Chinese medical perspective. Of course, I went to my GP, too, but in many ways I was looking for an alternative rather than their solution. I felt like I was navigating through a sea of treacle every day.

I was prescribed an SSRI.

Selective Serotonin Reuptake Inhibitors... or in layman's terms Prozac.

I took them for about four months and boarded a roller coaster in the process. I was up and down the whole time!

I felt great, then suicidal. One minute I retained a gym-like energy, the next my mind took me to the darkest of places and I began to visualise checking out altogether.

In a rare moment of clarity after months of struggle, I went back to the GP and told him that the depression was far better than the way I was feeling on these tablets. With the low mood at least I knew how I felt, and that was a pretty good baseline to work from. With these bloody tablets I was all over the shop.

The doctor suggested that I taper off from them, slowly reducing the dose every few days. That indeed is the right thing to do. But me being me, I did it my own way. I was having no more of that junk, I just threw them in the bin.

The withdrawal from it was vicious. I had two weeks from Hell.

It was like I was wired up to some kind of electric shock implement, designed to torture people. Walking around permanently attached to a game show buzzer. One minute I am OK, the next minute sparks are flying up my spine and out the top of my head. I might have found this interesting back in 1992 when I was dancing around the Ministry of Sound, but not now.

If that is what this pharmaceutical can do when it's coming out of your system, what the hell is it doing when it's going in? I was so done with this kind of medicine. It simply didn't work for me, and I began to resent the one-size-fits-all approach that so much of healthcare presents. It was a seed that was planted.

I knew that I had to throw myself at alternative medicine.

Everything was on the table.

By 2003 I was at a place and a point few knew about. Those close to me had witnessed the darkness, but there was another crossroads that I had approached virtually alone.

I had begun having secret meetings with the Vocations Director for the Westminster Diocese. It was an ongoing covert operation! I would rarely tell anyone where I was going. I know that I was finding myself again. I began to believe that it was time to fulfil something which had looked like my calling for much of my life.

I felt ready to take a final look and possibly make the transition.

'When you're ready, come to Allen Hall Seminary,' he had said.

The monastery said the same – come when you are ready.

I was constantly at odds with myself, asking where God wanted me to be.

I had wrestled with this since my teens. Do I stay in the world or in a way leave it all behind? Some people may see this as running away and I am sure many do run away from it. I think this world is beautiful, I don't have a problem with it, but I do have a problem with the people running it.

I confided in James and another family friend named Evan Carby, of Jamaican descent and a big soul music lover. Evan and I would sit for hours in my lounge listening to album after album. He was originally my dad's friend after Dad did some building work on his house years ago and they became good mates.

Evan and James said I should follow my heart, but this wasn't without them protesting the idea. They believed that I should never give up making music and that being a singer was my mission in life. It was Evan who prompted me to follow my dreams and pursue music way back when I was eighteen years old.

237

This was a big and difficult decision to make, but I felt ready to give it a go.

I attended some weekends away, retreats designed to help guys like me get a greater understanding of the vocation and discern the path ahead. This was a good experience.

I wanted to do it.

But then I didn't.

The doubts I had were not about giving everything up and taking the plunge. I could do that. The truth is that the one thing which stopped me progressing was Dad's health. He required some sort of daily attention without yet being in the hands of the care system. So, when I did ask the question of where God wanted me to be, the answer just came back as looking after my father.

The force was strong, but it never challenged the love and responsibility needed unconditionally to look after Dad. I couldn't abandon Dad: he needed me.

Even though he then lived on for another decade, I knew that it was his one final look at the world and that God's plan for me was there.

That did not mean that my commitment or belief waned. It just meant that I couldn't make that total sacrifice and I would have been deceiving myself if I had taken that route. Dad came first. Otherwise, there is no doubt I would have gone.

As it transpired, I now understand that I would have encountered difficulties at the seminary.

I wouldn't have toed the party line.

And that means...

One of the beauties through all my conversations with men of the Church over the years is when they do deviate slightly from the script. It would never deter my faith, but even those early conversations with Father Hanshell at the start of my pop career stay with me for their real-world nature which found context and understanding without being religiously robotic. Here I was, deeply religious, confessing to a man of the Church and yet there was no judgement, no trotting out of cliché, no 'I've got an answer for everything'... Instead there was a tranquillity and pragmatism *against* a religious backdrop.

238

And so, it was now.

A traditionalist priest friend told me:

'You'll have to study and write what they want to hear.'

'Just get through it and afterwards forget the stuff that is heterodox.'

My character would simply not allow that.

This meant I would have had to endure the spurious *Nouvelle Théologie* (New Theology) of Henri de Lubac and Yves Congar, or even worse the teachings of Hans Urs von Balthasar or Karl Rahner. If I told them I was into neo-Thomism and the teachings of theologians such as Réginald Garrigou-Lagrange, I would probably have had to pack my bags and call a taxi.

In short, I'm not a modernist.

That did not mean I could not take direction. It just was not who I was. I could not *not* explore another view. I love discovering opposing mindsets, as long as you can differentiate the trash from the treasure.

There was no way I could live, serve and keep a lid on what I wouldn't be able to tell.

I was grateful for that viewpoint, even though it came after Dad's decline had pretty much made up my mind. Even religion wasn't perfect and within its inner circle there were critics and there was criticism.

The very strange thing is how rumours spread. I had kept this aspect of my life so very discreet.

I began working again at a later date with Eliot Kennedy on the beautiful track 'I Will'.

'I heard a rumour you left everything and had gone off to join a monastery,' he said. 'I thought, yeah that's sounds like Kenny, that does make sense.'

I have no idea how something so private had spread so far, though it was untrue, and yet Eliot clearly knew me well enough to believe it a possibility.

'No, I don't know where you heard that, El,' I replied. 'I was considering it, but I am going to stay in the world for now and let it beat me up a bit more.'

And that was that.

The moment passed.

But it came so very near.

From my own experience and from beginning to find my way back to me, it was clear that hundreds of thousands of people were taking medication like SSRIs, really unaware of the consequences, but often were so poorly that their trust was blind and oblivious to the multi-billion-dollar industry that it had become.

In short, your illness lined someone's pocket.

And there *was* more than one way to skin a cat. The acupuncture alone had indicated so.

By 2007, my mind was in a better place and indeed had been for some time. I finally enrolled to study traditional Chinese medicine. This clearly was a left-field decision to a casual observer. To myself, it was perfectly logical and a first conclusion in response to a lifetime of curiosity. I didn't know how I was going to go. I was so far out of any discipline that education required and had never really given it much credibility at school, but I thought I would give it a go and see where it took me.

Where did it take me?

It took over.

I was often up until 4 in the morning studying formulas in foreign languages and listening to experts speaking in accents from Asia I struggled to follow. By the second year of the course, I began to get to grips with the whole process from being a serious student attending lectures, to empowering myself in pursuit of further knowledge, from sticking needles here and there, to understanding the herbs.

I began to reshape my philosophies. Crazy moments like being at that birthday party in Los Angeles now jarred with the idea that there really was a medical use for MDMA in a controlled environment, not the bedding department of a shopping mall. Experimentally, those days had long since passed me by. Occasionally I might be in the company of friends who smoked a joint but all those influences, including having a drink

241

which I pretty much stopped on New Year's Day 2005, were all gone.

I didn't think Chinese medicine was the only way, but I certainly was clear now that there were *other* ways. A Bachelor of Science was really only just a good start, but the lectures told me that I far from knew everything. Amongst my students were people learning, with still so much life ahead and looking to make careers out of this. I had some real medical context to give to its understanding, and there lay the difference in motivation. I was not about to graduate to save the world. I wanted to pass to explore the argument and to entertain a broader outlook.

But of course, I had seen it in practice. For myself and amongst my friends. From a starting position of mumbo-jumbo, I learned that it really was scientific, and aside from own introduction in 1999 with the irritable bowel syndrome, I also witnessed it cure my friend's chronic sciatica.

Of course, I started to become very receptive, too, towards medical professionals who had to toe the line but had a concept of where that line might actually be in reality. One of them over a beer confessed to me that the problem with Western medicine is that it thinks it knows everything when the reality might be just that it understands only 10% of what there is to know.

It is quite a logical thing to say, and it stuck with me. You are brought up to believe a certain way and, if you are trained and in the system, to deliver that certain way. Yet the UK is a very small island and there are other communities out there. The history of medicine is all about seeking cures for disease and illness, and you only find those answers by finding a way outside the status quo. That is the simple definition of discovery – something new. It is blindingly simple *if* you can challenge the narrative. The problem, though, is that unless we are scientists or studying science, many of us only think about such possibilities in or after our weakest hour. It follows that the time when the average person analyses medicine is around when you need it most and therefore are in the worst possible place and against the clock to debate another way.

242

One area that I found particularly of concern and fascinating was the lack of research into how one vaccine might interact with another. Babies are jabbed with a multitude of them from birth, yet very little science exists to determine the safety of so many of them being given at once. It was all very well having the right answer, but if you needed more than one and it did not work in tandem with something else, then where did that leave you?

Apart from the obvious, with a whole lot more questions.

Clearly, I am now in a different place. I have come through bad years where I was still able to perform but had barely been in a position to record. Despite mental and physical strength which I associated with who I was, grief and depression beat me for a while.

It was nothing I could have ever seen coming despite my mantra for life looking like it wanted to consume every physical pursuit and any mental stance. I loved having fun, being fit and engaging, but there is little you can do when a powerful dark force consumes you for whatever reason, and that is what grief had done to me in the early Noughties.

Naturally, coming out the other side and opening my mind to acupuncture and another way altogether, whilst finding the discipline to study for my own self-improvement rather than a piece of paper, all draws a line on that dark period.

I hold those memories in a little compartment in my mind, but I felt ready to go again and unfazed by challenges that lay ahead.

In order for me to tell you all the things that happened in the Noughties I have to rewind back to 1998. After the dissolution of Cooltempo Records, Ken Grunbaum and I stayed in touch, speaking every now and then. He started working with Danny D who had a new independent label called Delirious. Scoring a top ten hit in 1997 with the two-step club track 'Never Gonna Let You Go' by Tina Moore.

Ken introduced me to Michael Gray and Jon Pearn, two brilliant record producers who go out under the name of Full Intention. At the time they were working with a singer-songwriter called Nick Clow and were sitting on a bunch of very good songs. One of those songs was 'Crazy World'. When I first heard it, I knew I had to have it, and Ken, being the good A&R that he was, recognised that it would suit my voice perfectly.

Jon and Michael were up for it and even allowed me to make some lyrical changes to the song. I went over to their studio and attempted to lay down a vocal. Mum was ill at the time, and to be honest my mind was somewhere else and my confidence low. I didn't think I had done anything spectacular in the studio that day and planned to tackle the vocal again another time.

One of the strangest things about singing is that you may not feel like you are delivering the goods, and you are utterly convinced that you are having a bad day in the office, but somehow despite those subjective thoughts you still manage to capture something really special. Something that will not happen at any other time. The sadness and darkness that enveloped me that day produced an emotion and a vibe in the vocal that suited the song so well. The end result was amazing.

Now I was in possession of a new record, and it was undoubtedly one of the best I had made in a long time. It was guaranteed to blow up on the soul scene at least.

Ken and Danny D wanted to sign it to their Delirious label. They offered me a deal, which was very nice of them, not forgetting of course that Ken had made the introduction to Full Intention and essentially put the record together. The proposed deal would have tied me up and locked me in for some considerable time. I didn't want that. The problem was that I didn't want to be signed to anyone. I was glad to be out of EMI and was enjoying my freedom. Mum was very ill, and the road ahead was going to be a hard one in that respect, so I had to turn it down. 'Crazy World' would now join the other songs consigned to perpetual limbo, never to see the light of day. Or so I thought.

Fast-forward to 2004...

I had an idea. I wanted to get 'Crazy World' out there. It had been on my mind. I needed to put it into the hands of someone I could trust. I knew a lot of people in the game, but to be honest most of them were about as reliable as a politician's promise.

I took a drive to see DJ Bigger (Colin Bartlett) and Flip.

'Bruv, that is seriously good. How long you been sitting on this one?' Bigger asked.

'Biggs, it's been burning a hole in my pocket for some time, and now I want to get it out there.'

'OK leave it with me, bruv, I'll get some heat on this track no problem.'

Bigger was without a doubt the best person to give the track to. He knew all the DJs on the scene, the whole length and breadth of the country.

He put it into the hands of just a few of the so-called specialist 'taste-maker' DJs and this created an enormous buzz and demand for it. 'Crazy World' exploded onto the soul scene. It even managed to cross over to the followers of Northern Soul which was something none of my previous tracks had ever done. If this record had been around in the days of my Cooltempo deal, I am sure it would have been a commercial hit for me.

I was contacted by a good friend of mine named Everton Webbe. He had been in the music business for years, working alongside Jazz Summers at Big Life Records. Everton ran a label with Neil Rushton called suSU (Soul Underground Soul Unity). They absolutely loved the track and wanted to put it out. So,

245

after discussing things with the Full Intention guys, we all agreed to let suSU release it on limited edition 12" vinyl.

The demand for the record was so great that we had to manufacture a load more – in fact they couldn't make them fast enough, so I am not sure how limited that release was in the end.

It is now regarded as a modern soul rare groove. Rare only because it is so difficult to get hold of a copy. I remember once being sent a link to it on eBay. Someone was selling it for over one hundred quid. That is insane! I should have held back a few boxes.

Tony Blackburn played it often on his show on Radio London, saying he thought it was the best record I had ever made, adding that I was without a doubt one of the UK's most underrated singers. Thank you, Tony!

By now Ken Grunbaum and I had lost touch, I had not spoken to him in a long time. He got to hear it on Smooth Radio when Richard Searling played it on his weekly soul show. And it was through Richard that Ken and I got back in touch with each other.

'I told you it was a big record,' he said.

'Yes, you were right, Ken, just a shame we didn't have it back in the Cooltempo days,' I replied, acknowledging that this song was his idea to begin with.

It wasn't a chart hit, that is true, but that is not the only measure of a good song. It just felt great to have a track back out there being loved and supported by the very scene I started out from. I remain proud of it, and it confirmed as always that soul music is where my heart is.

What about those tracks from the third album that had never been released? That for a number of years now had been gathering dust in an EMI storeroom.

I had the finished masters of those at home on a DAT tape. I didn't own the recordings, so I wasn't able to sign them to a label or release them, but I did think they needed to be heard. Would be such an injustice if they remained hidden away forever. With the kind of reception 'Crazy World' had I became even more determined to make sure those unheard tracks got a fair hearing.

246

I had another idea…

'Stick that in your CD player and give it a listen, it's the title track of the third album that never came out. It's called "Him",' I said.

'Bruv, that track is unbelievable. Seriously, it's massive,' said Bigger with a stunned but excited look on his face.

'I can't believe EMI let that one go,' said Flip.

'Right, leave it to me, I'll come up with a plan,' Bigger announced as he tucked the CD away into his bag.

I knew we were limited on what we were able to do with the recording, and technically it wasn't exactly legal because I didn't own it. But that was OK because I didn't intend to sell it or make any money from it. I just knew it deserved to be heard and enjoyed by the people out there who love proper soul music.

Bigger once again placed it into the hands of just a few DJs who carried some clout on the scene, but this time he told no one who the artist was. He said it was 'Him' by Him. This was a very clever move because not only did the song go ballistic, it was also surrounded by mystery. They all wanted to know who the singer was and if he was from the UK or the US. Bigger left them sweating for weeks as the momentum grew and grew.

Eventually he revealed that the singer was me. This was met with such surprise by many, and my phone did not stop ringing. It was my biggest tune yet on the modern soul scene and one that some DJs said was the best soul record ever made by a UK artist. That is quite a statement and not one I would say, but I was happy to hear it.

The payback for being such a naughty boy in allowing Bigger to spread that song around was that my gigs went through the roof. 'Crazy World' and 'Him' produced as many, if not more, than I had back in the early 90s. I was now playing at some very credible Soul Weekenders and festivals that previously my pop hits had excluded me from.

I am not sure if Jonathan Butler, the co-writer of 'Him', and Simon Law, its producer, ever knew what became of that track. They had both moved out of the UK by the time I sneakily introduced it to the soul scene. But it is a credit to them that it finally got to be heard and their work received the appreciation it deserved.

Ken Grunbaum and I were now back in regular contact, and he still wanted to continue the work we began in 1990. He was the man who first signed me, and he still believed in me. So, he thought I should release an album and he had just the label in mind.

One of his old industry chums was the head of Curb Records. It is quite possible that you have never heard of them. They are most famous for breaking LeAnn Rimes in America where she rose to fame with hits like 'Can't Fight the Moonlight' and 'How Do I Live'.

And at the time not a huge amount else.

Well, this was the UK division of Curb Records so their artiste roster and chart success were nothing to write home about. Still, it was an opportunity to put an album out, and with Ken guiding it I felt reasonably comfortable with the whole thing. My commercial success was a decade over my shoulder so the chance of having another stab at it seemed like a good idea at the time.

So, I took the decision to sign to Curb – even though I always had a suspicion I was getting screwed over – because you are either in the race or out of the race, and here I was just about somewhere in it! Equally, I knew that I would get a lot of gigs out of it.

We recorded some new songs and when I say *some*, I mean not many. The other songs on the album were… get this… from the unreleased third EMI album. Yes, that is right. You read that correctly.

Ken went to EMI and asked if we could license some of the tracks from that album. That took some balls to do, but quite unbelievably he pulled it off. To my utter surprise they said yes and agreed to so with no questions asked, no fee required. It was as if no one at EMI remembered the writ I served on them back in 1995. What a mad game this is.

So, the release really ended up being a kind of compilation and not the new album I hoped it would be.

I *did* enjoy the freedom and lack of pressure, but this absence of intensity is probably directly related to what I could only describe as modest returns from that label. It was probably just as well that I only signed for one album. And when I say modest returns, I actually mean Jack squat, nothing, or in Spanish 'nada'.

At least the songs 'Him' and 'Let It Rain' got the chance to be released properly on CD. I am sure whoever bought the album probably bought it for those songs. And how many bought it? How do I know!? I've never seen a royalty statement from Curb. No wonder they released country music on that label because this was the Wild West.

The company just disappeared overnight in the UK. No calls answered, office space cleared. Everything and everyone went to ground.

So, like most things in life, you have to take the rough with the smooth and learn from every experience. One good thing of this was that I have always managed my expectations. I expect nothing, so when nothing happens, I am never disappointed, but when something does, I take it for what it is and enjoy the moment.

If I were to give Curb Records a strapline, words that sum up the brand, it would be this… 'Curb one step up from the gutter'.

However, three key things happened while I was signed to them. One resulted in a friend for life, the other left me scarred forever:

Since I really had done so well on the soul scene, I had built up special relationships with the promoters and DJs. DJs like Bigger and Flip were instrumental helping me promote my music to that audience and I had a steady flow of gigs.

Flip took me to see the owner of a venue in Essex who wanted to book me for a show. That was the first time I met Mark Aaron absolutely by chance, if there is such a thing.

We entered the Epping Forest Country Club by a side entrance, walking up a flight of steps that we never normally used. Coming towards me down those steps at the same time was this big guy. Flip and he exchanged greetings then introduced me.

'It's good to meet you, Kenny, I've been following your career,' Mark announced. It was always really lovely when people said that phrase, especially when it didn't really look like you still had one.

'I am looking after Alexander O'Neal. Take my number and give me a call,' he said.

And with that, he established his credentials with me and went on to become a friend for life. A good East London Jewish boy with an incredible knowledge of boxing that was second to none. Name a fighter from any year and Mark could tell you all the fights they had in the finest of detail. A real wheeler-dealer character who would do anything for you, and he did so much for me and my family. His generous spirit changed my life in so many ways.

Mark got me more gigs than any agent I have ever known, sometimes three in one night. At a time in my life when live work normally slows down, it went full throttle. I did many shows with Alexander O'Neal and we became friends. This is something I would never have dreamed of when I went to see him in concert at the Hammersmith Odeon in my teens and sat there thinking that I'd like to be on that stage someday. Alex inspired me through the 80s.

I sang for Muhammad Ali in Manchester when he came over to the UK. Twice I sang for Mike Tyson and hung out with Roberto Durán 'Hands of Stone'. With Mark, singing and boxing met each other in a big way. He introduced me to his good friend Silky (Barry Silkman) and this led onto gigs with Eddie Holman, Tavares, Patrice Rushen, The Womacks and a tour with Shalamar. Through Silky I met David Gest which in turn led onto more gigs, one of them with Sheila Ferguson from The Three Degrees. To crown it all, Mark got me a private show where I shared the stage with Alex, Lisa Stansfield and one of the greatest soul singers of all time, Bobby Womack. So, I was getting to perform alongside the artistes I had admired all my life and meet the boxing legends I had watched on TV with my dad when I was a youngster.

250

Always smart with his knowledge and tips, Mark persuaded me to start hoarding memorabilia for a rainy day and helping me source that rare, autographed picture of the legendary heavyweight boxer Joe Louis for my dad.

So, if Flip and I had gone to that meeting in Epping and gone through the front entrance, instead of the side, I would have missed Mark coming down those stairs and maybe we would never have met. I can't stress enough how much I believe in the connectedness of everything, and how things in life are mapped out in the minutest detail.

Next, I was asked to appear on ITV's *Hit Me Baby One More Time*. The early Noughties had seen a rebirth in TV talent shows with *Pop Idol, Fame Academy* and *X Factor*, and the network were also cashing in with all the artists of yesteryear with shows like this and *Reborn in the USA*. On the one hand they were trying to create the next big thing; on the other trying to resurrect the last big thing.

I really had nothing to lose. Again, I only anticipated a little profile and a lot of gigs on the back of it.

The show was a farce.

Right at the start, the musical director told me that I was one of just a few artists who had not dropped the key of their track. That was how averagely some of the acts had aged, but it was also the last piece of transparency because I learned from the producers afterwards that in fact everyone who voted for me in the studio actually nominated Nathan Moore from Brother Beyond! There was a glitch with the studio voting system, so my votes were stolen. The show producer did apologise to me, but it was too late. You can't run the vote twice.

When 911 won on the public vote, they were just as shocked:

'Kenny is an amazing singer,' they said. 'We can't believe it.'

In the final, the winner was Shakin' Stevens.

Shaky had an album out. The production company behind the show were also the same one behind Shaky.

All in all, it looked very shaky.

But it was good for me, and very good for Curb.

251

The public learned three things: that I was still alive… I still had a voice and I my 90s quiff hairstyle was long gone!

Some friends asked me why I did that show. I just replied, 'Because they asked me to.' I saw no risk – I knew that I could come on and do what I do best. That was singing. Dodgy studio votes were out of my hands. In fact, I even persuaded Junior Giscombe and Errol Reid from China Black to appear. At first, they were not 100% convinced it was the right show to appear on, but I told them that we had nothing to lose. Adding that it was probably rigged anyway and there was no chance any of us would win! This wasn't pessimism, this was me being realistic, and I was right. It was as rigged as an election in Bogotá, Colombia.

There *was* nothing to lose, though it did serve as a reminder that I did not wish to be back in 1991. There were now a couple of memories of what that was like when I would once again go to the supermarket and the cashier would say that they had seen me on the telly. I had stepped away from that. People no longer camped outside my house, and I was able to get on with life, but this brought it all back and the gentle nudge that fame was an unfortunate by-product of success in the music business. That brief dalliance with it for that show came and went. It did me no harm whatsoever and I don't think winning it changed anyone's life.

However, the final point of significance at Curb was the police. That is not to say Sting's band but the boys in blue.

One day I received the most extraordinary phone call from the label:

'Kenny, the police want to talk to you,' someone rang to say.

'Maybe they want you to sing at the next Policeman's Ball,' they joked.

So, I phoned them. They asked if they could come and see me, so I told them where I lived and invited them round.

I had no idea why.

'We'll cut to the chase. Your name and someone else's have come up in a conversation in a public house in Tottenham,' they began.

252

My radar was telling me straight away that this was undercover work, and someone had been mouthing off not realising who they were talking to. That was the London I grew up in.

'In what way has my name come up?' I replied.

'We were told that you and another guy called Animal murdered PC Blakelock in the Tottenham Riots.'

Wow. I was completely stunned by this.

I knew somebody had it in for me. Those strange conversations, like the one at the urinal in the nightclub, were coming home to roost. The thing is – I can remember exactly where I was that night and let us have some context here.

Keith Blakelock died in October 1985. I was seventeen and had just started dating a girl called Barbara. I was one of the head altar boys at St Ignatius Church at the time. My life was either Barbara, church, boxing, buying music or roller skating with the lads! I actually remember that evening and Barbara's brother David shouting out to me from the living room, telling me to come downstairs to watch the news. We saw the images of the rioting, knowing it was all happening only two miles away from where we were.

Civil unrest was rife in the country – a racial tension simmering.

But no, I was not there.

'Are you really looking for someone that young?' I asked the police.

'You and someone called Animal,' they replied.

'Animal? I don't know anyone called Animal.'

They were just doing their job. They didn't speak with any conviction or aggression. In fact, when they left, they simply told me:

'Do yourself a favour, forget we have even been here.'

But I didn't and I couldn't.

I rang Dave Sassoon immediately; he was as shocked as me.

'Who the hell is Animal?' I asked him.

'Don't you remember?' he responded. 'It's the old nickname we gave Derrick.'

253

I had completely forgotten that we called him that for a short while back in the 80s. This was when he decided to relax his hair and give it that 'Coming to America' wet look, very fashionable at the time. On the days when his hair was not so wet it stuck up in the air and he resembled Animal, the drummer from *The Muppets* shows.

I thought I had better call Derrick to warn him. He was another deeply religious person.

He found the whole thing to be quite unbelievable.

'Get the police to give me a call,' he said.

I called the detective on the number he had given me and told him that I now remembered who Animal was. He then contacted Derrick.

'I was at Dave's house that night,' he confirmed after the police got a train out to see him. And that was the end of that.

The police had to act on the information they were given and follow it up. How else can they eliminate the innocent and find the person or persons who committed this crime? A few years later, the police did arrest a guy who would have been fifteen years old at the time of the riot. He was subsequently released and the charges dropped. The case remains open and unsolved.

They had been sent on a wild goose chase in my direction. It was, of course, nonsense but it did leave me feeling very uncomfortable. What became so apparent to me was that the person who had told the police it was Animal and myself who had committed the murder must have been very close to us, part of our inner circle. Derrick was called Animal only for a short period of time in the mid-80s and just a handful of us knew that and used that nickname.

Whoever it was, they had put me in the frame. I could have been pinpointed for anything.

I knew somebody *did* have it in for me.

Rock'n'roll can have its perks. Many memoirs offer nothing but excess.

It was not a place I rarely toured.

But I did play that venue once or twice!

In 1992 at the height of my 'fame', I was in the Canaries with my mates Phil, Tony and Paul aka 'Woody' on a lads' holiday. Word was spreading that there was a major party at Bobby's Bar! You know – that world-famous location. *Then* we heard a rumour that 'Kenny Thomas was on the island, and he is gonna be there'.

Lying there in the sun on Playa de las Américas, a guy approached us and began his sales pitch for the party by saying that I was going to be in attendance.

'Kenny Thomas is gonna be at the party and no doubt a load of girls, too,' he said, not knowing who he was talking to.

'What do you reckon, lads, should we go to this party?' I said.

'Anyway, what does this Kenny geezer look like? I heard he is about as tall as Danny DeVito and really full of himself,' I added.

At that point Tony, Phil and Woody couldn't control themselves and began to laugh.

'What are you laughing for?' he asked us.

'That is Kenny,' said Phil, pointing at me with tears in his eyes.

The penny dropped.

'No way! Oh no! I feel like a complete twat now,' said the guy as he also roared with laughter.

He sat there on the beach having a chat with us for some time. His blunder remains one of the most memorable.

We went to the party.

It was in full swing and everyone was having a great time. Well, almost everyone.

I left the lads on the dance floor and went into the toilets. It was quite busy in there, but there was a young guy holding onto the sink, in a right state. He was panicking and clearly in serious trouble. He needed immediate help. People are coming in and out and nobody is doing anything, either because they didn't care, or they were too out of their heads to even notice him.

He was alone with no mates. He had taken something for sure and had no idea what was going on, barely able to talk.

'Hi, mate, are you OK? Tell me, what have you taken?' I asked him.

'I took an E,' he replied.

'Who are you here with?'

'No one, I'm on my own.'

'OK, I'm Kenny,' I said. 'You're gonna be fine, just come with me.'

I'd seen this before. I've been there before. Dragonflies and bowler hats.

I had to get him out of that noisy, claustrophobic environment before he really started freaking out. I told my mates I had to go, and holding him by his arm I walked him out of the club and down to the beach. I just sat there with him for ages, all the time reassuring him that he will be OK and to just relax.

'You're safe with me, mate, I'll look after you,' I told him.

'Thanks, mate, I don't know what's happening. One minute I was feeling OK and then...' He managed to mumble, as his eyes rolled about, and he struggled to keep it together.

His mates hadn't wanted to go out that night, so he decided to go it alone. He scored a pill off some street dealer not knowing how strong it was, plus he was unfamiliar with the hallucinogenic effects of the drug. So, when it hit him in the club he literally didn't know what day it was. Added to that, the fact that he was all alone made for a double dangerous situation.

The dark world of dance music and ecstasy pills is not all mirrorballs and disco dancing. This is the other side of it when it goes wrong and can have disastrous consequences.

I stayed with him the whole night just chatting, making sure he had some water to drink and checking, always checking.

There was no way I was leaving his side until he was completely back to normal. Slowly but surely, he returned to planet Earth and began to straighten out, but he wasn't quite there yet.

Phil, Tony and Woody came out of the club and joined us on the beach, as the sun was coming up. He came with us back to our apartment where he was able to chill out and have a good old cup of tea. When we could see he was back to himself and out the other side of it, he left us and made his way back to his place.

Later that afternoon me and the lads were sitting on the beach when he came bouncing along with his mates.

'Guys, meet Kenny, this is the bloke who saved my life last night.'

'Thank you so much for looking after me. I was in a bad way,' he said.

'Mate, it was nothing, I'm just glad you're OK,' I replied.

'I wouldn't do it again,' I urged caution. 'It is probably not for you.'

Maybe in some way I had saved his life. All I know is, I just happened to be in the right place at the right time.

But I was good creatively, too. It was here that I wrote the lyrics and melody for 'Wait For Me' in the midst of a lads' holiday but clearly at peace and in a good enough place to create.

As you know, I made a lot of friends in unusual circumstances – and many outside of the business. I was performing at a Northern Soul Weekender at a campsite near Fleetwood and took James with me. Wow – I didn't actually realise that when the music ends, the fun starts. What happened next we laughingly referred to as the Night of the Abduction!

When I came off-stage, I got talking to some of the people there and having a few beers with them. I signal that I am off to bed when I am told in no uncertain terms:

'You're going nowhere, you're coming with us,' one of them said.

I find myself in a chalet with Neeta and Ed, music pumping all night and drinks aplenty. There's a steady flow of people coming in and out of the chalet all night. I remember little more except surfacing the next day after 11! I had never met these fans before, but now Neeta and Ed are dear friends. I am not sure that many musicians cross the line over to the fan side and stay there, but it is a good place to be and humbling, too. You remember that for a long time you were on that side of the fence and then you had a few hits. Why would there be any line to cross?

One thing is true: I remember the people – less so the gigs.

But these were special moments. There can be a kind of loneliness when you're on the road doing gigs, even more so in those days of being a popstar, which is why I never wanted any boundaries unless they were absolutely necessary. Nowadays, of course, social media makes you accessible in a mostly good way, but more so then, people were quick to say, 'Oh, he's become a popstar now' (in other words, he doesn't want to know) or they would often hear 'he's so busy' which *was* often the truth.

For however long it lasts, it is a blast and you can be seduced by the whole experience, but it does end and some people do get trapped in another decade – socially, financially and mentally.

I tried to stay level. As Father Hanshell would say to me, 'You are called to love everybody in this life, but it is impossible to like everybody.' It is true that there were times in the 90s when I did not recognise myself. I hope that I have the self-awareness today to adhere to my old mantra – don't let who you are today stop you from being who you can be in the future.

If you've taken a few blows and you're on the ropes, you are still in the fight. Tomorrow is always another day.

When Arsenal's 'Invincibles' won the the cup and the league in 2003–04, I was officially missing in action for a fortnight with my friends Johnny Boy and Louie. The night before Arsenal scored the winning goal, me, John and Louie were invited to a house party in Wood Green for someone's birthday. We bowled into the party, larger than life, and positioned ourselves close to the food and drinks table in the kitchen, right in front of a rather large birthday cake. Within an hour of being there, John, having overdone it on the herbal cigarettes, suddenly turned a whiter shade of pale and fell forwards, crashing face first onto the floor, making a sound that would have been a good addition to any heavyweight boxing match. The paramedics came, and off we went to the North Middlesex Hospital. After a few hours and an X-ray, we all went home, John in his newly acquired neck collar. Louie and I concluded that had John been standing only another 8 inches further forward he would have landed face first into the birthday cake and none of this would have happened. It would have been a nice soft landing.

Not being one to let a neck collar stand in his way, John joined us the next day as we watched the match on the big screen at our local boozer. No sooner did Arsenal win, we immediately employed the skills of a local cab driver, Nutty Neil, to take us as fast as possible (*Italian Job*-style) down to the Drayton Arms in Islington, so we could really soak up the atmosphere. We cheered as an inflatable trophy was passed around the pub and held up high and joined in with the tribal chants and watched as some fans swung from the chandeliers.

And that is how its ceiling came down.

Chandeliers are not the best things to hang from!

The following weekend, Johnny Boy took a well-earned rest while Louie and I met Chad at The Old Parrs Head on Upper Street. We stood outside the pub, soaked up the sunshine, and joined in one of the best North London street parties I have ever seen. Despite all the gigs I have done, I don't think I have ever sung as much as I did that weekend. Come on, you Gunners!

In 2005, I had been touring with Level 42 which I absolutely loved. I am a big fan of their music, so getting to see them play every night was such a privilege.

After the show at the Albert Hall, I am invited to the box of an Arabic guy called Abdullah (Abudy) – an extremely wealthy man with an enormous musical knowledge, and whose dad had been the first to own a jazz club in Lebanon in the days when that city was one of the jewels of the Middle East.

He asked me what I was doing later that evening and invited me back to his apartment adjacent to the Albert Hall. I accepted.

I have never been in more palatial surroundings, and when you come from a council estate you notice these things!

'You must come to Cairo,' he urged.

I thought little more of it and a considerable period of time passed and I hadn't made it out to Cairo.

Then out of the blue:

'You're coming to Cairo... I am booking you a flight... Bring your girlfriend,' he told me.

'No, we've split,' I replied.

But I did go one better and took my friend James.

Money clearly was no object. We are met by a chauffeur, taken to a top-drawer hotel on the banks of the Nile, given mobiles and told that whatever we wanted was ours. The chauffeur would take us.

So, we *didn't* decline visiting the pyramids on horseback, and going to every museum in town in a contrast to how I would normally see cities which was a treadmill of arrive at venue, soundcheck, find hotel, do gig, go home.

This was something else and simply because Abudy was a fan and a very kind and generous person. Every once in a while, a moment like this comes along.

It happened again in the Gulf – and obviously there is serious cash in places like these. I had been gigging in Bahrain and ran into Mick Hucknall at the after-show party to one of his concerts. We were the guests of one of the bosses of Gulf Air.

The music agent Paul Fitzgerald was with me – as were many other well-to-do people from the island – and more champagne than you could ever drink... Enough to put you off for life.

'When you go to Dubai in a few weeks' time, why don't you come back over to Bahrain to see us?' said Ali, the Gulf Air exec.

So, we did. The next time we were there, we took a few days off and they flew us over to Bahrain. Paul and I stayed at their house, and they gave Paul a key to the front door. This came in handy because we went off partying with a load of Gulf Air hostesses and came back about 6am. We then tried to creep in by stealth and get back to our rooms undetected, but this failed miserably when we were rumbled by one of their maids. After barely an hour's sleep Ali comes into the room...

'Right, it's time to get up: we're leaving in an hour.'

'We're going to spend the day on the yacht,' he said.

The party continues on the yacht with a living room in it bigger than most people's houses. And more champagne, despite my vow the previous evening never to touch it again.

As Paul and I bombed it out on jet skis, so we were no more than a speck on the horizon, I turned to him and asked jokingly:

'Do we do this for a living?'

'Yeah, we do,' he answered. 'We are in a meeting!'

For a moment I pinched myself. It wasn't real of course and it certainly wasn't that boy from that council estate. This is a different world, one enjoyed by the super wealthy and those invited guests whom they briefly allow to participate in the high-spirited shenanigans.

Then an even bigger yacht pulls up alongside.

It belonged to the son of the Minister of Oil for Saudi Arabia. Not even the actual guy, just the son!

His yacht had a nice speedboat attached to it.

It wasn't long before I was zooming around the Gulf on that piece of kit.

It was a whole lot of fun. They were all lovely people who made me feel so welcome and went out of their way to make my time there as enjoyable as possible.

When I arrived back at Heathrow, I made my way to North London on the Piccadilly line. The whole thing seemed very surreal. One minute I'm on the Persian Gulf bombing around on a speedboat, steering wheel in one hand, a bottle of champagne in the other, and the next I am back on the tube making my way to Arnos Grove.

I called my mate Johnny Boy and told him:

'You would not believe the last few days I've had.'

And I am not sure I can remember it all, either.

But it wasn't really me, as brilliant as it was. I was often told in the music business that I was too reserved and that I should take what I can when I can. That attitude of self-entitlement and the ego required to fit that stereotype is a dangerous thing. Yes, you might gain much materially but you'll lose yourself in the process. Bar the odd wild moment or two, I was just *me*, so I never took anything for granted nor expected.

And this – years after my peak – was totally unexpected.

34 Francisca

What a voice.

It is 6 December 2007. I am booked to do a charity gig at Shrigley Hall in Macclesfield, Cheshire. The agent has brought a South African girl and her sisters over from Cape Town to perform on the show. They are also scheduled to do backing vocals for me at a subsequent event at StarCity in Birmingham.

I instantly connect with her South African humour.

But then I learn a little more.

Her name is Francisca.

She made her first TV appearance at the age of seven and has since carved out a name for herself in the Western Cape. Her dad Joe is a tough guy and into boxing – his ancestors were white immigrants from Croatia and Trieste in Italy.

Her mum Christina is Capetonian and her ancestors were no doubt brought to South Africa against their will by the Dutch colonialists who subjugated the region. These invaders helped themselves to vast amounts of gold, diamonds and minerals, and when they had finished robbing the country, they handed it over to the British who did the same.

Francisca is of mixed ethnic background.

Her mum and dad married in secret back in the bad old days of apartheid and went on to have four girls who all sang. They were born with microphones in their hands. The Jackson Four!

Then I learn that Francisca starred on second season of South African *Pop Idol* and was one of the favourites tipped to win the whole contest until she pulled out… when the bosses of the show began questioning her about how she identifies herself and her ethnicity.

She had an inkling of what was coming when they sat her down and asked her, 'What are you?'

'I'm a singer,' she replied.

'No, what colour are you?'

'What has colour got to do with a singing competition?' she asked them.

At that point she quit. And was forced into hiding when the press got hold of this news. The winner *was* a white girl, though the following year a girl from a mixed ethnic background did triumph. Of course – standard talent show obligation – Francisca was locked in a deal with EMI but, when free, chose to tour, picking up a lot of work in Egypt, Dubai and the Balearic Islands.

I guess that is how we met!

After the gig, we spent many hours chatting on the mobile – the usual kind of flirting and then I asked her straight:

'Let's go on a date.'

So we did. I travelled up to Manchester and it went brilliantly.

I called my old mate Shane Richie who was appearing in *Scrooge,* and he got us some tickets to the show. As he is leaving the stage – still with his mic on – he suddenly breaks into 'Outstanding'! He is such a character. Love him.

Then Shane invites us out with the cast afterwards. It was as though I had choreographed the whole thing.

But we got on brilliantly, and as they say, the rest is... destiny.

The more we talked, the more I liked her and the more we connected.

'Hey, you know I am a Christian,' I dropped in casually.

'So am I,' she replied. 'I was brought up that way, too.'

'Well, to be more precise I'm a Catholic Christian,' I added.

I was waiting for her weirdo alarm to go off... It didn't.

'Me, too, my dad's a Catholic so we were raised in the faith,' she confirmed.

I don't know if it would have mattered. I doubt it. It definitely did place us on a new level together. Life certainly did begin at 40.

The more I also realised what a crap deal she had been sold. I asked her what she was getting paid for her gigs and she was clearly being ripped off. I learned that their manager was driving them around half-pissed most of the time and trying to get it on with them – and I had known this guy for many years. I knew this was exploitation and highly dangerous. They were nothing short of musician slaves.

She told me that he was going on holiday soon and was leaving them stuck in the house. I knew this was the perfect opportunity. So, as soon as he left, I arranged to get them out of his house and back to South Africa. When he returned, he couldn't believe what I had done. I was now public enemy number one. No more gigs from him. But I didn't give a hoot. No doubt he moved on and began the whole process again with some 'fresh' talent.

When Francisca returned to Cape Town, I made my ex-employer BT very wealthy by spending hours on the phone whispering sweet nothings down the line. We got to know each other a little more this way, but a long-distance relationship such as this usually doesn't last very long. It is not like I could jump on an aeroplane and nip over to Alicante for the weekend – this was Cape Town, thousands of miles away. We didn't really have a plan as to how to proceed from here, but we knew we wanted to be together.

By 2008 it was clear that there was only two ways we could make that happen. Either I had to go to Cape Town, or we needed to get her a fiancée visa. So, we set about sorting out the visa so she could return to the UK.

Well – I did know within a month of meeting her that I was going to marry her and spend the rest of my life with her. Now I can see that *we* remind *me* of my mum and dad, which is really heart-warming. There is that international feel again and her fiery spirit like Mum's Spanish passion and a lot of humour and wind-ups. When Francisca rolls her Rs as she speaks, I hear Mum and the Latin accentuation she would put on English vowels! Yes – we have an age difference, but the dynamic was always strong. I see history repeating itself – and not in a bad way! I hadn't been looking. In fact, I almost felt the chance to have a family was passing me by and that had always been something I thought about, but a connection is a connection and we had that.

265

Music was one of those connections and what I didn't fully know at the time of meeting her was how good she was, not only at singing, but also at songwriting. When she sat down at the piano and played me some of her ideas I was blown away. I knew I could introduce her to some credible people so I took her straight round to see Bluey from Incognito who simply said that she could join the group anytime she liked, but he thought she should pursue a solo career and get her songs out there. He was right. I wanted Bluey to make a record with her and he said he wanted that, too, so we planned to make it happen when the time was right.

Back to the visa drama...

Anyone who has ever applied for a fiancée visa will tell you that it is enough to test a relationship whatever the chemistry. The madness had begun. At times we were made to feel like criminals sitting there at the immigration offices in Croydon. We had to jump through hoops and prove that we were the genuine article and not a passport-for-cash scenario. It was so intrusive and, in some ways, very humiliating, and of course there is the money. Nothing comes for free. With every form filled out there is some kind of payment required and if your application is unsuccessful you have to start all over again and pay for it all over again. Nothing is more important to the British government than money. It's all about the wonga!

Of course, we had to back it all up by setting a date, so picked one considerably in the future so if, for some reason, the chemistry no longer gelled then we had a get-out clause and Francisca could return to Cape Town. But I knew that wasn't going to happen. I had never been so sure in all my life.

Now, when I say, 'set a date' what that actually means is following almost in the footsteps of my mum and dad. This was a 'Home Office wedding' with a handful of friends, and James as my best man. This was enough to satisfy the authorities but neither of us saw it as a true marriage. In the eyes of the Catholic Church, for us to go to a registry office was not valid. We were not really married until it was done sacramentally in the presence of a priest.

That was always at the back of our minds, but this is not to say that the 'marriage' was therefore completely meaningless. No, it was still significant, and it did mean something to us. In the eyes of the United Kingdom, she was legally Mrs Thomas and that gave us a base to proceed from. It was clearly the first step to get to where we needed to be. In the eyes of the Church, she was not, and the latter was more important to us.

But we had cleared the preliminary hoops. Francisca had indefinite leave to remain. That meant a very long process was underway. A few months of instruction needed to be reintroduced because she had never received the Sacrament of Confirmation and that is a requirement for marriage in the Church. So, she attended the weekly classes and I kept a close eye on what they were teaching her just in case they threw in some of that hippie 60s theological nonsense. And they did.

It was as though we were back at square one when, of course, we weren't but these things were fundamental to who we were and we knew we had to be patient, and of course, if your heart and head are telling you that, whatever the bit of paper says, it is incomplete, then you are nowhere in life. If that is your moral code, as it was ours, then it wasn't even up for discussion.

I realise not everybody who comes to the United Kingdom is legitimate but when you unleash the process, you are on a treadmill at maximum incline. Occasional trips to the interrogation, sorry, immigration offices in Croydon were both laughable and deadly serious – an irritation at times in between gigs, recording my *Breathe* album and attempting to establish what normality was. However chilled you are in life and regardless of how much faith may light up the path ahead for you, it does put everything on hold. You do feel under suspicion. Borderline criminal.

There was only one thing to do.
Have a baby.

It had been a crazy time. Those kind people who bought the *Voices* album in droves would really have no idea of where I was and what I was up to. By 2010, I had been studying my backside off with books everywhere, 35 modules and a huge dissertation to complete while going into studios late at night with my technique still getting better after 20 odd years, gigging anywhere and everywhere and of course, writing.

All of this had put me on the cusp of where I wanted to be, and meeting Francisca really sealed the deal. I knew almost immediately that there was something greater to live for in my life and that was her. But musically, I understood now that I wanted to put something out independently. Unless there was a mega deal on the table – and you never say never – I really wanted to be in control of my own destiny. I didn't want to wake up in the morning with someone telling me that I needed to be seen at this event whilst I was wondering who was screwing me over. Those days were gone.

I identified two key areas where I wanted to be: I needed to sell independently at my own shows and, at all costs, must retain copyright. Plus, I wanted to keep the soul scene satisfied. That was my bread and butter and my icing on the cake.

So, with Mark Aaron providing a steady flow of gigs, I made the *Breathe* album with my own dough. In a micro-fashion, I had already formed my own little record label Solus with my friend Nick Adams. I had begun setting up studio at home and recorded all of the vocals there. I thought it would take me years to learn that process and would regularly speak to engineers. Very soon I only wanted to record at home and couldn't find a sound to compare to it wherever I worked. Some producers wanted me to fly here and there to see them – I once went to Denmark for just one track, but I could see those days were over and there was no need. It was a mini-cottage industry! We were starting to explore revenue streams many artists didn't really know a lot about. Not because I doubted the material but more so because I was not really likely to make radio playlists anymore, I was stunned and delighted when both Smooth FM and Jazz FM got behind the single 'The Show Is Over', which was written by Francisca. The Controller at Smooth, Jamie Griffiths, told me that I was being more heavily scheduled than a Lionel Richie comeback track. That was enough of a badge of honour if nothing else became of this project except further knowledge.

Of course, by this point the charts have long since ceased to mean what they did, and we were moving into an era of digital accountability, too. The game had changed. I learned a lot, such as what to spend money on and what to avoid and despite not being hugely successful, it did me no harm whatsoever. In fact, I had never been busier, was in control, and doing everything from the heart plus there was zero pressure from the music industry. I also developed a very strong friendship with Mark Aaron who became extremely wise counsel to me. Business-wise, he got it.

But it was also a tough year.

Francisca was constantly sick, she had morning sickness around the clock for the entire nine months. We were up every hour of the day and night but when little Angela finally arrived on 12 August 2010 it became the happiest day of my life. She was the most beautiful baby I had ever seen. I would say that, and all parents say it about their babies, because it is true. There is nothing greater than a new life arriving into the world, and Angela changed my life forever. However, I didn't legislate for about fifteen further months of not sleeping but I was delighted to name her after my own mum.

Things were pretty close to perfect. Just exhausting!

That also meant that when we finally got married at the Church of the Assumption, Old Harlow, in 2011, Angela was there, and also starring on the cake in miniatures alongside Francisca and me holding microphones, together with our two dogs Bongo and Boot! We had got there in stages, although not exactly in the right order, and now with a baby in tow. Lifelong friends Dave Sassoon and John Sander (Johnny Boy) were my best men.

Francisca was ridiculously late – to the tune of 45 minutes.

Growing up in London with so many African and Caribbean mates around me, I had got used to lateness. The phrase GMT – Ghanaian Maybe Time – was given to me by an old Benedictine monk friend, Br. John Davies OSB, who lived in a monastery with other Ghanaian monks who he said were late for Mass, late for vespers and will be late for their own funerals. Nobody ever turned up when they said they would. Francisca was showing a little bit of Ghanaian style.

I later found out that as the photographer had been taking pictures of her getting ready at the hotel, his assistant spilt a bottle of Moët. The whole bottle went over the wedding dress and veil. It took a while for it to dry out: about 45 minutes, I reckon.

I didn't know until after the ceremony because I simply did not turn around when she finally made it up the aisle.

Only later did I have the chance to ask her where the hell she had been.

The only other question it raises is this: Why was a whole bottle of champagne open at that time in the morning? Very worrying!

It was a truly magical day – bar the Moët. It had begun with rain but once we were inside the church, the atmospherics changed considerably, developing into a picture-perfect gorgeous setting.

I think some of the guests thought I was about to wheel out a cast list from *Top of the Pops* to perform afterwards. It is pretty standard to invite a few friends who can sing, but I was absolutely clear this was about us and not a chapter in pop's history. Knowing how much Francisca loves her salsa dancing, Mark Aaron took me some weeks earlier to see the Roberto Pla Latin Ensemble perform in London. So, I booked Roberto and his twelve-piece Latin band.

We could have been in Cuba.

We finally had our day. The little marriage certificates were for the passports. This was the one we wanted for life.

It seemed, too, that we were now reproducing every couple of years!

In February 2012 we discovered that Christina was on the way.

36 James

James was my travelling companion. He came to all my gigs and practically lived at mine. He was my co-pilot in every sense. Older than me, but looking younger, we were the tightest of friends from an early age.

We shared everything.

He had been one of the first to get a driving licence. I don't know how! In his first outing in his 'flash' new Granada Ghia, he took me for a spin (literally) which sent us flying into a 360 turn with my feet on the dashboard and my body pinned to the side window.

'I'm gonna die, I'm gonna die!' I screamed.

The vehicle turned around and came to a standstill.

'Take me home,' I told him.

And I never got back in that car for some time! But we always laughed.

A doctor once said to me that a good belly laugh two or three times a year was very beneficial medically. I was overdosing with James on a daily basis.

His entire adult life, though, meant that he was in and out of hospital and later travelling to Germany for a revolutionary treatment. I knew of course, from Mum, that other mindsets and different medicines were available in other countries. There is another narrative to the NHS.

James – you may recall – suffered from the little-known illness called sickle-cell anaemia. In short, this disease is an inherited red blood cell disorder in which there are not enough healthy red cells to carry oxygen around your body. If you Google it, you will see the suggestion that no more than 15,000 people suffer from it in the UK. Equally, it just says: 'Symptoms – pain.' He had also undergone a heart operation.

And that was what I recognised regularly in my friend once I had seen it at first-hand:

James was staying over one evening when late at night I heard a murmur from his room. I knew he was in trouble. When

I saw him lying there, he was in so much agony that he couldn't even raise his voice to alert me. He must have been lying there like that for some time.

This was so frightening, even for me who was used to watching people deteriorate in front of you. If we are honest, much of what we see through the eyes of a hospital is the aftermath. Quite often you do not see tragedy evolving at such speed in front of you. This was James's life.

I managed to get him in the car and down to University College Hospital in Euston. It was 5 in the morning. On this occasion he did recover and would be up and about in days. As soon as he could make me laugh again, he would.

But once again, the spell is cast and people that I love are struck early by conditions they seem most unfortunate to have – and yet here I was lucky enough to have never been seriously physically poorly. I knew I was fortunate, but it was no consolation.

Having James in my life made me live life. He was a massive Formula 1 and Michael Schumacher fan, so I made sure we made it to the Monaco Grand Prix one year. James always told me that he would not live past the age of 44. I took that very much at face value, even though my standard reply to him was: 'What makes you think you are going to get off that easy? You've gotta do your time like the rest of us.'

Secretly, it hurt to hear him say that, but I hid it and buried it deep.

'If you do go, James, please make sure I'm on the guest list up there,' I would often add.

'Don't worry, K, you'll be on it, I'll get that sorted,' he would reply.

He always seemed to bounce back. *We* always seemed to be having fun. We really did live every moment that we could.

Whilst we were in Monaco with our friends Tony Maffeo and Anthony Borg for the F1 race, James had a crisis. That is the correct language for taking a turn for the worse. There is only one way to deal with it and that is to head straight for hospital. His tolerance levels were extraordinary, often prescribed an amount of morphine that would be too much for you and me.

273

When we arrived at hospital, nobody knew what to do. They had never seen anyone with sickle-cell anaemia before. Nor did they know how to treat him when he said that he needed pain management.

Tony tried his best in Italian to explain to them the nature of the disease and the amount of pain medication required, but they really struggled to get a grasp of things and were quite understandably unwilling to give such a large dose of morphine. Tony spoke to the doctors at the UCLH (University College London Hospital) to see if we could find common areas of understanding. It was that rare.

James, as always, bounced back from this crisis, and we got to enjoy the rest of our time away. But it was a clear reminder that this can happen at any point, and it *will* happen again. James learned to live with that, but it never stopped him from enjoying life to the full and he always managed to keep smiling.

When he bought a huge antenna for his CB radio I bought a massive one, too: it was over 20 feet high, much to the surprise and annoyance of my neighbours on the council estate. The signal transmitted from our aerials made the neighbours TVs play up. How we loved those monster antennas. When we were roller skating with our four-wheeled skates in the early 80s, James was the first person I ever saw using in-line skates which he brought back from America. I couldn't match that one. But when he got his first dog *Zoltan* the Dobermann, I got my first dog: *Bomber,* an English Bull Terrier. We copied each other and enjoyed all of the similitudes.

If I was to write down every story about James and all the crazy times we had together, it would fill this entire book. But one that I will never forget was the time James, Bradley, Frazer and myself went up to the Southport Weekender and were staying at a boutique hotel. After a very long night of pounding the dance floor we headed back to the hotel. James went to his room to have a shower and get his head down. Upon leaving the bathroom he became somewhat disoriented, and wearing only a towel around his waist walked out of the room, down the stairs and out of the hotel, locking himself out in the process. When Bradley called me to say that James was missing, I went looking for him. Wearing only boxer shorts and a T-shirt, I did exactly the same thing. It was around 4am and now we were both locked out, standing in the street, in the freezing cold, looking like a right pair of idiots. I had to wake up the hotel owner who was none too pleased. After he gave us a good telling-off, he let us back in. So close were we that we even copied each other in being foolish.

James did not make 44.

He was right all along.

Another gone too soon.

Often we take much for granted. And then the moment has passed.

The day James fell ill for the final time I called his mobile phone many times, but he never answered. I was worried.

I tried it one more time later that day and his brother Albert answered. He told me James was really unwell and he was about to take him to the hospital. He asked me if I wanted to speak to him. I told him not to worry, just get him to the hospital and I'll call him later when he is feeling a bit better.

I never did to speak to him again.

James did not recover this time, falling unconscious and succumbing to a form of meningitis.

Over the next few days there was a steady stream of visitors to his bedside. He was loved by so many that there was never a moment that he was alone. All of us were there, the North London Crew: Dave Chamberlain (aka Armos), Wallace (aka Socket), DJ Ramsey, Miles (aka Mr Buzzard), Richard (aka Fox), Liza and Romany to name just a few of the friends. We all kept vigil.

We had all seen James bounce back so many times, but this time it was different. Somehow we all knew the end was near. And I knew the signs well enough by now.

His brother Albert called me.

'Kenny, I've got some bad news. The doctors said that James has had a catastrophic bleed on the brain, and there's nothing they can do to save him: he is not going to make it. Tonight, they are going to switch off the life support and my family really want you to be there.'

275

I was totally heartbroken, but I felt very honoured that they wanted me present. They also asked his other best friend Dave Chamberlain who had known James even longer than I had. Dave and I would join his family at the hospital later that evening.

James had been a fighter all of his life. He fought to survive every day.

Why would it be any different now?

So, when they switched off the life support he survived for a number of hours unassisted by any equipment.

His heart beat for the last time on 24 February 2009. The time was 0036.

He was 43 years old. Just two and a half months short of his 44th birthday.

I stayed for a while.

There was nothing more to do and life goes on routinely for the nurses. But equally, you don't just leave. And when you do, there is no turning back. They are gone.

At around 0115, I called home to let Francisca know.

Earlier that day I had called Myra, Dave Sassoon's nan, to tell her that I was on my way to the hospital, and that James was going to pass away. She had known him since he was a youngster.

So, after I had spoken to my wife I then called Myra.

'Hi, Myra, it's Kenny, James has gone,' I said.

'Yes, I know. Was it at around 25 to one?' she asked.

'Yes, it was, how do you know that?'

'At 0035, all the lights went off, there was a power cut here in my flat,' she elaborated. 'Two minutes later, everything came back on, and the fuse box never tripped.'

Turns out that no other flat in that block experienced any kind of power cut at that time. Only her flat. And that was the moment James had died.

For Myra and me no explanation was needed. We knew.

Exactly a year later to the day, I was driving from Cape Point back up to Cape Town with Francisca. It was the first anniversary of James's death. It was late in the day, and I wanted to find a church so I could light a candle and say a prayer for him. I had no idea where I was on that route, but I told my wife that we would stop at the first church we find. After some time, I spotted one in the distance so we made our way to it. It was open, so we parked up, went in and lit a candle. On the way out I looked at the name sign outside of the church: it was 'St. James'. I thought, 'Nice one, James, you led me to the right place.'

In the book of condolences for James's funeral I wrote…

'Rest in peace, my brother, make sure you get me on the guest list.'

37 The Little Miracle

We weren't planning on having another baby this soon. I had come from thinking I might not ever have any to now having a second one on the way.

I *had* always wanted a girl. That was Angela.

Eliot Kennedy had once said to me out of the blue in the car, 'You'll make a great dad one day,' but for a long time it looked like I was only ever going to be a decent uncle. I watched my sister Sandra having kids and often thought it all a bit crazy. But I wasn't without some experience in this field.

When Sandra's marriage broke down in the early 90s she went through an acrimonious divorce. Like so many women out there, she found herself alone with her three children, Natalie, Luke and Tess and zero support from the ex. I was in a position to help, so I did. I got her and the kids out of Hackney and into a property near me. So, between Mum and myself, we could give her the support she needed. In a way I became their only father figure, providing clothing, school uniforms and making sure their birthdays and Christmases were as magical as possible. I cared for them as if they were my own. I loved taking them out, but boy, I loved giving them back, too!

They were brilliant but I always knew when I left that I could duck in and out, and didn't have that 24/7 exhaustion that she was having.

Some years later she would go on to remarry and have two more children, Louis and Charlie. But history repeated itself... No, it was worse this time. Her new partner thought it was OK to have another secret parallel family on the go just a few miles away from where they lived. For a while he managed to flit between the two homes and kept the plates spinning, but, like most liars, he was unable to sustain this double life and it all came crashing down. Sandra found herself on her own again now with five children and Mum was no longer around to help. It was extremely tough for her. I was still single and again able to help, so I stepped in again and resumed a supporting role. Somehow

278

we all got through it. Her kids are all adults now and some of them have children of their own. The Thomas family pulled together during those testing times and did what we do best… Survive!

So, despite my best efforts to be a good father figure to her kids I had some natural insecurities and really didn't know if I would be a good dad when my time came. I honestly thought I had left it too late. I did know this. Francisca the solo artist was on hold and Angela's arrival meant that finally, despite a life's pursuit looking for answers to complicated questions, I had now entered the real world. I was no longer the centre of my own universe. And that was wonderful and gave me a clarity which I hadn't seen coming and whose effect I could never have predicted. On a very superficial level – late nights in recording studios would in time end up crashing into a school run, whereas they had previously just led to … crashing out.

But first Angela and then another on the way.

We were seriously churning them out!

Whilst I had always had that sense that I belonged in a big family, Francisca and I were just living and thought that if we were gifted with a new life, then we were open to it.

Then one day came the text – yes, the text!

This was a modern woman.

Attached an image from Clearblue.

I was shocked. Delighted. Unprepared.

We hadn't slept in fourteen months from Angela's colic.

But it was perfect.

And then we almost lost the baby.

On Francisca's 30th birthday, she suffered a massive bleed.

We were certain that she had had a miscarriage at two months.

We were resigned to our loss.

The doctors told us to come back in a couple of days and they would double-check the ultrasound just to confirm, but the reality is that everybody knew. The little one was gone.

As they begin to run the scan, I am staring at the screen. They pointed out the area of damage to the womb from the bleed.

There was a minute dot on the monitor.

'Is that what I think it is?' I asked, ever the amateur medic.

I was correct. There *was* still a live baby in there.

I knew that this was going to be a risky pregnancy but there was everything to live for. She was very much alive and kicking.

We never forgot this moment, but of course were nervous through the remaining months until her birth.

But then the most perfect baby arrived on 16 November, sharing the same birthday as my brother Steve. She was super cute, sleeping well and latching onto the teat. Everything was in order. She is our miracle baby.

I gave her the nickname *Cheeky Chops*, but because Angela was unable to pronounce this it changed to *Cheepy Chops*.

We named her after Francisca's mother, continuing that very Latin tradition we had started with Angela, but of course we had no clue what lay ahead for my little Christina.

Losing James was a terrible blow that cut right through me. It added itself to an ever-increasing list of reasons why staying in London was no longer what I wanted to do. Bar the move out to Hertfordshire, I had only ever lived there, and Dad was now in such a condition that he would really not know if I had driven 20 minutes or two hours to see him.

I had incredible experiences and am proud and a benefactor of my multicultural upbringing with its mix of war stories and young immigrant friends who became soulmates. Dad's influence had been huge, too – the boxing was colossal in not just my own life, but also in the lives of so many people he had nurtured from street fighting to the ring where the focus was only positive.

My music career had its roots in that Caribbean and soul diversity. I had lived the dream and partied hard. I had made some money and met my heroes. When I sang at an *audience with* the legendary producer Quincy Jones, he said to me, 'You're a great singer.' This has to be the icing on the cake for any vocalist. Through boxing, I had met Steve Finan and made a friend for life. Now I was pretty much free to plot my own musical journey as well as my family's.

In so many ways we were moving on.

However, there was something strange going on which was almost the final sign.

After Angela was born, Francisca started to tell me stuff. Weird stuff. There were noises in the house. My attitude to life was that almost everything was pretty much scientifically explainable. There would be a logical and sound explanation to everything.

But once I had dismissed it, the conversation had become very real, and we both started to notice it a little more.

One night both our dogs were looking and growling at something in the corner of the room.

'It's just a shadow.' I tried to dismiss it.

Then, as if I was not giving it enough credence, Francisca said she often heard footsteps upstairs.

'Noise travels,' I offered, well aware that our house was attached to another.

I continually found a suitable explanation for everything Francisca came up with. This frustrated her because she was convinced something unexplainable was happening in that house. I was having none of it.

One night Angela and Christina were asleep upstairs, when Angela begins crying hard. She is making noises that no child makes and certainly not her. You get to know an infant's cry and it sounded *like* her. But this was a distressed wail.

I flew up the stairs to go to check on her and she is sound asleep. Weird!

I mentioned this to Francisca.

'I told you there were strange noises in this house,' she said.

'OK, it was a strange noise and it was loud, but maybe it came from outside of the house,' I replied still unwilling to accept any preternatural possibilities.

Then the game changed…

I was home alone with the dogs, Francisca was out salsa dancing, and the girls were again asleep in bed. I was at the kitchen sink doing some washing up and that was the only thing I was doing in there.

I heard crying once more; I went upstairs and again there was nothing.

When I came back down, I turned towards the kitchen, I froze. The oven door to our cooker always had to be yanked open. You really had to pull on it.

It was now wide open.

I had been nowhere near it. I was previously positioned by the sink, and the dogs were not in the habit of opening the oven door, as clever as Jack Russells are.

This really spooked me out.

When Francisca came home, I finally conceded:

'There is something going on in this house,' I told her.

And from there it just got worse.

282

The room above the lounge was where I did my Chinese medicine. It had a desk in there and a heavy office chair with wheels. There was no carpet in that room. It had vinyl flooring, so you heard everything. Some nights the office chair would wheel across the floor up there. I would bomb it up the stairs complete with baseball bat, convinced there was a burglar on the loose. Nothing! Just an empty room and an office chair in a new position. No kids or dogs to blame, so no way of explaining it. We were really starting to get freaked out.

All this activity continued on and off for some time and it seemed to intensify as more of our children arrived on the scene. There were times when it quietened down altogether, and I thought it had gone away, only to start up again when there was a new arrival.

We were having a baby every two years. Angela in 2010, Christina in 2012, and it was now 2014 which can mean only one thing... Another baby. I do nothing by halves. If you're gonna go for it... Go big. I would like to supersize that order please!

We found out we were having a boy. Perfect! We named him after both of our dads... Joseph Kenneth. I nicknamed him *Smiley Pops* because he only ever smiled. He was adorable and almost edible.

When Francisca was pregnant with Joe – in fact throughout all her pregnancies – she had a habit of snoring heavily. I don't do snoring. When Dad snored when I was a kid, I would get up from my bed in the middle of the night go into his room and nudge the side of his bed with my knee to stop it. I couldn't stand that noise.

So, one night I left Francisca sleeping and snoring in the loft conversion and I went to the spare bedroom downstairs. That house had very thick internal fire doors. I had them especially installed so that they would be 30-minute fire-resistant. There were no windows open in the house that night.

Only a hurricane could close those doors.

I was lying in the bed slowly dozing off when suddenly the door went BANG as it slammed into the door frame.

'Is that the best you can do?' I attempted to out-banter whatever this entity was as I sat up in the bed.

My emotions had gone from disbelieving to fear and awareness to wary sarcasm.

Francisca came down:

'Kenny, the kids are asleep… Why did you slam the door like that?'

She ripped into me.

I told her I was nowhere near the door. I was still in the bed.

I did not know what to do. I was certain of one thing. This is a poltergeist.

I begin to do my own research, and I learn that poltergeists have about 20 moves and these range from making noises and moving objects right through to physical attacks such as scratching, hair pulling and choking a person. That is the full range of their armoury.

Some years earlier I had the pleasure of meeting the paranormal researcher Maurice Grosse, famous for his involvement in the Enfield poltergeist case from 1977 to 1979. He has been portrayed in several films and television series, including *The Enfield Haunting* (2015) by Timothy Spall and *The Conjuring 2* (2016) by Simon McBurney. He was a family friend of my mate Johnny Boy and his wife Shelley. He had since passed away, but if he had still been alive at the time, I would have sought his advice.

Having read my fair share of books on demonology over the years, I was aware of the various forms preternatural activity can take, such as demonic oppression, obsession and possession. The most serious of these being the first one. However, what was happening in our home was attached not to us, but to the building itself and this would come under the sphere of diabolical infestation. Another thing that made me lean towards this conclusion was that I recalled something very odd which happened way back in 1994.

The house was originally built in the 1930s and had not been modified very much in any way. The roof was the original structure and needed replacing. So, I hired one of Dad's friends, a roofer named Eric, to put a new lid on the place. I had not lived there for very long and had never used the loft. I think I popped my head up through the hatch once and closed it very quickly, because it was dark, dirty and it smelled like 1930. I never stored anything up there.

Eric began work on it and started to take off the old tiles. In the very far corner of the loft he discovered a very old, late 1920s bassinet pram which was quite big with huge wheels on it.

'Kenny, something doesn't make sense here,' he said.

'The roof is the original roof. The loft hatch is the original hatch, but the opening is far too small to get this pram through it,' he concluded.

'So whoever put this pram up here must have placed it in this loft before the roof went on and that was in 1930. I have never seen anything as strange as this before.

Was that pram placed in the loft by the people who first occupied the house? Did they maybe lose a child, and this was their way of preserving the memory? Could this be the reason why the poltergeist kicked off when my children entered the house? It was all very weird.

I decide to contact a good friend of mine in the church. Suddenly I am handed an address and instructed to write a letter. I have now been put in touch with the chief exorcist for the Westminster Diocese.

This is all very hush-hush.

I begin composing a very long note. It is not the actual address for him, but mail was forwarded from there. Their identity and their location are kept secret because if it gets into the hands of some Devil-worshipping nut job the exorcists can come under attack as has happened in the past.

I receive confirmation that my letter has arrived, and I am invited to a meeting. I am told I will be seen for an hour and then my wife will be met separately. For me to even go this far is serious.

I learn that at the root of everything is 'obsession, oppression and possession'.

'Has your family been into the occult?' I am asked.

'Have your parents ever been associated with occult practices?'

285

'Since this began in your house, who has been in that building?'

I reply that it is only various nannies from the babysitting agency.

'Have you found anything in that house that shouldn't be there?'

'Any objects that do not belong there? Possibly placed in less obvious places?'

I interrupted the priest.

'Father, are you telling me that cursed objects and things like hexes are real?' I asked him.

'Oh yes,' he replied.

He was trying to establish if the problem originated from us or from an external source. Above all he had to rule out if this was psychological in nature, i.e. was Francisca or myself a few cards short of a full deck?

No, this was real. Doors smashing shut and office chairs wheeling across the room are far from normal. I begin to understand that there could be nothing wrong with your house, but it could have something to do with an individual who enters the property and brings this malign entity with them.

We had been thinking about moving house so I start to look for a buyer. I move quickly.

In the street I meet an elderly woman who lives in the adjacent road near me. She actually knew the original owners from the 1930s.

'Did anyone ever die in that house?' I ask her, now not ruling anything out.

'Why, have you got a ghost? How exciting,' she replied.

It could have been an instinctive response or one with knowledge.

Then she confirmed that she did not know anyone who had passed away there.

At least that was now eliminated.

In my head, I remember what Eliot Kennedy had told me once about the studio we first used in Sheffield. Now that was a creepy building. The premises had been knocked from two buildings into one and included a labyrinth of corridors.

They would often come in to find faders on the mixer, which had been deliberately left in a precise position, but now were all down and the studio stool upside down with a matchbox balanced on one of the legs. He told me of an artist who came in to record one day, who was a bit of a new age type. She picked up a bad vibe in that place and announced that she had to leave and could not stay there one minute longer.

One day, Eliot received a call out of the blue from an old lady who enquired about the place, and she asked him if there was anything odd going on in there. She then told him that when it used to be to separate buildings many years ago, she had lived there until she was sixteen but couldn't wait to get out of there. She told him that someone was murdered in that building.

Eliot did some historical research into the old lady's story and sure enough, it was true. Someone had been murdered there and the person who committed the crime was hanged for it. Late one evening he told me about some of the spooky experiences he had experienced, and one thing about Eliot: he is brilliant at narrating a story. All I can say is that I never slept very well that night.

The priest decided that he would perform the solemn rite of exorcism on both Francisca and me. So, he arranged a time for us to meet him at the church and it was done according to the old rite in Latin. There was no levitating, strange languages or green projectile vomit like in the movies, although I am told this has been known to happen. It was simply peaceful and prayerful.

Things now pointed to the house, and the next move was for the priest to come there and say Mass and bless each room. We never managed to get this done because we found a buyer for the house. We sold it, lock, stock and barrel... Oh, and one resident poltergeist.

It was time to go.

39 Norfolk

A few people I knew had moved here. Not many. My brother Gary and his wife Jan lived in Suffolk. From the many books I had read over the years I was aware that in times past there were four big pilgrimage journeys: Jerusalem, Rome, Santiago de Compostela and... Walsingham, Norfolk – famous for its medieval shrine to the Virgin Mary. The magnificent old shrine and the priory no longer exist, because they were destroyed by Henry VIII in 1538. Part of the abbey ruins remains standing today, and pilgrims continue to go there despite Henry's attempts to end that.

All roads therefore led to Walsingham! Or Norwich, which is close enough.

I had been here once with an elderly Benedictine monk friend of mine named John Davies. When I told him that I was relocating the family to Norfolk, he reminded me of what I had told him at the time – 'I could never live somewhere like this, it's too quiet and out of the way.'

The arrival of my son Joe probably clinched the deal.

Collectively, though, we were now five, and Francisca really was concerned that we were in the wrong place to bring them up.

Certainly, a number of signs had been building up. Laugh at your peril, but the poltergeists left me aghast. Or maybe left me a ghost.

Plus, James and the new life. It felt the right thing at the right time. The London I grew up in did not exist anymore but even so, despite the rich influences on my upbringing, the experience of years told me that I did not want my kids growing up there.

What I thrived on was what I now feared – as a parent. Being mature.

In short, I had seen enough of various children not making it to teenage years. Stabbings and shootings were never as often reported as they were common. Francisca, from Cape

Town and all that brings, was honest enough to tell me that in the brief time that she had lived in London, she had noticed how much worse it had become in Finchley.

Francisca became frank.

So, I started to look. I began in Essex and then realised what was on offer if you went just an hour or so further afield. I wasn't looking for the *Famous Five,* but I really did want to extend their innocence. I wanted them to experience many of the things I didn't as a child. Yes, I had the local park as a kid but nothing like the great expanse of open countryside where you can ride your mountain bike for hours, filling your lungs with clean air, and really connect with nature. From an early age Angela was into horses and that is something there is no shortage of in Norfolk. Horse riding lessons were one of the first things she did after we moved. When I was a youngster the only time I saw a horse, it either had a policeman on the back of it or it was pulling a stiff to the cemetery.

Norfolk ticked a lot of boxes.

The crime rate was low. You got decent value and London was only a train away. I never feared leaving the capital. Now I breathe a sigh of relief when returning home.

It did take a little adjustment. I noticed often what Norfolk did not have rather than what it did – I called a mate of mine in London and told him to get up here straight away and open a Turkish restaurant. There were none.

Now six years on there is one, only a fifteen-minute drive from our house. And where did they come from? Good old North London.

I had to make the transition, too, from being a Londoner always in a rush to standing in a queue for a counter where people could readily exchange their life stories before they were served. But that was what we signed up for. It was different: people drive slowly, eat slowly, I bet they even sleep slowly.

Physically moving was horrendous! This was serious.

I had no idea how much stuff I had kept. That loft really did hold secrets.

And a lot of crap.

Of course, packing up and then unpacking took that extra bit of time as I lingered, flicking through my archive and discovered the wonderful *Blues & Soul magazine* and *Music Week*, plus zillions of records and books which I had loved at the time but had temporarily parked as I moved onto the next intellectual theory or musical discovery. I realise that I am not alone in having such sentiments during a house move but the enormity of the exodus and the volume of hoarding was a massive moment of reflection. To this day, much of that is still in storage.

On 5 August 2015 we finally made the move.

In embracing something new and seeking a fresh tranquillity that was in keeping with all the philosophies that I had accumulated in my personal study of life, I really now was saying goodbye to so much of what I knew.

And within 20 days of moving, I was also saying goodbye to so much of what that life meant.

Francisca and I were in the car, about to go on our wedding anniversary night out when the phone rang. It was almost the call that I had received many times… except it wasn't.

I understand what fight or flight mode was.

'Everything OK?' I asked as I had a million times before.

'No, it's not,' came the reply.

But I *had* had the conversation so many times.

'Your dad is not good,' the nurse said.

They told me he was not responding well and that they were going to keep him there. When I realised that he had not had much to drink for the last 24 hours I told them, 'No – call an ambulance.'

They insisted they could look after him.

I disagreed.

We went out to the restaurant, quickly ate something and came home. I packed some clothes and my rosary beads in a way that now sadly seemed all too familiar, and left for London at the crack of dawn.

I called my friend Carol because, of course, as of 20 days previously, I no longer had anywhere to stay in London. I had owned a house there just three weeks before. I realised quickly that Dad had acquired pneumonia. And that he had got it from the nursing home.

Gary met me there and together we sat by Dad's bed.

It was obvious very quickly that Dad was in a bad way.

He was in and out of consciousness and the doctor told us that he was not going to make it. Late that night I went back to Carol's, fearing the worst in the morning.

The next day, I went straight back in and never returned to Carol's. I couldn't take the chance. I would keep a bedside vigil and sleep in my car.

'He's not going to make it,' Gary and I reiterated to each other.

He was slipping in and out.

Somehow he hung on, but the quality of life was gone.

The end was near.

We stayed by his bedside the whole night. Eventually Gary had to go home to get some rest, but I had gone past the point of sleeping so I stayed there.

By the Saturday afternoon, Dad was still halfway between this world and the next yet I now faced one of the biggest calls of my career. I was due to perform that night in Birmingham and I hadn't slept at all. I was not in a good way.

I really was not, under any circumstances, the kind of person to cancel. Promoters put a lot of hard work and money into their shows, and they really lose a lot if you let them down. I couldn't do that to this promoter. I was also scared. There was no way in the world that I was capable of driving to Birmingham and back in this state, and life had a way of dishing out cruel blows. What are the chances that Dad would go the moment I left? Who knows? I prayed about it, and like in Lourdes with Mum, I had this inner feeling that Dad was not about to go just yet... he had more time. I had to dig deep and trust.

I called my mate Chad.

He is the guy who will always come. Whatever the mess, whatever the circumstances, I could rely on him. He simply had a heart of gold and has always got my back.

'I need to get to Birmingham,' I told him. 'I'm not with it, Chad. I am in a terrible state. I need to get to the gig, straight in and out, but I can't do it myself.'

'No worries, Ken, I'll be there,' he replied.

I gave my dad a kiss. He was now unconscious and remained that way.

'Dad, don't leave without me being here. I'll be back by your side in a few hours.'

Chad turned up at Barnet Hospital with Mason. They had only got back that day from a holiday in Ibiza. I grabbed some clothes from the boot of my car along with my backing tracks on a CD and off we went to Birmingham.

The set was only about 45 minutes. The promoter could not believe I had made it and did not expect me to be there under the circumstances. I got through the gig on autopilot... It felt very strange, like some kind of dream, which I guess was a combination of the extreme stress and not having slept. Chad got me straight back in the car and sped me back to London.

Thankfully, I made it safely back to Barnet Hospital. There was no change in Dad's condition. He had waited for me. But no change obviously meant we were still hanging on.

Racing back from Birmingham was an anxious dash, worried in my head that I wouldn't get there in time. When I arrived and everything was as it had been, that event just became a blur – something which hadn't taken place and if it did, it felt like a long time ago.

Time went from racing to erasing.

Even my new surroundings and home in Norfolk were almost something that hadn't happened. To set off in pursuit of a new life and upbringing for the children and then to be tearing back within the first month was not bad luck, but certainly was bad timing. I have asked myself many times if somehow Dad had got the message that we had gone, even though he retained little, and his own mind was frozen in time. You really do not know what connection they have when dementia or Alzheimer's arrives. My experience to date was that he could go way back into his past, but anything recent was a struggle. So even if I told him that we had moved then he would not retain it, but you just don't know, do you? When you get to that stage in life as people start to pass away with more frequency than in your younger years you often hear talk of those on the brink of dying hanging on just enough until an event in their loved ones' lives passed.

I was soon enough back in my car, but only for a few hours of broken sleep. I knew the next morning that the end was very near. It was not necessarily that Dad had deteriorated overnight but you just knew it was only a matter of time. I recall Uncle Leslie himself saying to me, 'He's just going now,' as I arrived to say goodbye to my grandad just as my career was on the cusp of getting going.

Now I knew that Dad was in the same place.

Most of the time I was alone with Dad in that hospital room. People came up to see him, to say their goodbyes... My sister, my brother Steve and his wife Deb, but they left and I was alone again for hours. Just praying, watching and waiting. I spoke to him at length. In reality, I don't know if I spoke to him or at him. I have no idea if he could hear me, but I like to think he *could*.

'Dad, how did we get here so fast?' were my disbelieving words.

And I couldn't figure it all out.

'Wasn't it yesterday that I was about twelve years old, sitting next to you in the car and you were taking me to the boxing gym?'

They say that life flashes before you when you are dying. I was in permanent flashback knowing that Dad was leaving us.

'It seems just a moment ago that I was sixteen and we were pulling down some of the nastiest ceilings in London and working on building sites together...'

I was really struggling. I accepted that he was on his way out of this world but again, measuring that passage of time cut me wide open.

How did we get here so fast? I felt cheated that it was going to be over in a blink but enriched, too, that we had spent our lives together.

Dad would often say... 'Son, enjoy your life, because it goes by fast, and it's over like that.' With the word *that* he would

293

click his fingers. That was etched into my memory and now here we were, and it does indeed *go by fast*.

Every parent tells a child to enjoy life. I was now that parent *and* that child and would inevitably tell my own the same. Time had raced along but I had never taken any day for granted. My faith made certain of that.

On the Monday my brother Gary returned to the hospital. Together we kept vigil by his bedside. This, though, was Dad's last day.

I had been prepared for it for over a decade. There is no preparation for it.

He passed away in the early hours of 25 August 2015.

'Rest easy, Champ,' said Gary, as he closed Dad's eyes.

A new house. A new baby.

A friend had reminded me of the old saying.

And it was correct.

But also a nod and a wink to the past. And exorcising it.

Dad always told me that if there were ever a fire in the house, to 'grab those cases'.

Inside one, the insurance documents, in the other his Masonic stuff.

In Catholicism, Dad joined with Mum. Finally closing the door on his 43 years of being a Mason. Many years before, at the age of thirteen and out of curiosity, I sneaked a look inside this case.

The ceremonial white gloves, the infamous apron and some mysterious books… the lot. I had been in possession of it for a long time while Dad was in the nursing homes, but out of respect to him I never opened it until he passed away.

At the moment he had been baptised, all this was over. You can't be a Catholic and a Freemason! Despite the fact that Masonry would like you to think that the two can coexist, they are in fact ideologically and theologically irreconcilable.

The former was more important to me than the latter.

It was time to end this.

I took to the wood-burner and made a decision instantly that I had been thinking about for some time. Whilst that reads as a contradiction, it took a spontaneous moment to end something which had been building up within me for some time.

In went the apron and the white gloves.

They burned with a furious bright blue flame. Gone!

It had meant something to my dad but now, where he was resting, I knew that he would understand. He came late in the day to conversion. He would have accepted that there was no place for this in my memories.

Jude David is born 9 December 2016 – and named after the patron saint of impossible causes and my best friend David Sassoon.

Obviously, Dad is no longer there to share the moment.

I was over the moon at Jude's birth but that was it for now! That big family I wanted had produced one more than I had expected. It was time to take a break and start subscribing to Netflix! Of course, like any new dad (though not so new at this point) I was learning on the go and fast. That meant understanding that kids can be lethal, too.

I love wrestling. I love play-wrestling like my dad did with me. One day before the move, I had placed my head on Christina's belly and took a finger right in the eye.

'Oh no, my eye,' I cried out, as I rolled around in pain.

But we had to go. It was time for pre-school, so I drove with just half of my vision, somehow able to park the car. My cornea had been sheared off by her fingernail. When I got back home, I handed the children to Francisca and ran as fast as I could to the nearest tube station. As the wind caught my eye, I could feel the front of my eyeball flapping about. On the tube I was writhing around in my seat like a complete nut job. The pain was off the Richter scale.

I finally made it to Moorfields Eye Hospital near Old Street, London, where they immediately administered some anaesthetic eye drops. This was instant Heaven.

For a month, my right eye felt like I was looking through a crystal chandelier. Only after three separate trips to a specialist did it begin to heal. I had learned the hard way. When play-wrestling with kids you really need safety goggles and a hard hat.

But my extended family was equally my world and to have neither Dad nor Dave Sassoon in my life for Jude's birth hurt.

Clearly, I was in a whirlwind of emotions at losing those I loved and loving those who were left. Every high with Jude came with that tinge of sadness. I was over the moon with the family. Norfolk had very quickly become the correct decision. That just left the career...

2016 will certainly go down as full on.

I was weighing up what to do next musically beyond gigging and writing when I got a call out of the blue from Marcus Vere.

I had met him a few times down the years. We were stablemates at Chrysalis. Would I like to join Living In A Box?

I didn't know what to make of it – if it was a good or a bad thing, if I looked desperate or savvy. The band had a few storming hits just before I broke through – songs like 'Living In A Box' and 'Room In Your Heart'.

You do get approaches every now and then. I was probably now at my most flexible and pragmatic, and concluded that there was nothing to lose after I spoke with him.

'Tich and I would love you to join us,' he said. 'You are the only singer we thought of.'

And we connected. He was very intelligent, eloquent and extremely clued up. He knew this would be a good fit.

'I need to know why Richard Darbyshire is not doing it.' I aired my only real concern now. 'I have the maximum respect for him'.

'Richard is out – he doesn't want to do it anymore,' Marcus explained.

Richard had been the original other member of the band, and such a great singer, but the band was no longer where he wanted to be – and it had been some time.

So, I was in. I didn't think of it as a career move but I knew it could be good. It just felt right.

'Let's get together and try some tracks out,' he suggested.

And it was like forming a new band again back when you were just starting out. We were off and it worked so well. So, you had Marcus Vere and Anthony Critchlow (aka Tich) the original members and now me on lead vocals in place of Richard. I got on so well with the guys and the songs were so good, that I knew this was going to be fun. Career move or not, this was something I wanted to do purely because I knew I would enjoy it.

I was essentially a 90s artist and Living In A Box were pretty much perceived as from the previous decade. That meant I was reaching a new audience and sometimes the band was, too. I

297

found myself getting onto 80s festival line-ups now which was a good place to be.

I also knew that I was singing as well as ever – just with a lot less hair.

And so, Living In A Box featuring Kenny Thomas were up and running, and the beauty of it was the freedom. I could still gig alone or with the band or somebody else. Before his death, Mark Aaron had previously asked me to do a big band night with a seventeen-piece orchestra and deliver what was essentially a crooner set.

Why not? Do what feels right. With no record company to stand in your way.

That is where my head was at. I was up for new challenges and even new genres.

So, when Laurie Jay, the former manager of Billy Ocean, introduced me to the pianist and record producer Wayne Brown, suggesting that we make a record together, I jumped at the opportunity. We recorded a piano vocal album of classic covers but with a jazz vibe. Choosing songs that you would not ordinarily expect to hear in that style. We called ourselves The Thomas Brown Affair and the album title track was 'Just the Two of Us', a song originally sung by Bill Withers on the Grover Washington Jr album of 1980 named *Winelight*.

The album was well received, getting airplay from Jazz FM and this in turn generated a number of gigs for us. I really enjoyed performing with Wayne, who became a dear friend of mine. Making that album was a whole new experience. I was singing songs I would not normally attempt to tackle and recording them live in one take.

As always with my career and my life in general, tragedy reared its ugly head once again and all future plans for our jazz duo sadly came to an end when Wayne passed away from a brain tumour. He was one of the best pianists I have ever worked with. A very humble but extremely talented musician who taught me so much in a very short space of time.

As wonderful as this new lease of life was in the Living in a Box band, I think it means more than this. I know everything happens for a reason and Marcus walked into my life at actually the right time.

Neither of us knew what lay ahead, but he was to play a significant and hugely supportive role in what was to come.

By the end of 2016, Francisca and I received confirmation of something that really would change our lives forever. At the end of a year which had tested us like no other emotionally, we were thrown one huge curve ball that remains with us today and will always now shape every single day that we are here.

We had no warning and no idea.

Retrospectively, I have often asked myself about the time everyone was certain that Francisca had miscarried but in fact hadn't.

We were about to face our greatest challenge ever and there was little knowledge or education with which to proceed.

Christina was seriously ill.

I promise to tell you the truth, the whole truth and nothing but the truth. From this point on, I can't quite do that. Everything I write that follows is in fact, the truth, the partial truth and nothing but the truth.

I simply cannot take you through every detail. I have to summarise and I must omit. This is largely because I want to protect the identity of certain individuals in the world of medicine who have asked to remain anonymous. But also to safeguard my family from incurring the wrath of the National Health Service who have already caused us so much unnecessary emotional distress over the last few years.

In short, if I had done everything their way, my daughter would not be here. Some names have been changed to protect the guilty. To be clear, though, I was never fighting an individual, more a system.

Everything had changed overnight. A social worker would begin randomly turning up at my house. I would learn of doctors in America who had spoken out against a certain narrative and then had been found mysteriously suicided.

I knew one thing. This would define me.

Everything had been going so well.

I was gigging with Living In A Box, performing at concerts like Let's Rock, Rewind and Flashback, plus I was doing my own shows. We were enjoying the new house and the first full summer, making friends and going to the beach. Life in Norfolk was starting to take shape.

Except, of course, people were still dying on me.

Dad had gone in the first month after the move.

Mark Aaron had passed away in the January.

My good friend Silky, the former footballer Barry Silkman, was struggling, too. He lost his wife Alison to cancer. She had already reintroduced me to the idea that there might be alternative ways to treat cancer. She was using various naturopathic medicines and Silky was regularly taking her to

Israel for revolutionary experimental treatments which did extend her life. She was a true fighter who never once gave up and kept a positive mindset all the way. I didn't realise it at the time but seeing the way she handled her illness made a huge impression on me. It greatly influenced the way I dealt with the battle that lay ahead of me.

But then on 14 May 2016, my best friend Dave died, too.

He had gone in literally a matter of seconds from a heart attack. He was only 47 years old.

'Have you heard about Dave?' my friend Bradley Isaacs said. 'It's bad news.'

'No, what's happened to him? Is he in hospital?' I replied.

'No, it's worse than that.'

'What do you mean worse than that? Tell me.'

'Mate, Dave's dead.'

I dropped to my knees, face down in the hotel room bed, still clutching the phone. I had sort of been prepared for Dad, Mark and James, but not Dave. No, no, no. Dave had been in my life *all* my life and even since the move he was still coming to my house, and we continued to laugh at the stuff that made us giggle when we were six or seven. We were that tight together.

I phoned Dave's Auntie Freda. She was in bits and my mind was all over the place as I tried to process what had happened. And now I had to get my act together and gig that very same evening in Birmingham with my good friend Jocelyn Brown. To say I was on autopilot is an understatement. She put her arms around me and somehow we got through. Jocelyn has had her fair share of losses over the years, and she is a very spiritual person with a deep faith. So with words of great wisdom, she helped me find the inner strength I needed to step onto the stage that night. I can't remember anything else about the gig except getting back to the hotel and then shooting off to London once more the following day.

I hadn't even got to tell Dave that we were expecting again – Jude arrived in December. And I always told Dave everything first and it was him that I went to when both Mum and Nan died. We literally were blood brothers, having done that thing as a kid where you prick each other's skin with a knife and then pressed our hands together!

In London I spent some time with Dave's family, his grandmother Myra, Freda, and his mum Angela. All of us devastated and in total shock. I sat there for a while in his bedroom, where he passed away: this made it all very real and final. Some days I still can't believe that he has gone.

I couldn't bring any of these people back, but overnight found myself in a situation where I could alter the fate of my little girl's life.

By October 2016, Christina had begun attending nursery but by Halloween and Bonfire Night, she simply was not the same person. Francisca took her and Angela to the big display nearby and she kept asking to be picked up. Walking was exhausting her.

We had never known her like this and, of course, the first time it happens you think that it is a one-off, but I have genuinely never seen someone go downhill so fast, and I had lost more than my fair share already in the previous fifteen months.

The next week I am driving her and Angela in the morning to nursery and school and she is sobbing all the way. Again she wants me to carry her.

This is now pretty much constant.

I take them to panto at Christmas, and she is asleep by the end of it. When the kids go trampolining, she can't keep up with it. It was clear that something was terribly wrong.

'Something is not right,' Francisca says. 'She is not walking properly.'

'Maybe she had hurt herself on the trampoline,' I offer knowing that, even if this were true, there had to be more to it. Her walk had started to appear very unusual; she was slightly dragging her right leg.

She was exhausted all through that Christmas.

By January 2017, having finally given up hope that it was a blip and having accepted that this was becoming worse, we went for a blood test and followed that with a specialist orthopaedic doctor who took some X-rays.

Nothing showed up – he couldn't see any problems in the hip or limbs.

'Something else is going on here, I am going to refer you to a neurologist,' he concluded.

I knew what that meant. Her muscles were not functioning properly but there was no evidence on a scan showing that. That meant it was quite possibly coming from the nervous system or brain and, worst-case scenario, that was going to be a lot harder to deal with than the bones of the lower body.

This was not getting any better anytime soon. But of course, life had to go on. We had three other little ones and I was trying still to gig. We waited for the appointment to see the neurologist, but this was not going to be forthcoming overnight.

By 5 February, I was at Butlins with Living In A Box for their sell-out 80s Weekender. While I was at Skegness Francisca called me to say that she had noticed that the limp was worse, the leg clearly was not right, and then her right hand had begun to weaken to the point of barely functioning. She simply couldn't hold objects properly. The hand was that weak.

I knew I needed to get home and get her to the hospital. I couldn't wait any longer for that appointment.

'Marcus, I have got a massive problem with Christina. I am going to need to move quickly.'

I warned him that gigs with Living In A Box might be up in the air. I also knew from that very first conversation that he was somebody I could talk to. I had no idea how generous and supportive he would become in time and indeed, remains so to this day.

'I need to organise a brain scan,' I confided.

'I can get you someone in the next 24 hours. It will cost a few bob, but we can make it happen.'

I had no choice. I was worried out of my mind.

I returned from the weekender in Skegness late that Sunday night, grabbed a few hours' sleep and the next morning rushed Christina to Norwich Hospital.

'She needs to be seen now,' I pleaded.

She was getting worse by the hour.

'Can you scan her today?' I asked.

303

'Not sure if we can do that today,' came the standard reply.

'Can you do it?' I repeated. 'If not, I am going to London now and will have it done privately.'

'OK let's get her seen by a doctor straight away,' they replied.

They did all the usual blood tests and observations along with a lengthy eye test. Christina complained that her vision was frizzy. If they had asked, I would have surmised so.

As you might expect, and perhaps you have this experience yourself, waiting around was now the norm. Hospitals are under enormous pressure and do their absolute best but there is nothing speedy about it. We all can relate to that feeling that 'surely the next name that they call will be yours', and more often than not it isn't. We were left hovering by her bed for hours.

I knew – because I had seen her rapid decline, and what it was leaving behind that time was something that we were running out of.

In the end, I had to stay overnight in the hospital. The next morning, they would do the scan.

Afterwards, we waited for hours and kept asking if they knew the results. They simply said they were waiting for her blood results to come back and would then tell us when they had all the information.

The way the doctors scurried around and talked among themselves about Christina felt very ominous. The lack of communication with us, her parents, and the hours of silence made me feel that 'no news was bad news'.

And then the verdict:

'Can you and Mrs Thomas please come…? We will see you in another room in 20 minutes,' someone asked.

We had by now been addressed by so many nameless people. You knew the verdict was coming. You could have cut the air with a knife – it felt sinister. Their cold, unemotional composure added to the drama and sense of gloom.

'The scan is showing a mass,' one of the team began and I instantly understood the terminology.

'Where is it?' I asked.

304

'In the middle of the brain, on the brainstem,' the consultant confirmed.

Then I began asking questions. Way too many for their liking.

'Are you in medicine?' another asked as their guard began to rise.

'No,' I answered.

'You are speaking with a lot of knowledge.' The consultant raised an eyebrow.

Generally, I found the people skills appalling – distant and icy. It reminded me of when Mum was dying, and nobody could use that word in front of me. But their language did change when they realised that I was *not* one of them but clearly had a greater level of understanding. They knew to be careful and not to trip up, but they could also talk more directly.

'We will be transferring Christina by ambulance to Addenbrooke's Hospital in Cambridge tonight. They are more specialised and better equipped to deal with this.'

Francisca and I were then left alone in that room to cry, to hold each other, and to try and get our heads around the most devastating news any parent could hear.

I knew we were in for the long haul and that a million more cagey conversations would follow. There were countless hours potentially ahead in hospital corridors.

For the time being, we were done with Norwich Hospital. I went home and grabbed some clothes and toiletries for Christina and myself and made my way back to the hospital. She was transferred immediately by ambulance to Addenbrooke's, the reported leader in this field. They weren't messing about – blue lights on and full speed all the way. In the ambulance I felt like my whole world was falling apart. I was literally hanging over the edge of the abyss, holding on by my fingertips, trying to keep it together and not completely lose my mind. My faith was tested like never before. Christina needed me in her corner for the fight ahead and collapsing into a heap of nothingness was not an option.

I looked over at my little girl during that journey and she gave me one of her smiles. In fact, she was smiling all the way as if nothing was happening, unaware of how serious this was.

When I used to carry her into nursery, I would always tell her, 'I love you so much,' and she would reply, 'I love you big much.' This has now become a saying in our family. So, when she smiled at me that night and told me that she *loved me big much*, that was my lifeline to sanity. I held onto those words and prayed like never before.

When we got there and settled Christina, they had already given her steroids. I left the room and cried and cried. I had to compose myself. There was a lot more to come. Nor did I want Christina to see me that way.

This was my lowest point to date – my own personal Ground Zero. The world was passing me by very, very quickly.

Christina then starts to feel sick, so they give her an injection. They are working as fast as they can. She still found time to smile like she always did and has no idea how sick she is. I know, though – they are running observations on her all the time.

I know I am here for a while, so I make up a bed next to her.

The surgeon came down to see me:

'You know about the tumour?' he asks.

'Yes,' I reply.

'It is a high-grade glioma, a diffused tumour,' he told me.

'You know we can't operate on this tumour, don't you?'

That left me staring reality in the face.

Except nobody was saying it out loud.

Christina's condition is terminal.

Our biggest option was gone. They couldn't operate on the tumour. That left radiation and chemotherapy as the next option. My guard was already up.

In the middle of the night, the nurse comes:

'We have got to wake her up,' she says.

'No, you can't,' I object. 'You've done all your observations. She has been pulled from pillar to post in the last 24 hours. She's not dying right now, is she? Let her sleep. Come back in two or three hours.'

I am beginning to stand up to what I know in my gut is wrong.

The next day, Christina tries to walk through the hospital. None of it is good. She is limping terribly and all around her are emaciated children who have lost their hair.

'This is Hell on earth,' I tell Francisca on the phone. 'We've got to get her out of here.'

Christina is now also very tearful. I have never known her so affected. I have never seen such a depressed four-year-old.

By the Wednesday of that week, Francisca comes up to the hospital. We are both ushered in to speak to one of the doctors.

'We can't operate,' she reiterates. 'It's terminal.'

'How long do you think she has got?' Francisca asks.

'Probably around six months,' she replies.

'Your only option is chemotherapy,' she continues.

'Let me stop you there,' I interrupt.

My tone is rising.

'We're not going for chemotherapy... Can you cure this tumour? No. So, why do it? Chemo would at best only manage the tumour and maybe buy more time but with increased suffering. Her last memories of this world are going to be nice things – not being stuck in this hospital with no hair and no immune system.'

The doctor did not know what to say. I know she can't have been expecting my level of knowledge or this amount of confrontation so early. I was showing her the courtesy of saving her time and cutting out the bullshit. The reality was that I had seen too much chemo and could recall no positive memory of it.

'I am taking her home,' I told her.

'But you really need to meet with the paediatric oncologist first to discuss the treatment options,' she tried to protest.

'There are no treatment options available here as far as I can tell and she is so depressed that she would be far better off at home,' I replied.

'She is on steroids,' the doctor continued.

'No problem, give me the steroids,' I concluded.

I knew that if they couldn't cure it, then they were simply managing death.

Managing death.

That was not for me.

I tell them that we will leave the next day – the Thursday. I am due to be gigging that night. It remains the only time in my career that I have pulled a show.

Instead, Christina is home and instantly a lot happier – that in itself has to be a lot healthier for you. I had already started to form a small plan whilst at Addenbrooke's. I already had a fair bit of knowledge from Irena, Alison and Graham Chandler (one of the doctors who taught me Chinese medicine). He had been managing his own cancer for years and defying all the odds given to him. So, I begin making phone calls and arranging my next move.

I know that I have to get my hands on certain immune-enhancing formulas such as Essiac, and other natural herbs like soursop and black seed oil to help with inflammation. So, I begin to research. I am already aware of what these can do to cancer cells. I start to make calls.

By now, the right side of Christina's mouth is drooping, and her speech is slurring very badly. Her right hand has lost its function and her right eyelid is not closing properly. Her behaviour dramatically altered, too. Clinically she was deteriorating fast, and the negative symptoms were increasing by the hour. At this rate I was beginning to wonder if the prognosis of six months might have been an overestimation.

I was contacted by a record producer friend of mine named Danny Kirsch, who is good friends with Chico, the former *X Factor* contestant. Chico is very clued up on alternative medicine. Chico tells Danny that I should visit a particular lady he knows who lives up north and that she will have some of the herbal meds I'm looking for.

So, before I'd even left Addenbrooke's, Chico made an introduction and I contacted the lady, and yes, she had exactly what I needed. Very early on the Friday morning my friend Andy Blake drove me up. I had not slept much all that week so I was definitely in no fit state to drive.

The herbal meds she had were a good start, but I needed to know more, and do more, and act quickly.

I start to talk privately with doctors, nutritionists, homeopaths and specialists in the field of alternative cancer therapy.

'Should sugar be cut out of her diet?' I ask.

The reply is absolutely, and that cancer thrives on it.

So, sugar goes – as do all dairy, animal fats and protein. We move to a more vegan, plant-based diet. I begin using my knowledge of Chinese medicine, focusing in particular on formulas derived from mushrooms. I get hold of some pure Ling zhi (Reishi mushroom, also known as Ganoderma lucidum) along with Lion's mane (Hericium erinaceus). These are good for the brain and the immune system. All the time I am checking in with other practitioners and consulting my books to determine dosages and making sure there were no contraindications.

I was advised to buy a water filter from the US to make sure Christina's drinking water is as pure as possible, also altering its pH value with drops. This was to make sure her body became less acidic. We incorporated a juicing regime, fresh organic leafy greens along with superfoods.

Christina took all of this in her stride and never complained or threw a tantrum as you would expect from a four-year-old. What was most amazing was the first time I gave her a capsule to swallow, she did it no problem. This was a mini game-changer and made it possible for us to get the much-needed nutrients into her system. It was as if in some way she knew we were engaged in the biggest fight of our lives, and she was ready to fight, too.

All the while we observe the golden rule, that is to *heal not harm*.

I am following strict guidelines and professional advice, talking to lots of people. The more I learned from them, the more they pass the conversation on. There was an incredible amount of insight out there from people who had experience ahead of me or who had the curiosity to believe there might be another way.

We needed a Plan B.

Over the years I stayed in touch with two of the girls I used to work with at British Telecom, my dear friends Caroline Fennelly and Debra Little. Plan B would come surprisingly via Debra. She mentioned Christina's situation to her friend Karen Bagnell, who happened to mention it to someone else during a business meeting in London. Quite randomly that person said:

'Your friend needs to talk to an Israeli guy called Ilan Slazenger.'

She took down Ilan's number and passed it on to Debra.

Debra then rang me and told me to call him.

I already know at this point that Israel's cancer knowledge was second to none. The first thing that Silky did when Alison fell ill was to take her to Tel Aviv. He often talked of their groundbreaking work.

I called Ilan and we spoke on the phone for a very long time. He has a vast amount of knowledge about medicine, nutrition and alternative cancer treatments. He asked me about all that I was doing with Christina, and he then began to tell me about a number of other things I should be using such as Poly-MVA (a lipoic acid mineral complex specifically created for gliomas). We also discussed vitamins and minerals, optimum dosages and her diet. This was a real eye-opener and a pivotal moment for me.

'You will get a package in the next 48 hours,' he said at the end of the call.

He was true to his word.

Ilan was sent to us at the right time, and he has stayed right by our side in the battle. Sharing his knowledge, giving us support and forming a solid friendship. In time Ilan and I would make inroads into whole new areas of alternative cancer therapies as we made contact with professors and doctors in some of the most far-flung corners of the world. Always sharing what we have learned with those in most need of it.

People began to approach *me*. There was a lot of info which seemed lost in an underworld of knowledge, but I knew was vital to get out there generally but would help me specifically.

I was now running an intense regime. Diet totally changed – even to the point that one recommendation led me to Germany to specifically buy a certain type of juicer. We began mixing stuff raw to extract the enzymes. I started to implement some stuff specifically to detox the body.

Then I began to share my info and get introduced to other parents, most of whom seemed savvier than many of the doctors I have spoken to. Social media was an instant journey of discovery and a little overwhelming. There is certainly more openness. I have already worked out that the professionals had a certain narrative that came from their *Big Pharma* training and education. There were risks for them not toeing the line. Steve Finan, though, soon warned me to be more careful on Facebook with the things I said. The doctors knew that there was a network out there all talking to one another. This was not like the old days when what the doctor told you was assumed to be the gospel truth and you blindly followed it. No, the world has changed and I was talking to other parents who were reading and sharing scientific peer-reviewed papers from PubMed and elsewhere, and they were very aware of other treatments available abroad. The internet is responsible for this change. That secret deposit of medical knowledge is no longer held tightly in the hands of the few who decide how much of it they choose to drip-feed you with. Now it's in the hands of the people and that gives them something that was previously unavailable – options.

There were also some crackpots. One guy told me that he could cure cancer in 21 days. Whilst you do look at anything and everything, I did ask him why he didn't have a Nobel Prize.

Soon I was back with them at Addenbrooke's.

Francisca and I sat there in the consulting room with at least five of them, all armed with their notebooks and Christina's scans. The paediatric oncologist, their top surgeon and some other medical professionals, all very keen to see where we were at. This might be intimidating for some, but not for me. I grew up on an estate where confrontation was a weekly thing and standing your ground was the default position.

My mind was already ahead of them. My position hadn't changed – they couldn't cure the tumour and had forecast a relatively short timeline ahead. I would take my chances and do it my way.

'About the steroids,' the consultant began.

'I have weened her off them,' I interrupted.

'I was going to tell you to do that,' he added.

'I've done that already,' I reiterated.

'We understand that you both wish to leave things as they are and are not in favour of doing chemotherapy?' he continued.

'No, that is correct. We have been told that she only has around six months to live and chemotherapy would only extend her life by a further three months at best. So, we'll take the six months and not put her through that,' I replied.

'We do think carrying out a biopsy would be a good idea so that we can determine the exact nature of the tumour and the genetic profile.'

'I'm right in thinking that doing a biopsy on a tumour in the brainstem carries certain risks, does it not?' I quizzed them.

At this point the surgeon stepped in and reassured us that he had conducted many biopsies on tumours such as this and the risks were minimal. Christina would spend one night in ICU after the procedure and then be able to return home.

'OK so let me get this straight, you do a biopsy which does have certain risks attached to it and then once that is done you still do not have a treatment that can cure this disease. So other than gathering medical information about the tumour, the point of the biopsy is exactly what? Can you show me another child like Christina with the same kind of tumour, which you have cured?'

'Cure is not a word we would use,' the oncologist flat-batted me back.

'Well, cure is the word I use because anything less than a cure is of no use to us and that is why we will not be subjecting Christina to a biopsy or chemotherapy. Unless you can prove it has a high probability of curing her and can show me evidence that you have achieved this with other patients, we intend to let her live out her remaining time in peace with quality of life,' I concluded.

'What would you do if this was your child?' Francisca asked.

This is the million-dollar question that no oncologist wants to hear.

There was no response. Just a mumble and a nervous British shuffling of papers.

They couldn't answer the question, or were trained not to.

'Mr and Mrs Thomas, we'll accept your decision and I have to say it is very brave of you both to have made this choice. In fact it is very refreshing to hear it, because most parents in your position ask us to do everything we can to save their child even when we know the outcome is still the same,' he said.

'We will arrange for the palliative care team to do a home visit and make sure you get all the help you need in the coming months. Of course, we are here should you change your minds and wish to consider what we have discussed today.'

We returned home with Christina knowing we had made a tough decision, but it was the right decision, albeit a heartbreaking one. We naturally assumed that they respected the choice we had made and that the matter would end there. We were wrong on that one.

That was the small amount of mistrust I was holding.

Of course, once the doubt sets in, it never goes away. I remained angry for some time. I was heartbroken, too, but sharp in my mind. Engaged with adrenaline and with a lot of information to process, I knew that I had to be on it.

A huge amount of me said at the time that I will need to recall this moment. Nobody actually had the balls to come out and say just how aggressive this cancer was. They simply used the term 'high-grade'. But judging from the poor prognosis and the pace with which the symptoms were marching ahead I knew it was bad. When I had digested that without hearing those words, I didn't actually eat for two days.

Communication was passive, almost cowardly – I lost count of the times I was handed a pamphlet. Disease and symptom management were at play. Time was always being bought.

Not by me – I knew it was in short supply.

I was never comfortable with the steroids that she was given and less so with the people around Christina. I did not want to see chemo going into her veins or tubes up her nose and remember that image forever.

We told Angela that Christina was not well, and to this day she has never mentioned it to her. Both of their lives had now changed forever. I knew from very early on that there was something different about Christina. I recall once, when she was around three years old, she ran to the door as I was leaving for a gig and gave me a big hug and said, 'I love you, Dada,' to which I replied, 'Christina, there's something very special about you, I just haven't worked it out yet.'

I have now.

Genetically, I always felt very close to her. We connected in a special way from the moment she was born. She was always the little comedian and when this rocked our world I thought that of any of the children she might be able to handle it.

But there was a long way ahead. And it was going to be our way.

The hospital could do nothing. It had echoes of when Francisca was pregnant and fell poorly and the doctors asked if we wanted *that* test for Down's Syndrome.

'No, we don't,' I had simply replied.

If she were, what would we have done?

Simply show her all the love in the world.

I needed to alert school, obviously. The left hand needed to know what the right hand was doing.

'Christina is facing the biggest fight of her life,' I told them, well aware that her life was at this point very young indeed.

Then everything descends on you.

The palliative care team visit, we are taken to see a children's hospice, the Norwich oncology doctor comes round, accompanied by some of the Addenbrooke's team. Our home had gone from a happy and peaceful place to an overwhelmingly invaded consulting room by medical people who all wanted to question and examine, prod and poke, and generally impose their plans on us. This was followed by a strategically placed social worker.

'Did you get my letter?' the latter asked.

'No,' I said, 'but come in anyway.'

I wanted to talk to them in the same way I had the religious cult Bible-bashers who knocked on the door when I was a kid!

I knew exactly why they were there. They are like the police. They were checking up on me because I had dared to reject the system.

I felt like a marked man. They, of course, were only doing their job, which they pretty much had taken as far as they could.

Christina is really uncomfortable with all these people around her and on many occasions had some of the biggest freak-out meltdowns I had ever seen. It was too much for her. I guess in her little mind she was trying to work out what was going on and why she was, all of a sudden, the centre of so much unusual and invasive attention. This resulted in Christina's sleep

315

pattern being affected. She would wake up at least three times each night and this pattern continued for three years.

The social worker was a nice enough person, but we knew she was closely observing things and checking us out, no doubt reporting back to head office. After all, we had refused the medical treatment on offer, but we had not refused life-saving medical treatment. Saving her life is something they were unable to do.

The palliative care team were all very good people, but they were in an end-of-life race, seeing tragedy every day to the point that it desensitises emotions. This was not their child and that was met with an often mechanical response. Simply, they were able to put the sad face on. You clearly get that vibe.

Visits were now almost daily. We felt completely overwhelmed.

Christina didn't understand but something in her body recognised the prying eyes. She regularly freaked out when they or anyone medical visited.

On one of those visits Christina was clearly tired and unresponsive. She probably just needed a good sleep.

'I am pretty sure she has hydrocephalus – a build-up of fluid in the brain – you need to get to Norwich Hospital right now,' she said. 'They will need to scan her and possibly perform an operation to insert a shunt in the brain.'

This caused us a huge amount of stress and panic, being led to believe that Christina was deteriorating much faster than we thought and that the end might be upon us. I put her in the car and raced over to Norwich Hospital.

When I got there, the oncologist examined her and asked me why I had come.

'I was sent here by the lady from palliative care,' I answered, really confused. 'You have to scan her apparently… she thinks she has hydrocephalus.'

And what was the response?

'No, I don't suspect that at all, she is absolutely fine,' the oncologist concluded.

I knew of course that it was better to be safe than sorry. I had never wasted any time if the kids were even the slightest bit poorly. But I was not happy that I had been sent to the hospital under such duress simply because the palliative care worker mistook tiredness for hydrocephalus when there was no real evidence for it. Where do you draw the line between caution, paranoia and misdiagnosis?

They then suggested that we should make plans to have a hospital type of bed in one of the downstairs rooms, and they gave us an enormous amount of drugs with specific instructions on what to do if Christina had a seizure which they told us was imminent. I got that they were only doing their job and that end-of-life care was their game, but they had not at all factored in that I was already going in the opposite direction to them with her diet, nutrition and the natural medicine. Plus, I was beginning to look at possible treatments abroad. I didn't want their drugs or their hospital bed, and as for those immanent seizures, they never happened.

'Enough,' I simply said. 'Enough. You need to go away now and give us some space.'

I was only just getting started:

'I will tell you what,' I continued. 'I really need you guys to back off now. I don't think we are at the stage where we need you. When we are, I will call you. Right now, we don't. You are better off spending your time with kids who do need you.'

'You are geared up for death.' I held my position. 'I am geared up for life.'

'My family and our home life have been turned upside down and now I need to restore it to some kind of normality. This is just as important for Christina's well-being, as are the hospital check-ups. Please respect that we now want to be left alone.'

As a family, we really needed to get back to where we were before she was diagnosed – as much as was possible. That was the medicine she needed right now.

They left. They backed off. They disappeared. Without protest. Every single one of them apart from the social worker who would still turn up unannounced. In time, they would call and conclude: 'You don't really need us, so we will remove Christina from our priority list.'

They admitted that we were a much lower priority, which leads me to conclude that any suspicion of me equalled mine of them, plus of course, protecting their own jobs. I told them it was fine to not be a priority.

Simply, if you were a priority, then you were clearly on your way out.

Everything around me was set up to accommodate the new parameters. But we had to go back to the hospital. They had had sufficient time to change their tune.

We are in a meeting with the paediatric oncologist – a very experienced person... one of the top brain tumour specialists. Somebody else is taking notes. There is always a somebody else.

'We really think you should reconsider giving her chemotherapy. If the tumour is found to be low-grade, chemo could be effective in shrinking it,' he said.

'No, we've made our decision and that has not changed,' I replied.

He knew that I had some knowledge.

'Chemo does not kill the cancer stem cells, the so-called mother cells, it only kills the daughter cells so this is purely disease management and not a cure,' I responded.

There was no answer to this. Scientific facts never go down that well.

'Look, I am not having my daughter spend her last days in this hospital suffering with the side effects of chemo such as losing her hair, nausea and mouth ulcers.'

'But she may not experience all of the side effects, some children don't,' they lamely replied. 'But yes, she would probably lose her hair.'

'Look, my daughter gets up in the morning, she brushes her hair, she puts ribbons and pretty Alice bands in and she will die with her hair,' I said as I looked him straight in the eye.

'If you could save my daughter's life and I was preventing you from doing that, then I would expect you to roll right over me and rightly so, but you can't save her life and you know it.'

'OK, Mr Thomas, I understand what you are saying,' he conceded.

'I'm looking into treatments abroad where they work with her immune system instead of wiping it out. I have no intention of just sitting back and letting her die. I'm going to do all I can to save my daughter,' I confided.

I knew, too, that they couldn't force it upon me, but they also couldn't support or endorse my idea of seeking treatment in another country. I had made myself familiar with the 1939 Cancer Act which means doctors are not legally allowed to offer or advise on alternative therapies for fear of criminal prosecution and the loss of their licence to practise. Unfortunately, their hands are tied and they can only provide you with the standard treatment that they have been authorised to use.

I did have a choice, though. Since they couldn't cure it, I could refuse it. If we had six months left, then I would take those six months on my terms and turn my attention fully towards the alternatives.

'We're all terminal, Doctor,' I signed off. 'It is just that some get longer than others.'

And we were done. For now.

In many ways, everything that I had experienced since Auntie Sole, Mum's rapid decline against Dad's slow ebbing away, Dave, Norman, Nick, James and Mark... It all felt like training. There is no preparation, of course and my goodness, I was now learning fast and every day, and well aware that I was being watched because I was thinking independently. That suspicion of healthcare, that raced alongside my spiritual beliefs which were forever being tested by the lottery of life, had led me here. My own daughter was staring death in the face.

Frankly, you would do anything you could – to answer Francisca's earlier question that nobody answered. They may have rules to stick to, but every rule is there to be broken. They didn't have all the answers – science from around the world and the anecdotal evidence reaching me confirmed just that.

These people *were* doing their job. But there were other ways to do it. They had to operate according to their training and prescribe drugs that big billion-dollar companies had persuaded some higher-ups to purchase. For the safety of their careers against that narrative, they could not deviate.

319

That is the background. That was the fight. Rules may dominate their lives.

For me, they were now all out of the window.

What I am unable to do here in the UK, I will do in another country where they are not shackled by the chains of organisations such as NICE (National Institute for Health and Care Excellence) and unreasonable man-made laws. Where they are free to use *all* medicines that heal and do not harm, where a person has the right to choose their preferred therapy, and where the bottom line is an individual's health and not the corporation's wealth.

So, I will fight for my little girl and do all that I can to save her *'By Any Means Necessary'*... to use the words of Malcolm X.

44 The New Normal

We have been in East Anglia for fourteen months. We have discovered new friends in the village and around the world through social media. There are enemies, too – I learn that Angela has been subject to playground bullying.

'My mum says your sister is going to die,' they taunted.

School friends were ignoring her, too.

She was just seven years old. I was straight in to the Head. They had to be aware, and they needed to manage it.

It wasn't just the kids. The adults were at it, as well.

At one local funeral word got back to me that a parent had openly said, 'We will be going to Christina's next.'

You won't be going anywhere near.

If and when.

Many messaged me in support; some were dissenting. Some so-called *friends* just disappeared off the face of the earth.

I was reminded of that time long before all this when I was forewarned: 'Have you factored in betrayal?'

In your moment of need some people step up and some step back.

The kindness of strangers and wagging tongues side by side were the new normal.

The doctors are still piling on the pressure and trying to dissuade us.

I kept thinking of Silky. I know he wished he had acted sooner and elsewhere. I never forgot how Mum had been so badly harmed at Barts Hospital and had never suffered more than at that point.

And I told them so.

Many conversations I had with them came to a natural stand-off. They tried to foist their treatment. I told them no.

I once walked off telling them, 'This ain't over.'

Eventually, I lost my cool:

'If you keep pushing this with me (referring to the biopsy and chemo), I will see every one of you in Hell.'

You note that my priority was justice in the eyes of God, rather than a court of law, though we did later have that conversation, too.

'Why don't you trust us?' one of them asked.

'Why should I trust anyone who says one thing one minute, and the complete opposite the next? At first you say you respect our decision and then you spend the following weeks and months trying to force us into it,' I replied.

Did they not realise the stress they were putting us through on top of the fact that according to them our daughter was going to die very soon?

'If you are thinking of taking her somewhere like Disneyland Paris then you need to do it quickly,' they said on one of their home visits.

And I am thinking... 'If I want my daughter to see Mickey Mouse, I'll bring her to you.'

It simply hammered down this thought-process that we don't have long.

The only place I was going to take her was to a hospital abroad. Disneyland will have to wait. I made it clear that I knew that there was another way and that frankly the Addenbrooke's way was never an option.

The knowledge that I was acquiring and the encouragement from people I would never meet confirmed that I was doing the right thing. The fact of the matter is that I didn't need anyone else's input to help me make a decision, but the support was immense.

To his credit, even Steve Finan called, as he had done when Mum and Dad died.

'Steve, this is my plan,' I confessed. 'I am going to do other treatments. I am looking at the USA.'

'Kenny, you're going to need to fundraise,' he replied swiftly as if he had already realised this.

'Really?' I questioned. 'I wouldn't even know where to start.'

It hadn't occurred to me that that answer was potentially right at my fingertips and certainly at Steve's.

Not long after Christina's diagnosis, I did a charity gig with Heather Small from M People, raising money for the family of a footballer who had tragically passed away. Their plight at the time seemed worse than ours. I never ever thought I would be in this position.

'I don't know how to go about raising money,' I reiterated.

Nor did I have any idea how much we were going to need. Flights and hotels would already start the bill off in thousands, let alone the treatments required.

'Leave it with me,' he said.

And the next day his son Joe was on the case. Being very savvy with all things internet-related he set up a JustGiving page.

'I am looking at a hospital in Texas,' I told him when the cost came up again. 'It is at least 50 grand per treatment and four of those is the norm, so we're looking at around 200k, plus travel and accommodation.'

That was a lot of dough and I felt really awkward going live with this. I knew there would be some nasty accusations as to why I couldn't pay for it myself. Well, the truth is that I did my best. The second and harsher truth is that once you start throwing money at this, there is no ceiling.

I remortgaged and had some money left from the house sale in London. I know I was lucky enough to be in a position to put a fair bit of dough in straight away. So, we decided that we would set the target at £80,000 to add to what I had.

Sure enough, I did receive an email from a journo at *The Sun* newspaper saying, 'We're *going* to run an article on your daughter's fundraising… Would you like to comment on it?'

I didn't even reply. And yes, they ran the story anyway as you would expect with no real knowledge.

To me it read as though a 90s popstar was desperate for money from complete strangers. I was never comfortable with putting a specific sum like 80 grand out there. It placed a price on life which was inappropriate and unfair.

No popstar ever forgets if a newspaper turns them over, nor do they ever let it leave their subconscious if they don't quite get trashed, but there is just that nasty little implied tone. That was this.

However, thankfully the public are smarter, and *The Sun* has its reputation. It drove more people than I ever could have imagined to the fundraising page. That also meant that when the *Mirror* rang and asked *if I would like to* do an interview, I was inclined to have a conversation and with a slightly better outcome.

I was then asked by someone if I would like to appear on breakfast television. I simply replied:

'I don't need that.'

I could handle the spotlight. I just didn't want it for my family. There was a limit to how public I was prepared to go with something so private.

There is no way in the world, though, that I could have even half-attempted this outside of the social media era and without my friends in the tight-knit soul scene.

It was clear early on that lots of artists were prepared to put on events for Christina and that every stranger who helped me who was in similar territory I would give back to as well. I was introduced to a lot of parents with children whose conditions mirrored Christina's, either medically or in a parallel way of little hope, enormous stress and financial requirements that could go through the roof. One such man was the inspirational Scott Lau, an incredible father who reached out to me at the same time as he and his wife Yang were taking their own daughter Kaleigh to Monterrey in Mexico where she was receiving intra-arterial therapy. This is a method of delivering concentrated doses of cancer-killing medicines directly to the brainstem via a network of arteries.

I learned an incredible amount from Scott. He had done his research and knew a lot about the various treatments available in other countries. He had chosen the Mexico option, but I was still at that early stage of trying to decide where to take Christina. He was also in touch with the daughter of the late MP Tessa Jowell, and it was through him that I first learned of dendritic cell therapy and eventually make contact with the professor in Germany who treated Tessa.

When I mentioned to the oncologist here in the UK that I was talking to the same people who looked after her, this was the reply:

'Why do you want to do that? Tessa Jowell is dead.'

'With all due respect,' I replied, inferring not much, 'Tessa Jowell was extremely unwell following her NHS treatment. Had she gone to Germany much earlier, maybe the outcome would have been very different. You need to realise, Doctor, that you are working with medicine of the past. I am looking into the medicine of the future.'

In her final days, Tessa Jowell made a moving speech in the House of Lords calling for patients with life-threatening conditions to have wider access to experimental treatments in the UK, allowing them to opt for innovative therapies, as they can in other countries.

How right she was.

Even those people for whom treatment came too late were determined to pass on what they knew. There was now a colossal network of information which you discovered through chance and from talking to people. There was no Yellow Pages to find the answers. You just had to keep talking. Real people had the answers, and they held a lot more weight than the leaflets they handed out to Francisca and myself at the hospital. How can you seriously sum all this up in a short pamphlet? Yes – there might have been a few numbers or a website on there, but it was posturing. It was propaganda. It was covering backsides. But mostly, it was limited thinking.

You joined other families at various stages of their struggles but without exception, everybody wanted to pass on their experiences and knowledge. We were all clutching at straws in the dark and lonely journey until we found each other. Scott is months ahead of me and I start to think about Mexico. You really are plunging into the unknown here, based almost entirely on what you can interpret from the internet so when somebody with first-hand experiences comes along, you bleed them dry for knowledge. That was Scott. I am also well aware that an individual's success rate can be simply down to a patient who may respond differently to another who is receiving the same treatment.

When one of the top brain surgeons in America tells me that he can't do anything for Christina, I really begin to think that Scott's thinking might be the *only* alternative. There were always going to be risks and there was always going to be the danger that you get so far down the line in a conversation before there is a problem, but now it looked like I would need to know the way to Monterrey.

The mooted costs were spiralling, though – Scott was intimating that I needed at least 300 grand to see it through. Within the first year post-diagnosis, I spoke to one parent who had already thrown £500,000 at treatments.

If part of you says, 'Lucky them for being able to,' then that is harsh. Most people I met had been backed by communities and similar fundraising and put every penny of their own money IN knowing in fact that they might not even save their children but merely prolong their lives.

How long was a piece of string? Boy, I had said that phrase so many times in life. Now it had context.

So, unless you are extremely wealthy, fundraising is the only way to make it happen. Scott and Yang Lau and all the parents I spoke to were fundraising and doing a great job of it. But many of them were also not in my position where I was able to call on my music biz friends to help me out. So, I offered my services to them, agreeing to sing at their events whenever they needed me to. On one occasion I called on my good friend Andy Abraham and he joined me onstage at a fundraiser for Kaleigh Lau.

That night was the first and last time I got to meet that brave and amazing little girl.

The eyes of the medical team were still watching. You cannot ask for help on social media and hope it be a success without expecting to appear on the radar.

The other thing that could not go unnoticed is the fact that Christina was not deteriorating as expected. The natural medicine packages continued to arrive at the house and new things were being introduced as per the advice of Ilan and the other specialists with whom we were consulting. The drooling had stopped, her speech improved, the right eye was now closing properly, and she was singing and laughing again. That cheeky little personality which had been absent for some time had returned. We got our little girl back.

That dreaded six-month point was approaching, too, and now I had some hope, and a reason to believe that we would go beyond it. I was even more determined to keep going, to keep fighting and to resist all attempts being made to undo it.

By month five, Francisca and I are asked to attend Birmingham Children's Hospital and are introduced to one of the UK's leading professors. They are keen to find out if the tumour is a high- or low-grade glioma. If it is high-grade then that is an aggressive tumour which starts to put time limits on life and once again throws out the argument for chemotherapy. If it is low-grade then this will provide Addenbrooke's with the information needed to argue and force their treatment on her. Obviously, we would like to know that it is a low-grade tumour, but here we are coming towards the period of expectancy that had been cagily admitted as six months and Christina was very slowly improving. A period of normality and stability had arrived against the odds. Well, against the predicted odds.

You can imagine that I have been working every day on this and my conversations extend from Mexico to India via Harley Street in London. You might be surprised to learn that the subcontinent was an option. I had been introduced to a friend called Steve White who was heading to Delhi and Chennai for dendritic cell therapy. It caught my attention briefly but again I felt that logistically it might be a nightmare taking blood samples one week and then cells the next. Germany was beginning to look like the best option.

The scan in Birmingham was one that would reveal great detail about the tumour, and through spectral analysis even show its precise chemical composition. I was told that this is the most high-tech MRI possible here in the UK.

It was a long and tough day for Christina, being examined all over again, going without food for the general anaesthetic but, as always, she got through it all with a smile.

I return to Birmingham two weeks later to discuss their findings.

The tumour is *both* high-grade and low-grade, and they detected the presence of an unusual chemical that they can't account for, but a chemical that when present can indicate a slightly better survival rate. I am questioned again as to why I don't want to give her chemotherapy, but at the same time I'm told *it will be ineffective* on the high-grade aspect of the tumour.

High-grade is not good news, but the professor's opinion was definitely bad news for Addenbrooke's. He had dealt a deadly blow to their chemo argument.

The professor said, 'This is probably a subcategory of tumour we have not seen before.'

That may be true, but a good doctor friend of mine who works for the NHS told me that this subcategory description was the best example of 'arse-covering' he had ever heard.

He said, 'They gave her six months and now if she survives beyond that they have covered their arses by saying it is an unknown subcategory.'

So, was their first diagnosis a misdiagnosis? Who knows? What I do know is that the many radiologists and doctors in Europe who looked at those same scans confirmed that it did show an aggressive high-grade aspect, and that in their opinion the original prognosis was a realistic one. They believed that somehow the alternative medicine we were using must have in some way slowed down or arrested its progression.

We are almost going through the motions in Birmingham, and whilst the professor does say to me, 'Whatever you are doing, keep doing it,' I was well aware that the NHS was under incredible pressure to be seen to be doing something. That was at the root of why – and now – they wanted a second opinion.

They didn't want to know about my methods which ranged from Chinese herbal formulas to Poly-MVA – all obviously totally legal and safe. They just had to avoid being compromised. Equally, despite those visits to the house, they must have been surprised to see that Christina was going to pass that initial six-month period.

All the time, of course, I was plotting my next move and my mind was shifting.

I had begun to hear that all was not going so well in Mexico – there seemed to be a few kids doing OK and many others not making it out of there. This was worrying news. But I had to bear in mind that the doctors over there, and elsewhere, are trying their best to find new ways to fight one of the deadliest forms of brain cancer.

It was also a great concern that it was a long flight and that might present problems; nor did you want to be that far away if the worst happened. Ultimately, only the care mattered, but these little issues were beginning to tot up. Plus, I was starting to hear real alarm bells ringing – when I discovered the colossal amount of money some parents were spending over there.

You can't help but think that there might be a Mexican doctor cruising around Monterrey in a new Bentley. But hey, most parents like me will be of the opinion: 'If you can cure my daughter then you deserve a Bentley – no, in fact have two.'

When I spoke to one of the professors over there, he was very well informed and brutally honest:

'Nothing is changing as fast as brain tumour research.'

He himself was in the process of developing a transdermal nanoparticle. He helped me make my decision when he said, 'If you're looking for the Holy Grail in brain tumour therapy, then you need to look to Germany.'

329

To date my friends in the music industry have come out in force and stood as one for Christina. I could not be more grateful, humbled or overwhelmed.

The first to really put their hands up were my old DJ pals Bigger and Flip who run the 'Smooth Grooves' nights, and they called on the services of Jocelyn Brown, Omar, Junior Giscombe, Bluey of Incognito, Drizabone, Pauline Henry (The Chimes), Sinclair, Cool Million feat. Eli Thompson, Bashiyra 'The Voice', Noel McKoy, Rose Vincent, Moni Tivony, along with DJs Greg Edwards, Bob Masters, James Anthony, Snowboy, Calvin Francis, Stretch Paul Taylor and Scott Savill.

Colin McMillan, former WBO Featherweight World Champion, undertook some fundraising through his boxing circles. It was through Colin that I met Danny Moloney, a Londoner now living in Norwich of all places. Danny is what I would call a *serial fundraiser*. He has done more fundraising for kids with cancer than anyone I know. Shortly after Christina became ill a young boy named Harry from a nearby village was also diagnosed with a brain tumour. Danny embarked on a huge mission to raise money for Harry to get treatment in the US and he asked Simon Webbe from the band Blue along with myself to sing at an event in Norwich. Danny then turned his attention to Christina, even training for weeks and completing a marathon for her, despite having undergone a knee operation some weeks earlier. He is an amazing person and, in my opinion, deserves one day to be recognised with some kind of award for his charitable works.

Kevin Bellamy started out as a fan of my music, and we became good friends when I was booked to sing at his 40th birthday party some years ago. He has been instrumental in organising several fundraising events such as the London Town Soul Boat Cruise with DJ Gary Spence spinning the tunes. His help has been simply amazing!

Dean Martin, John Parkes, Lee Lucraft and Mike Richards are loyal friends who stepped up and organised music events up and down the country, from Bromsgrove to Eye, and from Weymouth to Ware.

Making as many friends as I have over the years has stood me in good stead. They have all come to my aid in the darkest of hours. I met Mark 'Rosco' Robinson and his wife Alison when they booked me to sing at Mark's 50th birthday party up north. As you know by now, I am not one to just sing and leave, so I hung out with them that night and guess what, we became the best of friends. Mark is a great DJ and a walking encyclopaedia of soul music. So, when Francisca and I got married (our 'second' wedding) it was Mark who got the dance floor rocking that evening. When I dipped my toes into radio and presented a soul show it was Mark who provided me with a hard drive containing over 20,000 tunes to choose from. So, when I needed a DJ for the fundraisers up north, I called on him for help. When I had to travel to the Northwest to pick up naturopathic meds for Christina, a spare bed and a cooked breakfast always awaited me at their house.

I owe so much to so many for their kindness to me and most of it has come from the soul scene, and that is why we refer to ourselves on that scene as *The Soul Family*.

Other members of that family are my soul brothers Jon Jules and CJ Carlos. Two of the best DJs and nicest people I know. Jon Jules's wife Julia organised the *Crystals for Christina* event which included a sponsored walk and a night of music in Ascot, with DJ support from Ash Selector (Solar Radio), Mike Vitti (Mi-Soul Radio) Ian Reading (Zero Radio) and Ian Dee (Point Blank FM).

CJ Carlos held an event in Bromley and once again the soul family came out in force, with DJs Jon Jules, Mike Vitti, Brian Power, Ronnie Herel and Bigger, and performances from Georgie B, Phil Fearon (Galaxy), Baby D, Deborah Bell, Rebecca Scales and Everis.

If you ever have any doubts about humanity, then look no further than this aspect of my story. It should restore your faith in people and give you a small glimpse into the good things they do for one another. Sadly, we don't get to hear enough about this, instead bombarded daily with negative news in the media, and we often lose sight of the love that surrounds us.

Then came Marcus Vere from Living In A Box who rolled out the 'Big Guns' of the 80s family.

So far, there have been two 'A Night For Christina' sell-out concerts held at Under the Bridge, Chelsea, organised by Marcus. That is why I state that meeting Marcus was a much bigger deal than just me singing with him at festivals. He proved to be one of the most important people in Christina's journey, raising enough money to pay for several treatments abroad.

My thanks go to Kim Wilde, Tony Hadley, Martin Fry, Midge Ure, Nik Kershaw, Carol Decker of T'Pau, Heaven 17, Go West, Beverley Knight and of course Living In A Box. The first one was hosted by my pal Shane Richie, and the second by the Radio 2 broadcaster Gary Davies, and so many others gave their time across both fundraising gigs. Lewis Hamilton's dad Anthony was in attendance and promised to match whatever we raised in the raffle. He was true to his word.

Marcus is a man I owe enormous gratitude to – pulling the strings to co-ordinate these concerts for my little girl. Concerts that, according to those who were there, were the best they had ever seen. My wife and I were blown away by this outpouring of love and support, and we remain eternally grateful to all the artists and people involved in making it happen.

Marcus also took on the big fight with PRS – the Performing Right Society. Obviously, we wanted to reclaim the PRS from the gig. It has been a constant in the music business for years. You might recall Sir Bob Geldof taking on the Prime Minister Margaret Thatcher over the VAT on the Band Aid single. Eventually the Prime Minister caved in and around 500k was redirected to the charity.

We were simply trying to claw back a small amount of money that could benefit Christina. When you are dealing with stress and the huge admin of medical forms from doctors, you do not want to be filling in forms anywhere else, let alone in your own industry for a fundraiser, nor be part of some means-testing exercise that included such stupid questions as to whether I had a gardener or not.

That was what happened. So, I told the PRS to keep the money and stick their means-tested questionnaire where the sun don't shine.

On the first *Night 4 Christina* in June 2017, Bluey (aka Jean-Paul Maunick of Incognito) and his wife Takami arranged a concert at the Jazz Cafe, London, on the same evening, with many friends and artists I admired like Hamish Stuart (Average White Band), Natalie Williams, Tony Momrelle, Vula, Vanessa Haynes, Chris Ballin, Imaani and Moya Morris. I wish I could have been there, but I couldn't attend both.

Bluey was one of the first people in the music game to reach out, and calls us often to check in on things, and to let us know that he is willing to do the same again should we need it.

Here is a quote from an interview Bluey did with *Blues & Soul* magazine regarding that night:

In this life family is everything! We can only imagine what the Thomas family are going through. We in Incognito and the UK Soul Jazz Community are glad that we can do our little bit with great love for Christina. That brave little girl has become a symbol of unity to us all at a time when so much of the world is divided. We thank her for the opportunity to shine!

Ricky and Mandy Wilde were colossal. They host the Wilde Winter Ball every two years at Knebworth House. It's a star-studded event held in aid of the Hertfordshire Breast Cancer Appeal. I performed with Living In A Box at one of their events in 2017, and Marcus ingeniously suggested that I put one of my memorabilia items into their charity auction preceded by a few words from myself about Christina. Thankfully the Wildes agreed to this, and to my amazement it raised enough money to pay for a couple of treatments abroad.

That night Ricky and Mandy introduced me to two of their closest friends, Steve and Liz, a very successful couple who were very moved by Christina's story. They have helped us enormously over the last four years. Without them, we would not have been able to sustain the treatments abroad. Yes, there are caring people like that in this world, and we are truly blessed to have them in our lives.

'What am I going to do with all of this memorabilia stuff? I've got nowhere to put it,' I had said to my old manager Mark Aaron back in 2007.

'Kenny, take it, you never know when you will need to use it to raise money for something really important,' he replied.

How prophetic and right he was!

My pal Warren Thompson, the owner of Hoochie Coochie, the luxury bar and music venue in Newcastle, also held a benefit night for Christina. Warren's heart immediately went out to me and my family, especially as his own daughter has been battling cancer for some time now. People like Warren are one in a million and have their own stuff to deal with but they still make time to help you. The support from the soul family in the Northeast has been amazing, especially my dear friends Gill and Tom Robson.

Butlins also did their bit when the general manager of the Bognor venue Nick Joy gave the OK for the DJ Des Grant to organise a collection for Christina after my performance at one of their weekenders. Sadly, Des lost his own daughter Melanie to a brain tumour some years ago, so he knew from experience exactly what I was going through and wanted to help in any way he could.

My nephew Gareth undertook a wing walk; greatly supported by his work colleagues in the banking world of the city. My cousin Emma decided very courageously to have all of her hair shaved off to raise money. Our neighbours Simon and Alex, who had not long moved into the house next to ours decided to put on a summer fête to help the cause. My good friend David Gibbs used his 50th birthday party as an opportunity to benefit my daughter, and I helped him get Shalamar over from the US to make sure it was literally a night to remember.

Eliot Kennedy held a charity concert for his 50th birthday at Sheffield City Hall, with all proceeds going to local hospices. Gary Barlow, Mark Owen, Heather Small, Alfie Boe and myself performed there that evening and to my utter surprise

Eliot invited me back onstage to reveal that all the money raised from selling the programmes that night was being donated to Christina's fund. I was really lost for words!

My cousin Jackie was a great support to us, putting money into the fund and coming along to the *Night 4 Christina* concert. She was one of the very few who ventured up to Norfolk to see Christina, and her concern was evident from her consistent telephone calls to see how she was doing and to see if we were coping. Sadly, Jackie suddenly passed away of an aneurism in January 2019. She was a beautiful person and she is greatly missed.

I know what you must be thinking by now that this book contains an awful lot of death and bereavement. Unfortunately, I can only write my own story, so there is no getting away from it. As my friend Johnny Boy has often said to me: 'Kenny, I don't know anyone who has had as many losses as you.' He is right, but we all have to deal with loss at some point. The thing is that life has to go on, and as long as it does, you're still in the fight.

Michael Watson, one of the greatest fighters the UK has ever produced, recently attended a fundraiser organised by my friend Jim Hemmings. Michael has had to overcome great adversity when his career was cut short as a result of a near-fatal injury sustained during a boxing match with Chris Eubank for the WBO Super middleweight title in 1991. He told me that I was a warrior like him and that I should never give up fighting for my daughter. I would love to have one-tenth of Michael's courageous spirit. He is a source of inspiration for me!

The boxer Nigel Benn was one of the first to call and left a long message saying he was praying for Christina. He is a good friend of my mate Mark Peters who also arranged an event for my daughter, calling, once again, on the help of singers Phil Fearon and his wife Baby D. Nigel also donated some items for the auction that night.

Even some of my band members arranged a night of music for my daughter. The drummer Neil Bullock and his wife, the singer Louise Warren, put on a gig with Tommy Blaize (*Strictly Come Dancing*), Junior Giscombe, Hannah White and myself in Cheshunt. It was a great show that could have easily sat on any of the big stages in London, but it was done there in little old Cheshunt, and put together with a lot of love for Christina. I had known Junior Giscombe for many years and ironically I couldn't help but remember that the night we became real friends was when we were doing a fundraiser for a sickle cell charity back in the early 90s.

I even got involved with a joint fundraiser. My old mate Pete Walsh put together an event to raise money for Steve White and my daughter. That was at the time Steve was having dendritic cell therapy in India, and I was about to head to Europe with my little girl to do the same.

One of my dearest friends, Fr Jeff Woolnough, said Mass and held a prayer vigil in his parish church at Leigh-on-Sea, and word even reached Pope Emeritus Benedict XVI in Rome who sent us a letter saying that he would be praying for Christina.

Shovell from M People who follows the Buddhist faith told me that he is chanting for Christina every day. So, people from all walks of life and various faith traditions were all willing Christina well through their thoughts and actions. These good intentions and the power of prayer can never be underestimated. It operates on a much higher spiritual frequency, and when people come together in this way, great things – even seemingly impossible things – can happen.

I could see, though, that money would go out as fast as it would come in. But I was humbled. We would not be where we are today without all of their help. Equally, the fact that there were now these additional funds focused the mind even more. At one point, I became very aware that, having advertised a concert, we might not even make it to the date. I would always say that should the worst happen, those funds could be used for another child who needed it. I already knew a few who did, and I was beginning to share some of the naturopathic medicines I had with them.

I was always going to make a decision, but beyond all the obvious reasons, I had to be absolutely sure it was the right one. I was, after all, spending other people's money. That changes the level of responsibility.

One of the Christina gigs was attended by a top paediatric brain tumour surgeon who worked with a leading Harley Street professor in this field.

I had just one question for him.

'How many times have you biopsied a tumour and then the tumour has gone wild and begun to grow?' I asked.

The response was 'many'.

This was valuable information.

Major doubts were creeping in on all fronts.

'There is something in Mexico I'm unsure about,' I told Francisca. 'Some kids are not making it out of there.'

She knows that I have a fairly good knowledge of medicine and backs my judgement. We, are of course, united in whatever action we take. There were also personal case studies to note. We had seen people we loved deteriorate and die after chemo, and my brother was permanently suffering from peripheral neuropathy after being given the chemotherapy drug vincristine, which is well known to damage peripheral nerves.

When the oncologist had suggested vincristine for Christina, I simply declined. Unfortunate to be in this situation – yes, but very lucky in a strange way that I was benefiting from people's knowledge through their own adversity and negative experience.

Occasionally, some of the staff would try to play us, taking Francisca aside to work on her as I was often the most vocal. They knew that should she cave in and agree to their treatment plan, this would automatically overrule me. How devious and conniving is that?

'We speak with one voice,' I was forced to tell them.

Opening the lid that tiny bit more with every conversation at Addenbrooke's, I asked what their thoughts were on parents going to Mexico and being asked to sign NDAs (non-disclosure agreements).

I had to be careful what discussions I had with Addenbrooke's, and they equally were right to be guarded in their replies, but this was a broader discussion outside the parameters of an individual's treatment.

Then I concluded that there had to be something not quite right – what exactly are those chemicals going into the children's bodies over there in Monterrey? To me something didn't feel right at all.

I really did start to think that I could be stuck out there for three to four months and come back alone and that would be beyond grim. I was well aware, too, that even if we were to shrink the tumour, significant damage to the brainstem may have already occurred.

'The treatment can go various ways with varying degrees of success, and it is not without great risk,' I was told.

The oncologist was not going to say anything specific and whether it was real or something I just felt, I was consumed by pressure again.

On the one hand, have a biopsy and take chemo; on the other, we are brave and refreshing. Christina might lose her hair, get diarrhoea and vomit a lot… She might not. There were a lot of 'mights' and 'coulds'.

They were still pushing for that biopsy, and I was still pushing back.

On one occasion I told them, 'You really have picked the wrong parents to have this kind of fight with.'

I'm not sure if they liked me or not, but secretly I think there was some degree of respect for the fact that I was following my conscience and doing what I thought was best for my daughter. Nor were they particularly comfortable when I mentioned that I had had a conversation with that Harley Street brain surgeon.

I knew things were hotting up when Christina went past that six-month point. I immediately contacted Ilan to sound him out as to whether I could have legal advice and a barrister waiting in the wings. It got to that level.

The oncologist's assistant called me on my home phone. Such moments always delivered anxiety.

This was their final big push to get me to back down and let them dive in with their non-lifesaving therapeutics on what they themselves said was an incurable brain tumour.

'You just keep pushing chemo,' I lambasted the assistant. 'I am not interested in what you have in your bag of tricks.'

I have never experienced such internalised anger.

'Have you seen that peer-reviewed paper that has just been published from a study at Yeshiva University in New York?' I asked. 'Chemo can indeed shrink tumours in the short term… But it could also allow cancer to spread, and trigger more aggressive tumours.'

No, they hadn't seen it and they don't like it when you tell them knowledge that they alone are supposed to have.

'OK let me tell you now… I've absolutely had enough of all of you, and the pressure you keep putting us under. Go away and do your multidisciplinary team meeting and then come back and make your move, because I'm ready for you.'

24 hours later I received a call from the assistant.

'Mr Thomas, I've spoken with the doctors and we have decided to back off now,' she said.

'Good move,' I said. 'Now I can get on with trying to get my daughter the treatment she needs.'

I did allow them to perform routine scans, but I was going through the motions. I knew the answers were elsewhere and I think they had reached the end of the line. Pressure from above, a level of accountability and their own training were the reasons we had ended up here. I also knew by now that we were dealing with an outdated medical model, and it was almost frightening how informed I had become so quickly by not going down the prescribed route.

I had seen my brother Gary suffer, too. One of the reasons for moving to Norfolk was undoubtedly to be closer to him and his wife Jan. She was diagnosed with cancer about three weeks before Christina. She had all the conventional treatments and was given that infamous *All Clear*, but the cancer came back and she passed away in June 2019. She was spiritually strong, but a serene person who had a calming influence on us all. In her presence you always felt at peace. She was taken way too soon. Yet another terrible loss for my family. Gary has often said to me that if he had that diagnosis again, he would never go down that route.

339

Two parallel but different journeys.

At the same time, the house is essentially modified for a special needs child, adjusting props like the handrail on the stairs so Christina's left hand can grab it. Yes, there were mishaps – one bad fall had led to her chipping her teeth. And no, Francisca and I have barely seen a proper night's sleep in years – and remember we were a young family. Jude had arrived in the December of 2016 and Christina was diagnosed two months later.

Sometimes Christina would try to pull a fast one, so used to waking up in the night was she, that if she startled out of habit then she would still want comforting even on better nights. One thing was for sure: life had changed not ended and there was no going back to how it used to be.

I had just bought her a bicycle when she fell ill. To this day, it sits in the garage. Unused. On days that I would take Angela and Joe to school and Christina would accompany me, we would see her classmates running around freely in the playground.

It broke my heart.

However long that would be, she would need care of some sort for life – she had metamorphosed from a sharp child to a slower one with a lower attention span in weeks.

'Daddy, my bones are moving,' she would often say, giving us the only real insight into how she felt physically and how a child was understanding it.

We were throwing the kitchen sink at this and did see highs. Gradually, with the measures that I had implemented, I saw her face begin to change from that pale colour of illness to something much rosier. But by gradual, I mean over much of that initial six-month period. That touch of OCD from my childhood was now channelled into a better focus, stabilising this new random world that we were now in. We knew that the mere extension of life and the glimpses of managed quality meant that we had been right to reject chemo. There were the lows, too – almost permanently very little movement in her right hand.

The knock-on effect for the whole family was immense – little Jude only knew this world, Angela and Joe were old enough to understand that there had been a change, and neither Francisca nor I could really book any work in with certainty. Even though I did continue to go out and do some gigs, there was always that doubt of what you were leaving behind.

We needed some help. I can't deny it. It was almost impossible to do it all. Originally, we engaged a home assistant-cum-au pair, but this never worked out. Then Minki, a good friend of Francisca's from Cape Town, came over to visit us. When she saw the situation that we were in she quite unbelievably and selflessly decided to stay for a further five months to help us. Minki's real name is Nomathamsanqa Thole. This is a Xhosa name, and it has that unusual click sound in the middle of it. (Xhosa: a *Nguni Bantu* language and one of the official languages of South Africa.) It took me all of five months to try and master the click technique, and I say 'try' because I never really did nail it. One of our fondest memories was when Minki saw snow for the first time in her life and we all played in the garden and made a big snowman. She absolutely adored *The Lion King* musical when I took her to see it in the West End. Especially as many of the cast were South African and some of the songs were in her native tongue. She had never been to a theatre before. My kids loved Minki and she was very much part of our family. We will never forget what she did for us. She helped us through a very tough patch.

But, as time passes, you begin to tick off milestones. With every day that exceeds that six-month period, you take heart and a cautious confidence. We brought forward Christina's birthday from November to the August to share it with Angela just in case. But that September she had been able to complete her first day at school, even though we knew that there would be weeks when she might not go at all. Your relationship with the original advice, however, goes in the other direction.

And as days turned into weeks and months, I knew that for the NHS – who I accept were working hard and only following orders – the moment had passed where they had any sense of moral recall towards us. After that original bleak outlook of half a year for survival, they would struggle to make a case after she outlived that by ignoring everything that they had recommended. Three medical figures confirmed to me that this would be the thinking. It was important to understand how the system works from within.

I was told that system didn't like me resisting them, nor could it handle an alternative to it that seemed to be flourishing. Humility was not on the agenda.

They continued to push back at every opportunity, suggesting that we reconsider their option, despite saying that they would back off. But we held the line, and with even greater determination we stuck to our plan. They called us *brave and refreshing* to begin with, but soon forgot those words. I didn't care much for those kinds of compliments. All I know is this: they hit a brick wall when they came up against our unwavering focus.

While they predicted death, I focused on life.

From this moment on, I only gave them occasional updates.

It was time to go dark.

I would now say less and less, and provide limited information on social media.

I was heading to Germany.

Dendritic cell therapy can be described as a kind of anti-cancer vaccine made from your own blood. These dendritic cells are cultured from your own white blood cells, and for seven days they are transformed in the laboratory into a new generation of dendritic cells. These new cells are then reintroduced into the body and help the immune system recognise and attack abnormal cells such as cancer.

I knew my friend Steve White was getting good results with this particular therapy in India. He was defying all odds and living beyond the prognosis given to him by the UK doctors. So, this became my sole focus. I had abandoned the Mexico option and looked to Germany as suggested to me by the professor in Monterrey.

Steve told me all about the therapy, the procedure and reactions, and he gave me a good idea of what Christina would have to go through. I needed to act fast. Time is always against you and running at double speed when you find yourself in such dire circumstances.

As we progress, though, not everybody is as fortunate. 12 June 2018 was a sad day.

I got news that Scott and Yang Lau's daughter Kaleigh had peacefully passed away that morning, surrounded by her family including her younger brother Carson. They had fought the good fight and done all they could for Kaleigh, but now for her the fight was over and she was at peace. For Scott and his wife, the fight would never be over and they would continue to reach out to other parents like me, giving their support and advice. They are such amazing people and have never stopped doing all they can to create awareness of this disease. Recently they both did a 13,000-foot skydive to raise money for the hospice that cared for Kaleigh. Such inspirational people!

So even with all that he had gone through Scott still kept in touch with me and helped me navigate my way through the tsunami of information, providing me with the name of a professor in Cologne who was treating UK patients with DC therapy. I contacted the professor, but at the same time I kept researching other clinics and all possible options with the help of one of my wife's family members. Her cousin Celeste lives in Germany and is married to a German guy named Michael. He contacted various doctors throughout the country to check out what therapies they had available. This helped immensely, at least eliminating some options and pointing me back to Cologne.

The lengthy telephone conversation with the professor went OK and he outlined in greater detail the treatment protocol along with adverse reactions. Naturally we had to discuss the cost, but his overemphasis on money being paid upfront prior to starting the therapy did not sit comfortably with me. I knew of course that this would run into tens of thousands of pounds, and I will pay anything to make my daughter well. However, money is only a means to an end, and not an end within itself. There was also quite a hefty charge for the first consultation, just so that he could have a little look-see and then decide on Christina's eligibility for the therapy. Again, this did not sit well with me.

We were always faced with the possibility of what might happen if we did nothing, permanently prepared for deterioration, inflammation and seizures. Yet, the clock is always ticking and all you want is to minimise suffering and prolong life.

I make the decision to fly to Germany. I travel alone. I consider taking Christina, but she is vomiting and is not worth any risk. The empty seat next to me fills me with sadness. I should have been on my way to meet the professor, but the day before I left I made contact with a different clinic in Cologne. They were doing the same treatment, using the same labs and the cost was more or less the same. However, the conversation with them went very differently and the focus was on Christina, the therapy and not the money. I trusted my gut feeling, and at the last minute cancelled with the professor and switched the meeting.

It is now July 2018.

'Kenny, it's really very strange. I get the feeling that I am talking to a doctor,' Dr P told me very early on in our conversations.

'I'll take that as a compliment,' I smiled. 'But I can assure you that I am no doctor.'

I had heard similar sentiments back in the UK, but the same words had a different overtone now. In England, it induced a guard of caution. In Germany, it meant that we were one.

A Hispanic connection cemented that spirit, too.

I handed Dr P a huge number of medical reports along with Christina's MRI scans. He asked a lot of questions, all the while making notes. Then we discussed the cost, and this was when I knew I was putting my daughter into good and caring hands.

'We will do three dendritic cell infusions and then she will have an MRI scan to see what effect it has had on the tumour,' he said.

'Should I pay you for those now?' I replied.

'No, you can pay it as we do each one,' the doctor advised.

'If we can see after the third one that it is not working, we will discontinue and there is no need to spend any more money.'

'If there is a positive response then we will plan a further three DC vaccines and keep going as long as we are getting good results,' he concluded.

And that made me feel instantly better, especially as it was not just my money that I was spending. Dr P was all about the patient and getting positive results. From that first meeting with him I immediately sensed that he was a good man with pure intentions. He took his Hippocratic oath seriously and wanted only to *heal and do no harm*. I instantly felt happier and with enormous hope in Cologne.

It was a huge relief to have finally found the right place for Christina. The experience from other people and my own common sense told me that you can spend vast amounts of money and it might not ever go away. We go through everything in each last detail. I ask for the benefits and the negatives. Christina might live for a number of years – or she might not. Things can turn very quickly.

I passed on everything I learned to people in similar positions. Many could not afford what was required. I helped as many as I could.

I was introduced to Daren and Joanne Price whose daughter Amber also had a brain tumour, albeit a different type to Christina's. Daren had done a vast amount of medical research and we began to exchange information almost daily. I introduced him to Dr P, and they eventually followed us out to Cologne for DC therapy. The network of parents in the UK was growing each month, and with all of us constantly looking into new treatments around the world this meant that our options were also increasing. The more we all knew, the more we could share with others and enable them to make an informed decision and quickly swing into action.

This was the message I was hearing from the network. Do not make your move too late. Of course, you 'waste' a lot of time having those initial consultations in the UK but at that point you have no choice, nor do you have knowledge. It is a sad indictment that only through frustration and dead ends do you discover that there might be another way of thinking and it is equally distressing that you almost have to go underground to acquire this information and you are getting it often from people for whom it has been too late.

One thing is clear – England is a relatively small island. There are many other countries out there who do things differently and whose thought-processes approach science from a different angle. Being British and under UK healthcare does not mean that is the only way. I add to the contradiction that in a Britain that was part of Europe (as we were then) I am bound by European laws, yet I can't have access to certain medicines and experimental therapies, as in Germany? There is something not right with that.

Clearly, the people you were dealing with are a massive factor. If you felt no connection or were in any way uncomfortable, as I was with the oncologist in the UK, then you were going to react differently to the same piece of information. If you form that bond, you save a lot of negative energy, more effectively channel that helpless anger, and clearly have more faith. Plus, I liked the vibe of the clinic in Cologne. There was one guy in from Boston, USA, whose illness was similar to Christina's, and he was responding well. He had already lived way beyond his prognosis. This was evidence that it can and does work.

When I return home, I begin to reorganise my schedule. I have some gigs booked in that I need to honour, but I am wary about putting too much else in ahead. I lose a lot of work. I earmark October to get back out to Germany.

I need to arrange everything properly. We have been told by the UK doctors not to fly, so I book an apartment in Cologne and plan to go by Eurostar with my friend Chris Gallagher helping. Chris was born when I was ten years old. I remember holding him a few days after his birth. His parents lived in the flat above us on Hillside Estate. He is like a brother to me and has proved to be one of *the* most important people in Christina's journey over the last four years. Going to Germany for those treatments really was a two-man job and I could not have done it without him. I needed someone with me who is on the ball and can think like I do. There are very few people whom you can actually trust when you are in a potential life-and-death situation. I can trust him with my life.

We budget for two weeks. In between treatments we will take Christina to the water park and zoo, and make those special memories a year and a half on from when the doctor had patronised us by saying that if we wanted to take a trip to Disneyland then sooner would be better than later. Chris has already sacrificed a lot.

Of course, the purpose of the mission is concealed from Christina, notwithstanding that she has some awareness. She hated all the people around her, but has been very tolerant of the herbal medicines. Right at the start of this process, she has taken capsules and drunk liquids that taste like crap. The method was set early and, to her credit and bravery, has never been a problem. She enjoys the long train journey. It is one for a kid. That is how she sees it at this point.

Meanwhile, I hear that Steve White has slightly deteriorated and his brain tumour has progressed. He is not getting the same results from the India treatment as he did previously. He had to stop travelling there and undergo surgery again. I was very sad to hear this. But Steve was such a warrior that I knew he would keep going.

There is a very real chance that I may have to head back out to Germany twice a month. You have to think logistically, and you have to be prepared to put your whole life on hold. I even considered moving out there for a few months as flying was out of the question. Meanwhile, Francisca remains at home with the other three young tearaways to contend with. For a while, needs must, and we have to operate separately in a team. It does place an enormous strain especially with Jude so young and being unable to give your 100% to a newborn. Constantly running into brick walls and lack of sleep have depleted our energy levels. At times it has felt like we were being killed with 1000 cuts rather than one big stab. Now we have to be apart to keep the family together.

Francisca's cousin Celeste and her husband Michael agreed to drive across Germany and meet us in Cologne. Michael helped me with some of the forms that were written in German. Seeing them on that first day out there was a real emotional support.

When we arrive at the clinic, guess what? Dr P questions if somebody in the UK really said that we couldn't fly.

I confirm that there has been no operation to insert a shunt, but the oncologist in Addenbrooke's had said that they wouldn't be in favour of it and were not happy signing it off.

Dr P examined Christina.

'I do not see any reason why she cannot fly to Cologne and I'm not sure why you were advised against it,' he told me.

I was so happy to hear this. It was a real game-changer and would be much easier than taking the Eurostar twice a month or moving to Germany. There are at least sixteen further visits ahead – not that I know this at this point. That is therefore the last time that I take that advice from the UK doctors. I make a note to start looking at airline schedules out of Stansted and Heathrow.

An enormous amount of blood was taken from Christina. Some to extract the dendritic cells from the rest to check liver function and stuff like vitamin D3 levels. This was not comfortable for Christina but with her sitting on my lap and Chris gently holding her arm while Dr P got to work, we managed to get it done. She is such a brave little girl.

Every time we were at the clinic, be it for blood samples or the DC infusion, Dr P made sure he gave her an intravenous high-dose vitamin C. The benefits of this were visible almost immediately. In my opinion anyone with cancer should be given this regularly, no matter what country they are in. It is inexpensive and should be used much more.

Exactly a week later she is given her first dendritic cell vaccine along with the vitamin C infusion. One of the main side effects, or should I say the perfect immune response to the DC cells, is a flu-like fever. Within a few hours of receiving the injection Christina begins to become restless and sweaty. I have to stay up that night and take temperature readings every 30 minutes. I have to report back on things, so I am WhatsApping Dr P through the night and into the early hours of the morning. The care and the aftercare are exceptional. My gut feeling had been correct. The level of detail and attention is extraordinary. I shake my head to think that I would never be able to communicate on that level in the UK.

Dr P advised me to allow the temperature to go as high as it can naturally without intervening with paracetamol, allowing her immune system to respond to the millions of DC cells that have just gone into her body. It is never going to be comfortable for her. We manage things naturally by opening the windows, using a cold compress on her forehead, and even giving her a warm shower. I thought a warm shower would be the last thing to do, but Dr P assured me that after being exposed to warm water the body responds by lowering its temperature. He was right. It worked. If she reaches 39.5 that should be the peak. Everything is regulated and everything has a schedule. She reads 38, 38.2, 38.4, 38.6. The numbers are good and steady but gradually rising. Should she reach above 39.5, then Dr P said not to hesitate in giving her some paracetamol. That first time she

349

peaked at 39 and then it slowly came back down through the night, and she slept through. I didn't sleep because I continued checking with the thermometer until the morning.

She woke up as bright as a button, full of beans, laughing, singing and ready for action. It was a lovely sight, considering how she was not many hours ago. This we would have to do every month for many months to come, and often the fever was greater than that first time. Christina took it in her stride and even looked forward to her Germany trips, especially when we took her to see the famous Christmas markets in December.

I am reasonably confident that after months of painstaking research and personal stories I have made the correct decision. I hope and pray it is the right one. I did not have a million options.

Four months later Christina had an MRI scan in the UK. We were told that there was a slight progression. Here the language gets misleading as progression actually means deterioration: the tumour had slightly grown. I sent the scans to my cousin José; he was not so sure. He got two other medical professionals to look at the scans, one of them a paediatric brain tumour specialist. He said six eyes are better than two.

In the UK I was told that tumour had progressed – in other words got worse.

José told me that part of that tumour was now inactive.

'We can see inflammation which is the result of necrosis,' he said.

That meant cell *death*. This was good news. There was also in their opinion a slight reduction in size.

What I could not get my head around was why it was the complete opposite to what I was being told here at home. I guess six eyes were better than two.

My cousin's knowledge and analysis were so important. It gives you confidence when your own is shot to pieces. I had a little understanding and a lot of doubtful curiosity. I hope if you ever find yourself in a similar position with no knowledge, you take heart from this passage and remember your right to ask a second opinion and perhaps scour the internet for others' experiences outside the UK.

Dr P spoke directly with José and this they were able to do in Spanish which meant nothing was lost in translation. Dr P said to me that he wished he had someone like my cousin working with him.

We were very happy with this news, and this meant the DC infusions were having a positive effect and we should continue with them. So, I planned the next three months, flights and hotels with Chris, my right-hand man.

I feel like my life has been building to this in an odd kind of way. It is not the summit of my existence but all those early feelings from when Aunt Sole died and all those questions of the Church, philosophy and science were as though I was guided here and had been prepared and educated in advance of this moment. Lately I had been reading as much as when I did my degree.

I know I am doing the right thing in this particular moment in time, and you only have that context in hoping to *buy* time in the belief that something else or some breakthrough will become available as the clock ticks.

That said, I still wished that we had come here earlier – that sentiment I had heard from others so many times. Equally, to have lost her in that first six months would have been devastating. Nobody is ever prepared for the loss of a child, but by this stage we were as mentally aware as we could be. It gave me context – looking back at the idiot I was at times in the 1990s but now truly embracing time that I had wittered away in foolishness back then. It occupied my every thought and most of my dreams. On at least one occasion in my broken sleep, I dreamed that I heard Christina saying, 'Look at my hand, Daddy,' and it was moving normally when it hadn't done since diagnosis. There were times when I held Christina and rested my head against hers, secretly praying that her illness would come out of her and into my body instead – after all I had had a life and some of those years I wasted. Why her and not me?

I felt very merciful to a higher power that we were still here at all.

I think about what happens if Christina does not make it. I know the hospital at home will be straight on offering us condolences and telling us they did their best for us. I am way past that point, but should we find ourselves there I will simply thank them for their call and tell them how glad I am that they didn't get their hands on her.

I know that I have never been more driven or focused about anything in my life. I am running on empty but with tunnel vision.

Three people whom I knew went to Cologne after me. Steve White had reached the end of the road in India and considered Germany to be a better option. Steve had reached the point where he really needed something to turn things around fast. I had a long conversation with his wife Katheryn about the clinic in Cologne, and this helped them make the decision to come over. I met them out there and was deeply saddened to see how much Steve had deteriorated. I hoped and prayed that he would bounce back because no one had fought this disease harder than him.

Timing was everything, though.

The doctor treating Christina told me that most people who come to them are so far down a road where the likes of chemo and radiation have ravaged them that there are now limits as to what they can achieve.

This is an important point. I had resisted everything in the UK, so Christina came to them with a clean slate and was responding. The British narrative tells you that there is only one way. Clearly, this is not true but crucially most people have already taken steps in that direction and therefore when they find places like the clinic in Cologne it is often a little too late.

My friend Herc Eracli came over there, too. He was receiving a lot of advice from Ilan which did help. He had also unfortunately gone through many invasive and aggressive treatments in the UK which achieved very little. So, by the time he got to Cologne he was extremely weak and in a great deal of pain. When we saw him at the clinic, he always seemed so much more concerned about Christina than he did about himself. Such a lovely person who really didn't deserve to go through what he did.

Dr P did say to me that he was happy for me to recommend them, but did not want me to mention them on social media. They did not want to be famous; they may have to turn away people who do not stand a chance or they might not be able to cope with the volume of people turning to them. This is highly specialised work and the nature of it combined with that moment in individuals' lives when people turned to them would inevitably for some lead to disappointment.

That, in itself, is heartbreaking to declare. They have done wonders for Christina. That won't always be the case – possibly for her and certainly for others.

The whole process is exhausting for everyone involved.

I did recommend Cologne. My circle of friends grew. We had to share the knowledge because that knowledge was deprived through official channels and that was also the process through which I acquired knowledge!

Scott Lau brought two new things to my attention. TBL-12 and ONC201. TBL-12 is a natural product made out of marine ingredients, with the main ingredient being *bêche-de-mer* (sea cucumber). It works by modulating the immune system. It has been used for millennia in Chinese medicine, but it is not something I had used or had access to in my TCM studies. Scott put me in touch with the guy in New Zealand who made this product and he kindly sent me some to give to Christina.

ONC201 is a whole different thing. It is a new cancer drug and early results in brain cancer clinical trials suggest that it can kill cancer cells but not normal cells. It penetrates the blood brain barrier and engages proven anti-cancer pathways that lead to death in cancer cells. Scott gave me an idea of where and how I might be able to access this new drug. I got Michael on the case: he spoke German and would hopefully be more successful than me at getting a result. I gave him the name of a doctor and the rough location. He set to work and managed to track him down and made contact. It turns out that the drug was in a phase 2 trial and accessing it was not going to be easy. In fact, it looked almost impossible to access it, so I had to put it on the back burner. I needed to continue with the next round of DC infusions and come back to ONC201 and try again at a later date.

Thanks to Scott, I now knew about ONC201 and this would prove to be very important going forward, but for now I had to accept that I was unable to lay my hands on it.

I get a call from one of my close music industry mates, the record producer Brian 'Keys' Tharme. He tells me about this amazing guy named Graham Sweet who lives in Dorset, claiming that he is a genius with herbal medicine. He asked me if I would like to be put in touch with him to see if he can help Christina in any way. Yes, I would!

Graham and I became good friends and yes, he is a herbal medicine genius. He introduced me to a whole new side of natural medicine. Some things were very similar to Chinese medicine with slight variations, but other things were way outside all the boxes I knew. Through Graham and his contacts, I imported samambaia and graviola from Peru. At one point I even seriously considered travelling to Lima with him in search of a very rare herb known to cure cancer. I had visions of us being shacked up with some shaman out in the jungle trying to negotiate the best price in my broken Spanish.

Graham provided me with a lot of new herbal formulas which I introduced to Christina's regime over a period of many months. One thing I learned from him was to keep chopping and changing the protocol. Take things away, then reintroduce them, then go over to something completely new. He said disease can be very adaptive, so you have to be one step ahead, always coming at it unexpectedly with natural chemicals and powerful molecules. Never let it get used to any medicine because it will find a way around it. Graham is also importing fresh soursop plants from Sri Lanka and cat's claw, making a powerful tincture which Christina has twice a day in some fresh orange juice. All natural and so very good for the immune system. Recently I sent him one of my own herbal formulas to try out which he found to be very beneficial. So, we share our knowledge with each other, always with one aim in mind: 'healing disease with all the natural and wonderful things found in creation'.

I buy frankincense from a lady who travels to Oman and distils the best oil, well known for its anti-tumour properties, and from Ilan I get the ultimate green bee propolis straight from Brazil, which I then combine with pure organic royal jelly. Steve White introduced me to Jim Dickson from Vitacure Ltd who provides me with the best organic turmeric, serrapeptase, lumbrokinase and probiotics. My dear friend Stefano Leonardi, whom I have known for years from when I first moved to Finchley, is probably one of the most well informed people I know when it comes to alternative medicine. He is a bit of a scientist really and many times I have visited his house to find his kitchen looking like a scene from the TV series *Breaking Bad*. Making up the perfect colloidal silver solution, which I have to say I have had some great results with, once adding it to a nebuliser along with some dimethyl sulfoxide (DMSO) and eliminating a chest infection in no time at all.

I let Dr P know about all of these herbal meds. What I am using and when I am doing so. We keep an eye on Christina's liver function via the blood tests, making sure her system is never overloaded at any time. Safety is so important even with natural herbal medicine. I noticed that Christina's energy levels were up and she was looking well. Little positive interventions were nudging it all in the right direction, plus the dendritic cells were doing good things.

One night in Cologne, Christina was asleep next to me in the hotel room and my mind was so restless. For some reason I was unable to sleep. Then in the very early hours I get a text from Daren Price. Before I even opened the text to read it, I knew what it was. His sweet little daughter Amber had passed away. I was gutted for him and his wife Joanne. You share this journey with each other: when others grieve, you do so with them. When you receive some positive news, they encourage you. Daren, at the height of his own loss that night, messaged me saying, 'You keep going, pal, for Christina and for Amber.'

One small thing I was able to do for Amber which brought a huge smile to her face in those final days was getting Gary Barlow and Mark Owen to sign a get-well card for her when I met them at Eliot Kennedy's 50th birthday party. It made her so happy. She told all of her friends and showed them their kind words.

A few weeks later I get more bad news. Steve White and Herc Eracli have both passed away. I am very sad and emotionally numb. I'm on a roller coaster with highs and lows, but the lows seem to be dominating. I am also acutely aware that all of the people, the friends, who were fighting their illness alongside us are now gone. Christina, for now, is the last person standing. We are back on that lonely journey again.

I was unable to make Steve's funeral because I was in Germany, but I did attend Herc's. The church was packed with people, and I got to hear stories about him that confirmed my own thoughts that he was a very special person, as was Steve. This only raises one question which is difficult to answer, and one which I have always asked: 'Why do bad things happen to good people?'

After a number of DC infusions in Cologne, my cousin José confirmed from her scans that Christina's disease was stable. This is good, and I have no doubt that the dendritic cells played their part, but it was not achieving the shrinkage we hoped it would. It was time for me to consider a different treatment and look once again at ONC201. Some time had passed since I last tried to access this new drug, and I had heard that children from various countries were getting it from a particular doctor in Frankfurt.

To date as I write, Christina has been to Germany fifteen times. We may return again, of course, but for now she is doing well. We couldn't often see a daily improvement as we were too close to the situation, but she was still very much alive and way past that ominous prognosis of six months, and others whom we would see less often could chart that progress. Dr P, who had seen many people in decline, confirmed how well she was doing.

I finally cracked the Enigma code with ONC201 and made contact with Dr A in Frankfurt. The timing could not have been more perfect because he was now admitting new children onto the phase 2 trial of the drug at his clinic. I flew over there alone, armed with every scan and medical report on Christina, hoping she would be eligible for the drug. It was a long meeting with a huge amount of information to process, but the long and short of it is that her tumour met the criteria for this medicine. I left there with a three-month supply of it and an official letter allowing me to pass through Customs with the medicine. I had to move fast because it was in a cooler pack and was only good for a number of hours. I switched to an earlier flight, made it back to

Heathrow, then drove back to Norfolk and whacked it straight into the fridge. Mission accomplished!

Dr A told me that ONC201 does not work overnight but takes about three months to really get going. It might shrink her tumour, as it has done on some of his patients, or it might just slow things down and stabilise her disease. We won't know until we do further scans, but for now we would have to wait and see. There can be certain side effects with this drug, the most notable one being euphoria. I was happy to hear this because we had so far managed to avoid Christina's being subjected to unnecessary suffering and I wanted to keep it that way. So, on the days she took the ONC201 we noticed that her mood was more jovial and a few more raspberries were blown in my direction. To be honest this fitted in perfectly with our family because we are quite a silly bunch anyway, always joking and messing around. Living each day as it comes, keeping things as normal and happy as is possible.

I knew one thing. We were doing something right.

More scans. Little change.

For this type of tumour, no change is good news. The best news obviously was to see shrinkage. But stability was key. Her seizures haven't happened and Christina most days is singing, dancing and getting up to mischief with her sister and brothers.

You could even measure what she felt within herself by these words:

'When are we going back to Germany?' she began to say. 'I miss Germany.'

That meant a lot. I remember the doctor who said to get to Disneyland sooner or later, and how *I* wasn't going to stand for the poor quality of life that the proposed treatments had on offer. I wanted this to be a joyful time for her if indeed it didn't cure her.

She was enjoying her young life.

She continued to go to school in her special needs buggy. She was occasionally tired but never complained, although as time went on her energy was improving by the day.

358

Scott Lao then introduced me to a guy called Mike Watson. He is all over PEMF: pulsed electromagnetic field therapy. I thought it was an acronym for a boy band. Thank goodness that it wasn't. It is an amazing science.

I took a trip down to see Mike with Christina, and we tried out of the PEMF machines, which he then kindly allowed me to borrow for a while to continue the therapy. He really is the most knowledgeable person on PEMF here in the UK: his scientific mind and his understanding of this technology are second to none.

I mentioned the use of PEMF to Dr P in Cologne and he was very aware of its use in Germany and of its benefits in reducing inflammation and pain along with its many effective applications for cancer patients. So, it was a thumbs-up from him. It is sad to think that most doctors here in the UK have never heard of it, and if I would have mentioned it to them, they would no doubt have given me the 'Tin Foil Hat' Award.

Mike Watson is one of the few people to focus on EPEMF, enhanced pulsed electromagnetic field therapy, where two machines are used at the same time, using various frequencies doing different things at the same time.

I bought two machines from a company in Austria to use on Christina.

Does it cure cancer? This depends on who you ask. Some scientists claim to have killed cancer cells with this technology, but using much more powerful machines set at very strong frequencies.

Did it benefit her body?

Yes.

She slept better, her mobility was slightly improved, and her energy levels were elevated. We use it every night. She simply lies on her bed on the large PEMF mat and often within 20 minutes goes off into the most comfortable of sleeps. Her right leg often causes her some discomfort, and this is always resolved with PEMF. Most days Christina will now ask me, 'Daddy, can I go on the mat?'

Like most things I learned from Chinese medicine, it is good to implement these things when you are well and not wait until you are ill. So, I decided to use it on me and the rest of the family. Christina's illness did have benefits for all of us. My newly acquired knowledge of nutrition, supplements and herbal formulas has benefited us all. Over the last four years my children, Christina included, have not had one bout of cold or flu. This, I have no doubt, is down to my introduction of nutrients, supplements and dietary changes.

At the back of my mind, there is always still the very real possibility of the Doomsday scenario. Do I believe that we can win? Or will there not be a favourable outcome? I do not rest on my laurels.

I continue to research and learn as much as possible, even though Germany has calmed the situation and we have reached a general plateau of tranquillity. Many parents, too, from all around the world continue to get in touch with me. You have to keep your radar up. There could be a medical breakthrough just around the corner at any point. I was constantly looking for results and was determined not to see Christina fade and deteriorate like Mum had. I had listened too hard and for too long back then. Now I was listening to my heart and following that innate gut instinct.

It is easy to adopt a mindset and a position that this battle is 'you versus the tumour'. That is what I see often with the standard cancer treatments being used every day in most hospitals. That is wrong. There is a person with that tumour. It is not you versus the tumour. Removing the person in an abstract way from the disease can mean that they are disregarded, and this often results in greater suffering. You have to be mindful of the person and in my case that person is my little girl. So, I remain mindful of this reality and do my best to avoid focusing solely on the disease. Quality of life is what I have always wanted for her and so far have managed to achieve that.

When you hear her ask those questions that all children do, like 'when I grow up... when I am older...' it breaks you. Because you do not know if she will get there. More importantly, the innocence in the question tells you that she has no idea that it is in doubt.

It is difficult to answer. You just look for landmarks ahead, hoping that she will make them – such as her next birthday or Christmas.

Then she would come out with the sweetest things:

'I want to be a doctor when I'm older... I want to help people get better.'

For this pure and innocent little human being, it was pretty much all she really knew.

Roller skating was such a massive part of my life. I don't really expect it to be that big for my kids. For our CB radio – well they have, quite simply, mobile phones. But we moved to Norfolk for that simple life. Not simple as in superficial but simple as in stripped back, free from noise, safe, with space, where values could embed rather than being lost in the city.

You see the kindness of strangers in a close-knit community and the parochial curtain-twitching of village life. It is up to you how much you engage, though of course we have had to with the practicalities of Christina's life and in benefiting from neighbours' generosity.

But those ordinary elements in life and Christina's inability to engage can break your heart. She won't be roller skating anytime soon. When I take Angela and Joe out, I cannot help but be consumed with the thought that there is a child missing out who should be there with us. We have that bike in the garage that she has never ridden. It has been there for over four years. I would have taught her by now, but her disability had made that impossible. Instead, I bought a tricycle with a passenger seat which she now rides around in with Joe pedalling as fast as possible.

The last video of her before the tumour was discovered is of her trampolining. The kids love trampolining. She had started swimming lessons, too, and was a very fast learner. It places everything on hold.

Yet, you are living in three parallel universes. Your other children need normality, progress and development, and then you, yourself, still have to perform. For three years I gigged with a heavy heart – not a completely broken one, but a severely wounded one. Slugging it out and getting into some sort of zone onstage before, on some occasions, crying myself to sleep in a hotel room or pounding lonely roads back home into the early hours. Only now is Francisca beginning to make new music as well.

You have to function for yourself and the family and keep going for everyone. That means you still host and attend children's parties when it is one of the kids' birthdays, though Christina was not a regular on some of those guest lists. It was just too awkward for some people, but when invited and the bouncy castles would come out, I would invariably have to go on it with her and hold her hand. The knock-on effect was that sometimes Angela would be omitted from her age group's parties because they knew Christina would be coming with us. To be so young and excluded because people perceived there was baggage had become our cruel reality.

We often felt isolated, despite the goodwill of many. On the whole, school made her feel special and she was assigned a teacher one to one. They stepped up and made provisions and have done brilliantly, and if she is leaving for Germany then some of the kids have written cards before she goes. And Germany itself offers a much calmer, soothing process than the UK. Their clinics don't seem to have that spectre of doom and gloom which I associate with the hospitals here at home. The way they treat her has a tenderness to it. The tone, the vibe, the energy is all different, and it lends itself towards healing and more positive outcomes. I always tell them that I will go to Hell and back if that is what it takes. Christina, meanwhile, has a free will and nothing is forced upon her. She enjoyed going to see Dr P in Cologne, but she often freaked out when she was surrounded by a team of white coats at Addenbrooke's. Make of that what you will.

You remain on your guard, though – a permanent state of alert. There is no stopping of time. I very rarely drink alcohol these days, but I did invite the old London crew to Norfolk to my 50th birthday party in my garden. With my mate Bradley on the decks, he rocked that patio dance floor like it was Hedkandi at Rouge nightclub all over again. My kids enjoyed seeing us old boys throwing a few outdated shapes to our beloved house music. I kicked the last one of them out of the front door at around 4.30am. I have done enough socialising in the past and there is nothing that I haven't seen, but it was so good to blow off the cobwebs and host a banging party. A one-off.

It is so easy to not do anything when you are in the situation that my family and I find ourselves in. Easy to just give up and become scared of living. I often think of the words said by Tim Robbins and Morgan Freeman in my favourite movie *The Shawshank Redemption*: 'It comes down to a simple choice: get busy living or get busy dying'.

I am going to get busy living, and if that means finding another excuse to have a garden party to celebrate life with the people I love, then let's do it.

You still can't quite let yourself go, though. You have a complete perspective of what is necessary and unnecessary. Sleep is at a premium. Christina often comes looking for me in the night. When you do manage to nod off, those dreams are vivid. So very real – Christina running freely with expressive hands. When you wake up, it is a completely different world. Though we didn't know Christina's fate when we moved to Norfolk, I think the hermit lifestyle is understandable.

But there is no normal. There never will be. Every day has positives, and every day has negatives. They come in equal proportion, so you never get far ahead of yourself. The next inconsistency can be just around the corner. For Christina and for ourselves we live in the moment.

For Francisca it is tough. The bereavements that I have experienced, and have become almost accepting of, are new territory to her. She has never had a major loss. But you can't sit there and think, 'I am used to loss.' It doesn't work like that. People are individuals and, from Mum to David, many have gone early and for the cruellest of reasons. Maybe you can deal with any bereavement after the first major one with a slightly better coping mechanism. Maybe not. Perhaps it gets worse when you see those whom you love go so early and you are left questioning the research, care and advice they were given.

No, it doesn't get easier. You become more desensitised, and if left unchecked you get angrier. And no parent should lose a child.

Francisca loves salsa dancing and boxing and is able to go out to find that release. I rarely do. You have to dig really deep to find any normality. It leaves you numb. Your normal is different to other people's.

But you need inspiration – and you really only can take it from those still in a similar fight or those families where someone didn't make it and are kind enough to share their stories.

I met my dear friends Stella and Tony in the 90s and ended up being godfather to both Stella and their first child Francesca. They are now godparents to my son Joseph. Francesca was born perfectly normally but then was diagnosed with a neurological disorder and would never walk or talk. They went on to have two further children, Matthew and Samuel, now both at Cambridge University. I never knew until now how they managed to keep going all day after sleepless nights, modifying their home and with a nurse coming and going at all hours. They kept smiling and I would look at them, unable to understand. They knew by experience what was happening to us. It takes friendship and experience like that to see it clearly on your behalf and they lost Francesca in 2013. To sing the *Ave Maria* at her funeral was such an honour and a heartfelt moment, long before any of this happened to us. They have been a great support, often making the journey up to Norfolk to spend time with us.

It is a very lonely battle, but it teaches you how to conduct yourself. Stoicism sets in; the nonsense and noise of life are irrelevant.

The practicalities take over. Christina has her own mind and does not want everything that has been offered to her. The hospital made plastic splints for her legs and tried to get her to use a cumbersome frame to walk with. She was not interested in these things and she soon abandoned them. She is a free-spirited child.

Then the care and caution for Christina spill over towards the others. You look out twice as often to the garden if Angela, Joe and Jude are playing and you don't want to see history repeating itself – one minute normal on a trampoline or bike, the next knowing that may never happen again, and it is hard for Angela as she and Christina are very close. She adores her little sister.

I have to manage this for Angela, in particular, being the eldest.

I know that we have been sparring with the cancer all this time. It has consumed our life and every single manoeuvre is delicate. The decision to pause the dendritic cell treatment for now and switch to the ONC201 was not an easy one to make, but does appear to have been a wise move.

The good news is that the tumour is not altering much at all.

There was of course another huge curve ball incoming.

50 COVID

I began working on this book a long time ago. In the era of BC. Before COVID.

Now everything has changed. Forever.

Despite a hugely successful, brief crowdfunding campaign at Christmas 2020, I personally did not feel I could bring my story… our whole family's story up to date until there was some light at the end of the tunnel. Everybody is aware that one of the most decimated industries in the pandemic was entertainment and hospitality, and of course, I had gigs booked in, and under my new manager Ed Lewis had been making huge plans for the 30th anniversary release of *Voices*.

That excitement about meeting Ed had to be tempered. As for all of us, Zoom replaced every kind of meeting we ever knew. Ed had come into my life after a gig in Marbella, Spain, in June 2018 where I had been at lunch with my friend Darren Green and asked him if he could recommend a good manager. Darren knows a lot of people in the music biz, the movers and shakers, so he arranged for me to meet up with Ed back in London. Ed is a great guy, very switched on, extremely creative, well connected and super organised. We had only been working together just a few months when the pandemic hit.

Then everything stopped.

I had been so exhausted by gigging and going to Germany that I actually thought I could do with a few months off, but as you will know, too, that gear change we all felt often led to claustrophobia and every six weeks or so those emotions would become very intense and stifling.

It struck me early that any singer's story would remain unfinished if there was not a coming out of the other side chapter. For months I dithered as dates to tour got moved again. As I write, it is now over eighteen months since I began wondering if gigging would ever be as it always had been.

That remains, like most artists, the main source of income, so whatever you might have tucked away, you need to top it up and funds are only going one way – down. Plus, your relationship with the audience is what all of this is based on. Singing live in front of familiar faces, and every time making new friends, too.

However, as you will appreciate, it could not be my biggest concern.

How the hell was I going to get to Germany for Christina? Let alone homeschooling four kids and being cooped up in the house all day. We moved to Norfolk for peace and a certain degree of isolation. Nobody knew that self-isolation was about to be the norm.

I called Germany and asked if the medicine could be shipped to me. They told me no, that they couldn't send it. So, with lockdown looking so inevitable, I once again flew out to Frankfurt and back the same day and managed to get Francisca's family, who had been staying with us, out of the country and back to Cape Town. A tiring journey on all counts considering that I had to first get to Heathrow from Norfolk, but one that always left me feeling a real sense of achievement. Like a man on a mission, I was happy when it was accomplished, and I had got the medicine safely back home.

At this time I was in touch with the parents of two other children who had very similar brain tumours to Christina's: Craig and Lois Jackson and their daughter Edie, plus Sarat Afsar and his daughter Safa. We spoke often, sharing information and discussing possible treatment options. It is always an anxious race against time, and often I was able to put parents directly in touch with doctors abroad, thus avoiding some of the endless searching I experienced back in 2017.

Craig and I were constantly in communication with each other during the early days of the first lockdown. He and his wife Lois flew over to New York with Edie for a procedure called CED (convection-enhanced delivery). We became quite concerned that the pandemic would prevent us from accessing the medicine in Germany. So, when I made my way there Craig also travelled from New York to Frankfurt just a couple of days after me and collected a large supply of ONC201. He then flew back that same day to the US. So, this gives you an insight into the lengths parents go to just to get their hands on this medicine, and the sacrifices made trying to save their children. When our lockdown was temporarily lifted, I was straight back out there, even in the face of very tough restrictions in Germany.

I was always under the belief that I had to physically collect the medicine and take it with me, placed in a cooler pack, then plug in my little car refrigerator and get it back home. As the pandemic wore on – and I assume that I was not the only one making this request – it emerged that it *could* be sent. Sarat was the first person to confirm that Doctor A in Frankfurt had agreed to FedEx it over to the UK. I was of course happy to hear this, but at the same time really disappointed that it took a worldwide lockdown for them to change their position. So, I made my request and the shipments followed. This made the process a little easier for now.

At the back of my mind was the very reality that the NHS was becoming almost a 100% COVID service. I am tempted to say understandably so, but it is common knowledge that many people waiting on operations and treatments pre-COVID were being pushed back due to this international emergency. They were doing an incredible job in the pandemic under the greatest of pressure. Do not mis-understand my respect and admiration for them in this tough time.

In June 2020 I *had* begun leaning on the Health Service very hard for a scan for Christina, but they couldn't deliver due to COVID. I told them how badly I needed it and that the doctors in Germany had to get their eyes on it, too. I was not about to see all of the money I had spent on trips there (and all that entailed) disappear. I had tried to make those trips a holiday for Christina, as tough as life was. They will always remain Daddy and daughter moments.

I have never liked putting my little girl through those MRI scans where she has to go under a general anaesthetic and spend the day in hospital, and often feels so poorly afterwards, but it has to be done. It's the only way we can really know what's happening with the tumour in detail.

369

The British oncologists and myself had arrived at a peaceful place together, even wishing me good luck with Germany and noting that Christina had fared well.

'Mr Thomas, I think you made the right move,' I was told.

And grateful to hear it, too. But also slightly angry – mostly at the system which had tied *their* hands. Some of my irate mentality turned to compassion because I knew that they were interested in what was going on, and of course they wanted to see her do well, but they could not endorse it or put it in their reports.

I find that sad.

Equally, whilst we fought on and deliberately contradicted that narrative, yes, we did try to prepare ourselves for that day when Christina might not be there. But in all honesty, as much as you think you can be set for it, you can't. We will never be ready for that day.

For years, we have been running on empty, fighting the system and all to keep our daughter alive. Three years of broken sleep, at least, only really helped by Minki, when she came over from Cape Town for five months to help us.

It had been Francisca who reached out to palliative care during the lockdown. Christina *had* been noticeably deteriorating and the ONC201 takes about three months to get properly working – and there are always likely to be some negatives. Common sense told us to reunite with the hospice team and ask them to come and assess it.

They arrived at the house dressed head to toe in hazmat suits, gloves and masks, looking like Dustin Hoffman from the movie *Outbreak*. My kids were a little freaked out by their outfits, but they soon got used to it and quickly resumed their game of *Minecraft* on the Xbox. The doctor examined Christina and concluded that palliative care was not needed as she appeared to be quite stable. She has remained that way ever since. This all happened around that three-month mark of using ONC201, so I can only assume that this may have caused the downturn. So, we have to be vigilant and keep observing her daily, even the microchanges that take place. You live on a knife-edge. There is a level of stability, but you are *on that edge* all the time.

Furthermore, I had of course seen many parents, whom I had got to know through this process, lose their children. We were all on the journey at different stages. I had seen how, at the final moments, things went downhill extremely fast. The thought of this fills me with dread.

This reality would be hammered home once again when I received the very sad news that both Edie Jackson and Safa Afsar had passed away. May they rest in peace. I wanted nothing more than for these children to be healed, as I do my own. I honestly share and experience some of the pain these parents go through each time this happens. A dark cloud hangs over me for a number of days, accompanied by a deep sadness. At times I find it difficult to make sense of it all. Why them and not some of the evil people roaming about on this planet? No child should have to go through that. I guess this is a normal human reaction in the face of something so very difficult to understand. As a kid I always used to ask a million questions. I wanted to know the answers to everything, I still do. But you don't always get what you want, and I have to accept that.

One dilemma that I do have is: Why do the doctors here in the UK refer to these tumours as rare? From where I am sitting, they don't seem to be uncommon at all. You hear a lot more about them these days. Stop calling them 'rare'.

So once again I was *the last man standing*, ever aware that, as a father, I could be next, and constantly gutted at the loss experienced by people who had become my friends.

But I was not for giving up. To paraphrase Martin Luther King Jr... If a man has not found something worth dying for, then he hasn't found something worth living for.

Neither do these other parents who have lost their children ever give up. They keep going and they keep giving.

My wife and I were left absolutely speechless when Craig and Lois Jackson drove all the way out to Norfolk and gave us the ONC201 that they had bought for little Edie. They didn't want anything for it. They just wanted to help Christina continue her fight. Sarat also kindly gave us the remaining medicine he had purchased for Safa. Such amazing people who, in the midst of incredible great pain and loss, made time to think of another child who would benefit from that medicine.

There was one observable difference between Christina and the children who had passed away. They had all been operated on, received radiation or chemotherapy – the very thing I had resisted. Often I would hear these friends say that they had wished that they had spoken to me sooner and that they didn't realise that they had a choice or the power to resist. I find it very sad that they felt the obligation to accept the narrative. But when parents find themselves in that situation it is hard to think straight, and that narrative is often the only thing you hear, and it appears to be the only hope you have. Please remember that here I am talking mainly about inoperable paediatric brain tumours like DIPGs which unfortunately have the worst survival rates and are the least funded in research.

Things need to change, and these children deserve to have access to safe experimental medicine here in the UK and not have to travel around the world in search of a cure.

Christina will always be our miracle baby. Every day that she is here with us is in itself a small success. We live in the moment, one day at a time, counting each day as a blessing.

By October 2020 the NHS finally confirmed that they could do a scan and it would take place in December. It should have happened in July, so it was five months late. Better late than never.

A few days after the MRI I get a call from the oncologist at Norwich Hospital. It was bad news. The tumour has progressed. It has grown. We were gutted.

I then get a call some days later from the oncologist at Addenbrooke's. They had had another look at the scans and the tumour had not grown. It appeared to be more or less the same size as it was in the last scan eleven months ago. So, this was good news.

By now, Francisca and I are used to having our hopes dashed and then raised again in a matter of days. I don't even bother questioning them as to why they said one thing and then changed it later on. I simply sent the scans over to my cousin José so his team could have a proper look at them.

José admitted that, although he is not familiar with the exact mechanism at work with ONC201, it appears to have made the tumour less active and they could tell this from the highlighting in the MRI, the brightness or lack of it in the images. So again he confirmed that for now her disease appeared to be stable.

We have to accept that it is what it is, and the disease being stable might be as good as it gets right now. We have to keep going.

Many could not believe I had still been gigging up to the moment when the pandemic hit. You had to find a way, though, to achieve some sort of normality, or often escapism. Music and gigging are my own form of therapy.

Phone conversations with Bluey, Errol Reid, Junior Giscombe and soul singer Keni Stevens proved to be good medicine during the lockdown. Knowing that you are not alone and that others are in the same boat brought a welcome perspective. Keni and I spoke the most, and like typical old blokes we had a good old rant and proper moan about the whole affair.

Of course, all fundraising for Christina stopped overnight because of COVID-19. Creativity both waned and peaked. We all had time on our hands to dream up anything, but circumstance and atmosphere and creative inspiration *were* thin on the ground. Life was slightly numb and a tad boring. You know that. You were there, too.

As church-goers we were unhappy not to attend. A Sunday Mass and the Easter Triduum became virtual. Just like everything else.

I did not remain inactive. I started talking to Eliot Kennedy a lot and that is a very good place to be. Francisca, writing her own material prolifically, made a recording with Bluey from Incognito who rightly surmised that 'We have times on our hands… it is not as though we are touring the world.' We had been 'threatening' to make this record for a very long time but, with Richard Bull as co-producer and working remotely without

373

ever meeting up, including a big brass section, the pandemic facilitated the release of her track 'Fall Into My Love'.

She is a better songwriter than me, seeks no glory and I know that I married a genius. That fiery Cape Town spirit and my crazy Hispanic temperament, we are joined at the hip. She gets me, and I her.

To sum up the way I feel about Francisca I have to use the lyrics of Gladys Knight and the Pips, taken from the song chosen for our first dance on our wedding day. You're the best thing that ever happened to me.

She gave up everything for me – not Kenny Thomas the singer. Me. And yes, she misses Cape Town very much.

But, hey, let someone else decide on her skill as an artist and a songwriter. I asked Eliot Kennedy because I knew that he would never bullshit me.

'She's brilliant,' he responded, leaving me glowing with pride.

The industry was somehow working – just about.

A while back my friend Jon Jules put me in touch with the DJ and record producer Dr Packer. I am a big fan of his work and had always wanted to make a record with him. Lockdown meant that Dr Packer was not touring the globe and was finally able to get into the studio and finish our tune, a cover of The Fatback Band's 'I Found Lovin''. It is a song I often perform live with my band but had not recorded until now. The pandemic, as bad as it was and with all gigs cancelled, did force us to redirect our energies into other areas with positive results.

A podcast with Mark Wilkinson for his *Life Remixed* series enabled me to still connect with an audience and talk about music and, more importantly, Christina. Mark was so moved by her story that he decided to revisit and remix the track 'Sweet Sweet Music' which we wrote a few years ago. This time with Toni Economides in the mix the record would have a whole new vibe, with all proceeds going towards Christina's medical treatment.

Gary Barlow was online seemingly every night with his Crooner Sessions in what might have looked like he was somewhere between filling time and filling a void in people's lives by just giving something back for free that was warts and all and different. So, when he called me to duet on 'Thinking About Your Love', I couldn't have been happier. I came late to the Crooner Sessions party but I am very grateful that he invited me in for a sing-song. Then, when I clocked over 4 million views of it, I was blown away.

Thank you for your continued support.

Home was now absolutely everything – from a school to a studio, and we tried to keep everything as normal as possible for the kids. Like everyone, we improvised pretending to be geography teachers or simply putting up a mirrorball in the lounge for the kids to disco to. Impromptu was king.

We grew corn on the cob, lettuce, potatoes, tomatoes and runner beans on our vegetable patch, and sometimes barely bothered to get dressed – not unfamiliar to you, I am sure.

At one point, Christina was the only one going into school. She had been assigned one-to-one tuition, as she was now deemed special needs – and she loved it. The attention was all on her and we are respectfully grateful to the teaching staff charged with her education in moments that allowed us to breathe and dedicate some sort of normality to the other three.

As lockdown slowly lifted, everything was coming at a rush, including all of those 2020 gigs that had been moved often more than twice. Things were supposedly returning to some kind of normality, but it didn't feel that way.

I had placed so much on hold – including this memoir and a tour – that when it looked like we could come out to play again, that gear change and the pent-up energy had to be managed once more.

I raced straight to Sheffield to record with Eliot, Francisca went down to London to write with Peter Andre, and if there are benefits to have come out of the pandemic, then the reconnections with people and that notion that if we can get through this, then we will be truly grateful, were an excellent reset for everybody.

A new lease of life.

I knew, too, that the UK's 'Brexit' from Europe was also a little sleeping nightmare. Touring would now be bound up in paperwork, but we all wanted to get out on the road. You don't think of politics and pop being a lethal concoction bar those famous moments of Sir Bob Geldof fighting Maggie Thatcher over the Band Aid record and Tony Blair courting that era dubbed *Cool Britannia* but a wise soul in the music industry said to me, 'We were the last ones to be thought of in COVID and in Brexit,' and whilst that may sound self-pitying, I make the point for all working musicians out there. The arts make a lot of money for this country and its reputation. Brexit hasn't helped.

Jocelyn Brown summed it up to me when we finally met at a festival:

'The last eighteen months have been tough.'

We all knew that we would be the last thing to come back.

But we did – and we do as a human race.

When I 'resurfaced' I performed under the extraordinary conditions of a socially distanced concert. You would take anything just to start the ball rolling again. And that meant that the noise level had to be lowered, nobody was allowed to shout too loudly or come near the stage, and 'bubbles of six' were standard. When I drove home from that first gig, I thought, 'I can't do this, it's too weird, this is not gigging.'

When we did finally do a normal concert I vividly recalled the bass player in my new band looking at his guitar and saying, 'Ooh this is how it feels, it's all coming back to me.' Gigging is definitely not like riding a bike. You have to ease into it and get back in the groove.

As they say, the new normal.

An invitation to become an ambassador for the charity Children with Cancer UK by my good friend David Gibbs is something new and exciting which I accepted in a heartbeat. David is the Deputy Chairman of Trustees for the charity, and he has very big plans for their work going forward. I simply want to help as many children as possible, and being an ambassador for this charity is another way in which I believe can achieve that.

Now, as I pen these final thoughts, I am back travelling the length and breadth of the UK starting to see audiences whom I love and whom I have asked to *wait for me*. There is nothing sweeter in life than that connection through music and by which I have made so many genuine friends and, of course, realised my dreams.

It is the former that counts. My pop career was just a moment in time. If we remember where it started – and all those incredibly brilliant diverse influences which began with the union of my parents and embraced all of those London *commonwealth* factors, I couldn't have wished for a more rich and colourful tapestry. Nor could I be more grateful for the salient point, which is that, whilst pop opened many doors, I chose which ones to go through, and at the end of the corridor, so many beautiful kind people who have been consistent and true to me remain.

Notably, of course, Francisca who, miles from her childhood home, does not have the escape of being out on the road on a Friday night, even though she has the talent.

My story remains unfinished.

None of us know what lies ahead. From a pandemic to palliative care. COVID provides this additional chapter which was never meant to be. We are real enough to understand that there may be a time ahead when a further section is added depending on what happens with Christina, and of course, there is much of that story that at this point still remains private.

Some of the names have been changed to protect the innocent.

I am grateful that I can still make music. Steve Finan was right. You can gig for the rest of your life. I am sad that so many people in this story will not get to read it because they have already left us, and I have to acknowledge those new friends who came into my world because of Christina, who were themselves suffering and have since passed away. They went to great lengths in giving me as much information as they could, knowing all too well that time is always against us.

As I said to my dad, 'How did we get here so fast?'

I hope I have done you all justice.

And I am grateful to you, for your continued support to our family and our careers and for making it to this final page. That love is something which we cherish.

Thank you for understanding the importance of baring my soul.

A Debt of Thanks

A massive thank you to everyone who has helped Christina in so many ways over the last few years.

I'll do my best to try and remember all of you...

Steve Finan, Joseph O'Connor, Ricky and Mandy Wilde, Steve and Liz, Eliot Kennedy.

Ed Lewis.

Marcus Vere, Laetitia Vere, Tony Hadley, Beverley Knight, Kim Wilde, Midge Ure, Martin Fry, Go West, Nik Kershaw, Heaven 17, Living In A Box, T'Pau, Rusty Egan, Shane Richie, Gary Davies, Pete Faint, Steve Turner, Martin Cohen, Tim Bye, Mark Wraith, Billie Godfrey, Kelly Barnes, Rob Hughes, Dick Rabel, Tony Creaney, Andy Willsher, Ray Robinson, JJ Vere, Giselle Vere, Nina Vere, Lily Allen, Anthony and Jo Critchlow, Emma Robinson, Lennox Brown, Una Le Meur, James Le Meur, Rebi Merilion, Dawn Schenk, Louise Shaw, Caitlin Derer, The Ben Corfield Football Fund, Anthony Hamilton, Toby Baines and Elske Willenborg, Graham and Mia Wrigley, Daniel and Marcela Pinto, Revd. Peter Wolton, Bradley Wicks, Ilan Slazenger, Gary Smith, Paul Hayden.

Bluey aka Jean-Paul Maunick of Incognito and Citrus Sun, The Jazz Cafe organisation (The Columbo Group), Hamish Stuart, Omar Lye-Fook, Vula, Natalie Williams, Bashiyra 'The Voice', Moya Morris, Tom O'Grady (Resolution 88) and Nick Van Gelder, Chris Ballin, Joy Rose, Tony Momrelle, Vanessa Haynes, Imaani, Matt Cooper, Francis Hylton, Francesco Mendolia, Francisco Sales, Sid Gauld, Dominic Glover, Alistair White, Karl Vanden Bossche, Trevor Mires, Jim Hunt, Jamie Anderson, Russ Tarley.

Jocelyn Brown, Junior Giscombe, Drizabone, Pauline Henry (of The Chimes), Cool Million feat. Eli Thompson, Noel McKoy, Rose Vincent, Moni Tivony, Greg Edwards, Bigger, (DJ Set), Bob Masters, Flip Pearce, Tracy Pearce, James Anthony, Snowboy Mark Cotgrove, Calvin Francis, Stretch Paul Taylor, Scott Savill, Lee and Carla Lucraft, Alexander O'Neal, Jaki

Graham, Colin McMillan, Rick Astley, Peter Andre, Ben Ofoedu, Vinnie Jones, Louise Redknapp, Errol Reid, Andy Abraham, Les Spaine, Pete Walshe, Mark Wilkinson.

Jon Jules, Julia Jules, Rochelle Anderson, Melissa Pickard, Chelita Virdee, Ash Selector, The Crystals Ladies Team, Ian Reading, Ian Dee, Mike Vitti, CJ Carlos, Phil Fearon, Baby D, Georgie B, Deborah Bell, Rebecca Scales, Everis, Brian Power, Ronnie Herel.

Simon Dunmore and the Defected team.

Danny Moloney, Benny Macann, Alex McAllister, Gary Winter, Lucinda Ratcliffe, Nicky Burgis, Emma Deeba, Lucy Thompson, Adam Thompson, Chris Thompson, Stacey Matthews, Rae Williams, Mike Wiseman, Suzanne Steel, Gary Brannan.

Kevin and Lorraine Bellamy, Paul and Trudy at The Victoria Tavern E13, Al and Lorraine Webb at Monty's Bar Hornchurch, Tony Leigh and Mark Adams A&E Asbestos Ltd, Ashley Griffiths of DE Group Ltd, Colin Greyo Integral Environmental Solutions Ltd, John Meates, Matthew Dennis and Paul Shaw of Environtec Ltd, Gary and Debra Bude at Elite Tiling Ltd, Charlie Pigram – Spotless Locations Ltd, Steve and Jane Woollacott – The Pride of London, Gary Spence Solar Radio, Bobbie Shepherd, Lynne Walker, Sharon Worledge and all the Soul Boaters.

Neil Bullock, Louise Warren, Hannah White, Tommy Blaize, Pete Harris, Trevor Barry, Chris Taylor, Paul Pryor, Beebe Aldridge, Bryan Corbett, Chris Storr, Johnathon Bird, Mick Wilson.

José Santana Montesdeoca, Nathan Thomas, Gareth Thomas, Emma Harris, Amanda Harris, Barbara Harris, Christopher Gallagher, Andy Blake, David Gibbs, Rob and Netta Hubball, Joseph Zammit, Jim Hemmings, Mark and Alison Robinson, Warren Thompson, Tom and Gill Robson, Nick Joy, Des Grant, John McDade, Roy Dandy, Des Barber, Marco Martinelli, John Parkes, Mark Peters, Peta Moffitt from Stagecoach Bournemouth, Angela Roberts, Freda Robinson, Everyone at Best Nails in Brentwood, Nick Farmer, Simon Palmer, Alex Townshend, Darren Bance, Sarah Davies, Nicolas

Gale, Rob Gibson, John and Shelley Sander, Celia Sander, Alex Georgiou, Jimmy Lazarou, Steve Kurz aka Kurzsy, Fr Jeff Woolnough, Fr David Ward, Rev Bill Dimelow and the parishioners of Our Lady and St Walstan, DJ Beat, Stephen Barlow Linder, Diane Marsh, Mick and Christine Heaphy, Andy Geraghty, Glynn Carelse, Mansfield Mbeya, Paul and Julie Connaughton – JPC Community Farm, Mark Edmonds, Michaela Madden, Howard Bostridge, Alexander Bostridge, Mark Crawford, Matt Facer, Daniel Henshaw, Julie Barkley & Elaine Frost – Surrey Soul Train, Mike Richards, Richie Richh, Sarah Hood (The Fox and Hounds, Ramsden Heath), Mark Courtney OCDS, Antonio Raphael, Lorraine Pye, Rebecca Steward, Julie Pocock, Carole Button, Tanja Johnson, Dean Martin, Dr Brian and Donna Doherty, Vincent Lynch, Daryn Ferguson, Stel Charalambous, Sofia Charalambous, Christalla Pascal, Marc McAuley, Paz Perrotta, Chris Tofalli, Marie Gregory, Chris Thrall, Tom Wallace, Irene Mumba, Roxy Finch, Ann Cook, Andrew Randell, Jamie Callis, Shirley Phillips, Donna Martin.

And for help on this book: Matt at ProofProfessor and my editor Tony Horne (www.tonyhornebooks.com).

A heartfelt thankyou to those not mentioned or those not wishing to be mentioned: you know who you are.

Lots of love from the Thomas family xx